SHOW TRIALS

SHOW TRIALS

Stalinist Purges in Eastern Europe,
1948–1954

GEORGE H. HODOS

PRAEGER

New York
Westport, Connecticut
London

Library of Congress Cataloging-in-Publication Data
Hodos, George H.
 Show trials.

 Bibliography: p.
 Includes index.
√ 1. Trials (Political crimes and offenses)—Europe,
Eastern. 2. Soviet Union—Politics and government—
1936–1953. 3. Stalin, Joseph, 1879–1953. I. Title.
KJC67.P66H63 1987   345.47'0231   87-13769
                        344.705231
ISBN 0-275-92783-0 (alk. paper)

Library of Congress Catalog Card Number: 87-13769
ISBN: 0-275-92783-0

First published in 1987

Praeger Publishers, One Madison Avenue, New York, NY 10010
A division of Greenwood Press, Inc.

Printed in the United States of America

The paper used in this book complies with the
Permanent Paper Standard issued by the National
Information Standards Organization (Z39.48-1984).

10 9 8 7 6 5 4 3 2 1

To Marta

CONTENTS

LIST OF ABBREVIATIONS

AVH   Államvédelmi Hatóság [State Security Authority of Hungary]
CC   Central Committee of the communist party
CIA   Central Intelligence Agency
CP   Communist Party
DDR   Deutsche Demokratische Republik [German Democratic Republic]
GDR   German Democratic Republic
K5   Kommissariat 5 [the fifth (political) branch of the East German police under Soviet military administration]
KPD   Kommunistische Partei Deutschlands [Communist Party of Germany]
KRN   Krajowa Rada Narodowa [National Council for the Homeland]
MVD   Ministerstvo Vnutrennikh Del [Ministry of Internal Affairs, responsible for the Soviet state security organs, from 1946 to 1954]
NKVD   Narodnyi Komissariat Vnutrennikh Del [People's Commissariat of Internal Affairs, responsible for the Soviet state security organs, from 1934 to 1946]
OSS   Office of Strategic Services
PPR   Polska Partia Robotnicza [Polish Workers' Party]
SED   Sozialistische Einheitspartei [Socialist Unity Party of East Germany, after the merger of the communist and the Social Democratic parties in 1946]
SSD   Staatssicherheitsdienst [State Security Service of East Germany]
UDB   Uprava Drzavne Bezbednosti [State Security Directorate of Yugoslavia]
USC   Unitarian Service Committee
VVN   Vereinigung der Verfolgten des Naziregimes [Union of Victims of Nazi Persecution in East Germany]

PREFACE

"The Party is dead; it can neither move nor breathe, but its hair and nails continue to grow," said Rubashov to Colonel Ivanov of the NKVD, Stalin's security police, at the outset of his interrogation.

"We know more than men have ever known about mankind; that is why our revolution succeeded. And now you have buried it all again. . . . Everything is buried; the men, their wisdom and their hopes. You killed it, you destroyed it. . . ."[1]

Rubashov, Arthur Koestler's literary symbol of the victims of Stalin's purges, was a broken, disillusioned man, his revolution betrayed and converted into an instrument of personal power by Josef Stalin. Koestler modeled his tragic hero after Bukharin and placed Trotzky's pince-nez upon his nose, but he represented the entire Bolshevik old guard, Lenin's comrades in arms who, pushed into the opposition by Stalin, watched helplessly as their power was taken from them, their loyalty to the party mocked, and they, themselves, systematically and brutally destroyed. In his thirst for absolute power, Stalin used the right against the left, then left against right, and finally played off the center against both until, in the 1930s, he had them all slain in the Great Terror.

Ten to fifteen years later, after the war, a very different group was liquidated, the young guard of the communist leadership in Eastern Europe. These were not opponents of Stalin, but his faithful disciples. At the time they were chosen by their master to serve him as victims, they were at the height of their newly attained power. Rajk, Slánský, Gomułka, and their comrades were no Rubashovs; they were no less devoted to the policies of Moscow than their executioners.

The difference was also reflected in the methods of interrogation used to extort false confessions.

"I plead guilty to not having understood the fatal compulsion behind the policy of the government, and to have therefore held oppositional views," conceded Rubashov midway through his interrogation.

"I plead guilty to having followed sentimental impulses, and in so doing, to having been led into contradictions with historical necessity. . . to having placed the idea of man above the idea of mankind. . . . I admit that these points of view are, in the present situation, objectively harmful and, therefore, counterrevolutionary in character."[2]

The next step, from accepting subjective guilt to confessing to abominable crimes, consciously committed, followed with implacable logic. To accomplish this, Rubashov's second interrogator, Gletkin, needed only the blinding light of a desk lamp, the false testimony of another prisoner, and the exhaustion brought on by uninterrupted interrogations.

"The roles had been exchanged; it was not Gletkin but he, Rubashov, who had tried to muddle a clear case by splitting hairs. The accusation, which until now had seemed to him so absurd, in fact, merely inserted the missing links into a perfectly logical chain."[3]

But Rajk, Slánský, Kostov, Patrascanu, and Gomułka did not suffer from subjective guilt feelings that could be reinterpreted into objective crimes. When Rubashov was escorted to his first interrogation, Ivanov, an old friend, smiled at him from behind his desk.

" 'What a pleasant surprise,' said Rubashov, dryly. 'Sit down,' said Ivanov with a polite gesture."[4]

Perhaps, in 1937, a similar scenario greeted Bukharin at his arrest, his nerve having been broken during ten years of harassment and vilification. According to some witnesses, he had never been beaten or tortured. Maybe. But with the new victims, the executioner had no time to waste. It took only a few weeks of physical and psychological torture for communist leaders, at the height of power, to be transformed into helpless clumps of human flesh, robbed of their humanity and of the meaning of their lives. They were beaten with rubber truncheons and rifle butts, their nails were torn out, they were denied drinking water and forced to swallow the urine of their captors, they were subjected to water baths through which electrical currents were sent, they were confined to cages in which they could only crouch, they were threatened with the arrests of their wives and children—when these had not already been arrested—to the point where they felt hopelessly delivered to an incomprehensible fate: buried alive, robbed even of the possibility of committing suicide. The higher their position in the party, the more brutally they were tortured. Only rarely did the mechanism break down, when they were beaten to death or were driven insane by overzealous interrogators.

The philosophical conversations described by Koestler, the appeals to party loyalty, the requests to render a last service to world communism through confession, came only at the very end of the ordeal, after the process of physical and psychological destruction was complete.

Rajk and the other postwar victims of Stalin were no Bukharins. Neither were they "national communists," more loyal to their countries than to Stalin's demands, as they have often been described by Western observers. To invest them with Titoist tendencies is to completely misjudge their personalities and political careers. Drawing a mistaken analogy with the trials of the 1930s provides their hangmen with a perverse justification; if the victims were guilty of actually opposing Stalin, then they had to be liquidated. The distorting nature of the Western characterization of these people as national communists becomes clear in the cases of Gomułka, Kádár, and Husák, each of whom was first a victim of the postwar purges and survived to become faithful servants of Soviet imperial policies.

The show trials in Eastern Europe would have occurred even without the break between Stalin and Tito, probably even with the identical victims, as the device by which the brother parties of the postwar Soviet satellite states in Eastern Europe were subordinated to the Soviet party. Show trials were an integral part of Stalinism, and their introduction into the satellite states was a logical step, albeit with variants on the tested Soviet model. These differences were not merely geographic or periodic. In the factional, ideological, and power struggles of the 1930s, the victims were selected first and the necessary scenario written afterwards. In the Eastern Europe of the 1940s, the scenario was created before the victims were selected. The Stalinist terror in the satellite countries constituted a new chapter in the history of the show trials, distinctly different in character from those that preceded them, about whose differences little has yet been written. To fill this gap in our knowledge about and understanding of the later version is the purpose of this book.

*   *   *

The show trial is a propaganda arm of political terror. Its aim is to personalize an abstract political enemy, to place it in the dock in flesh and blood and, with the aid of a perverted system of justice, to transform abstract political-ideological differences into easily intelligible common crimes. It both incites the masses against the evil embodied by the defendants and frightens them away from supporting any potential opposition.

The concept is used here in a specifically narrow sense, restricted to the liquidation of communists by communists. It ignores the Stalinist show trials against real enemies of the system such as the leaders of the bourgeois and social democratic parties and of the Catholic church. On the other hand, it includes not only public trials before selected audiences and broadcasts on radio, but also secret trials, news of which was disseminated by clever whispering campaigns among the party membership. In their secrecy and with the silent disappearance of the accused, these were no less effective as instruments of terror than were the public trials.

The centerpiece of this book is the trial of the Hungarian communist leader László Rajk, not only because of my personal involvement in it, but also because the hanging court in Budapest provided a model for all of the subsequent bloody purges in the satellite countries. A detailed account is given of the relatively unimportant starting point of the purges in Tirana because in the relevant literature the analysis of postwar developments in Albania, culminating in the show trial of Koci Xoxe, receives only superficial treatment. Quite the opposite situation applies to the trials in Czechoslovakia, whose long and bloody course is amply documented in the memoirs of survivors as well as in the confidential report of the commission set up by the Central Committee, a copy of which has been published in the West. Consequently, the trials in Prague are examined here primarily in terms of how they related to the other East European trials and how they differed from them.

An examination of the show trials in Poland provides many opportunities to cast light on obscure and neglected aspects, to date mostly unexplored, as the existing literature is concerned mainly with the planned—but never staged—show trial of Wladisław Gomułka. The chapters dealing with the Stalinist purges in Bulgaria, Romania, and East Germany probe into territories hitherto scarcely documented. It is my hope that they offer a number of new suggestions for a much more detailed exploration of events still kept secret by a nearly total silence on the part of perpetrators and surviving victims alike.

This study would be incomplete without at least a cursory analysis of the rehabilitation of the purge victims that occurred during the period of de-Stalinization—that slow, uneven, contradictory process that saw those responsible attempt to extricate themselves from their crimes. This sudden confrontation of socialist ideology by factual reality had a decisive influence on the Polish and Hungarian uprisings and was one of the origins of the Prague Spring.

* * *

I was one of the fortunate survivors of the Rajk trial and thus had an opportunity to obtain, from the point of view of the victim, insight into the mechanism and the psychology of the model trial. From the moment of my arrest to the present day, I have been haunted by a single question: How and why could this have happened? When I began my research into this question I found, to my amazement, that there exists no book that offers a comprehensive study of the trials that swept Eastern Europe from 1948 to 1954. I was limited to a mosaic composed of fragments, and to piece them together into a coherent and understandable explanation became an inner necessity.

Some insight came from my own experiences. That, in turn, was enlarged and deepened by the relatively rich primary literature provided by victims who survived the Prague show trials. The best among them was the intelligent and honest report by Artur London, titled *Confession*. Many details were divulged in the two books by Eugene Loebl, *The Revolution Rehabilitates its Children* and *My Mind on Trial*. I also learned much by reading *Report on My Husband* by Josefa Slánská and *Truth Will Prevail* by Marian Šlingová, both stirring accounts of the persecution of the victims' families. Finally, among the personal reports, there was *Prisonnier politique à Prague* by the Israeli defendant, Mordecai Oren, which bore witness to the anti-Semitism of the purges. Especially valuable among the official documents were the report of the Czechoslovak Central Committee inquiring into the background of the Slánský trial, a work banned immediately after its publication, and an additional study, published only in Paris, *Dans les archives du Comité Central* by Karel Kaplan.

On the show trials in other countries, the primary literature is restricted to scattered articles in newspapers and periodicals and two books, *Volunteers for the Gallows* by Béla Szász, a personal account of the Rajk trial, and a deeply moving report, *Light at Midnight* by Erica Wallach, on the attempt to emulate the Hungarian trial in the German Democratic Republic. The survivors of the Kostov trial in Bulgaria and of the trials in Romania and Poland have kept their silence, the only direct but propagandistically distorted information on the latter coming from a defector, Security Colonel Josef Światło, in his broadcasts for Radio Free Europe.

The personal memoirs and reports, however, illuminate only part of the picture, and because of their restricted scope, do so in a necessarily subjective manner. The existing secondary literature is even less helpful. In contrast to the rich literature on the general phenomenon of Stalinism, there are relatively few comprehensive historical studies of Stalinist Eastern Europe. Even in the most outstanding of these, *The Balkans in our Time* by Robert Lee Wolff and *Histoire des démocraties populaires* by François Fejtő, the show trials receive cursory treatment as part of a general history rather than the thorough analysis they deserve. In the rather scarce literature about the Stalinist periods of the individual communist countries and their communist parties, the show trials are treated as mere copies of the Soviet purges. The authors content themselves with the obligatory reference to the Stalin-Tito break and explain the liquidation of thousands of East European communists by labeling them summarily but misleadingly as "national communists." The few studies in which the purges receive more than these brief references date mainly from the 1950s, a period during which the Stalin-Tito break, the spectacular confessions, and the rehabilitation of some of the victims in the Khrushchev era were still on everyone's mind. Missing is all of the information that has come to light during the last thirty years.

What were the global and domestic backgrounds of the postwar purges? What was the role of Stalin and his security organs? To what extent did Rákosi, Gottwald, Gheorghiu-Dej, Dimitrov, Bierut, and the other willing servants of the Soviet Union influence the trials? What role did Noel Field play—he whose ghostlike figure propelled the wave of purges from Budapest through Prague and Warsaw to East Berlin? Why were there no public show trials in Poland, Romania, and East Germany? Wherein lie the similarities and the differences among the trials and where did they interconnect? How were the victims chosen and how were the scenarios drawn up? The answers to these and similar questions that have haunted me for three decades cannot be found within the narrow limits of the individual trials.

The present book originated in my need to discover answers. This attempt is made in the full knowledge that, for the foreseeable future, it will not be possible to examine the secret archives of the communist security services. Therefore, it falls upon the survivors of the show trials, living in the West, to fill the void as best we can. Our generation is passing on and since, up to now, no one more competent has come forward to take up the task, I feel compelled to make the attempt. Soon there will not be anyone left to tell about this chapter of history with the intimate knowledge that comes from having been a participant.

* * *

In this book, I have inserted some of my personal experiences. They are intended to serve as illustrations, photographs in a travel book about a scarcely explored country. I began this long journey convinced that I and my fellow communists had found definitive answers to the world's problems. But the reality of communism destroyed for me the validity of these answers, and I am still groping to find new and satisfactory ones.

On orders of Stalin I have been thrown in prison, five years later Khrushchev gave me back my freedom, accomplices of the hangmen declared sanctimoniously that I am rehabilitated, legally as well as politically.

The thaw in the Soviet Union was soon frozen again. The strangled de-Stalinization of Khrushchev, his tanks in the streets of Budapest, Brezhnev's troops in Prague buried all the resurrected hopes for a better future.

The pessimism might have been premature. With Gorbachev, a new historical chance seems to be emerging to rid socialism of the strait-jacket of Stalinist legacy. Only then can the still open wounds of the show trials in eastern Europe be healed. Only then will their victims be truly rehabilitated.

* * *

A final remark: It is customary for an author to assume responsibility for all of the mistakes contained in his book, and certainly there are many errors in this one. I hope it will not sound presumptuous to ask for the indulgence of the reader if I shift part of the blame on to the East European governments that block any access to the secret party or to the security archives, and that wrap the details of the show trials in silence.

SHOW TRIALS

CHAPTER 1
INTRODUCTION

HISTORICAL BACKGROUND

It is not the purpose of this book to present a history of Stalinism, or even of the political terror that it unleashed against opposition movements in Eastern Europe. The scope of this work is limited to a history of the purges and show trials against communists that took place in the Soviet satellite nations during the early postwar years and that served as one of the main instruments by means of which the Soviet Union established domination over the satellite states and their communist parties, making them subservient to Stalin and his security services.[1] This work also establishes the connections, similarities, and differences among the events in the different countries without any attempt at a theoretical analysis of these events.

The historical background leading to the show trials is amply documented in the political literature dealing with those times.[2] But there is a need for a brief outline of the three elements that triggered the trials: the Cold War, Stalin's growing paranoia, and the Soviet-Yugoslav split.

At the end of World War II, the Soviet Union controlled all of Europe east of a line drawn from Stettin on the Baltic Sea, to Trieste on the Adriatic Sea. The West, led by the United States, was unwilling to accept total Soviet domination of this vast area and, fearing a further expansion of communism in Europe, countered with a "policy of containment." Step by step, the Cold War intensified; U.S. support for the Royalists in the Greek Civil War in 1946 was followed by the Truman Doctrine in March 1947, offering political, economic, and military aid to any nation threatened by communism. In June 1947, the U.S. proposed the Marshall Plan to rebuild Western Europe and enable it to withstand communist pressures from within. In June 1948, the decision was made by the Western powers to build up a strong, anti-Soviet West Germany, and in July 1949, NATO was forged out of the Brussels Union and thus completed the creation of a worldwide circle of strategic bases around the Soviet Union.

In the sphere of intelligence, President Truman in June 1948 broadened the role of the newly established Central Intelligence Agency (CIA) to include covert operations against the Soviet Union and its satellites in the fields of "propaganda and economic warfare; preventive direct action including sabotage; subversion

including assistance of underground resistance groups; and support for indige-
nous anti-communist elements.''[3]

The covert operations centered in Western Europe and provided secret sub-
sidies to buy or influence individual politicians, political parties, labor unions,
newspapers, and cultural organizations. Until the institution of total Stalinization
cut the East off from the West, the same methods were used in the satellite
countries: Clandestine channels were opened to finance and manipulate anticom-
munist factions and parties, churches, and civic groups. In Poland and in the
Ukraine, intelligence agents actively supported armed guerrilla movements. In
Albania, a secret British-U.S. paramilitary operation was foiled by the betrayal
of the double agent, Kim Philby.[4] The alleged efforts to recruit communist
leaders, of which so much was made in the show trials, belonged, however, to
the realm of Stalinist fantasy, doubtless fueled by an organized disinformation
campaign in the Western media, suggesting rifts between fictional nationalist and
Soviet, liberal and orthodox wings within the satellite leadership.

The policy of containment thwarted any possible Soviet aspiration to expand
further to the West. The Soviet Union found itself encircled and isolated. Stalin
reacted by turning the occupied countries into satellites, using them as a military
defense belt and forcing the Soviet pattern on every aspect of their political,
economic, and cultural lives.

Ideology became a powerful instrument in this policy of colonization. The
initial theory about the existence of different national roads to socialism was
banished, and in its place was instituted a Stalinist concept of imposed conformity,
the absolute primacy of Soviet interest, and the exclusive validity of the Soviet
example. The external Cold War was translated for internal use into the pseudo-
Marxist ''theory'' of the ''growing intensity of class struggle'' in the phase of
transition from capitalism to socialism. Vigilance became a paramount concern
because the theory implied that the enemy, beaten and cornered, finds covert,
desperate, devious methods to conspire against the people's democracies and to
sabotage the construction of socialism. The party was no exception; the paranoid
suspicions of Stalin saw the enemy infiltrate the top positions, imperialist agents
disguised as communists trying to subvert from within his newly won empire.
Soon the most dangerous enemy became the one who held a party card and
occupied a high position. Tito's revolt seemed to Stalin the proof of his patholog-
ical nightmare of spies and enemies everywhere; it led directly to the show trials.

*   *   *

The purges would have taken place even without Tito; the break merely
speeded up the process. The aging despot began to distrust his closest associates.
He accused Molotov, Voroshilov, Beria, Mikoyan, Zhukov, even his personal
secretary Poskrebyshev of being English spies,[5] the proofs of their guilt being
held in readiness by extorting false depositions and confessions from purge
victims in the prisons and concentration camps of the Gulag. He terrorized his

most servile courtiers by arresting their relatives, the wives of his head of state Kalinin, of Poskrebyshev, and of Molotov, and two sons of Mikoyan were thrown into prison as traitors; Kaganovitch's brother committed suicide in the interrogation room.[6] Chief ideologist Andrei Zhdanov, forced into early retirement died suddenly in Leningrad under mysterious circumstances; Stalin, who was probably responsible for his death, accused the top Jewish physicians in the Kremlin of his murder and concocted the infamous "doctors' plot" as the culmination of his anti-Semitic campaign. Thousands of Jews prominent in the political, scientific, and cultural life of the Soviet Union were liquidated and the deportation of the entire body of Soviet Jewry to Birobidjan in Central Asia was prepared.[7] In the "Leningrad affair," closely related to the death of Zhdanov, nearly the entire staff of that city's party organization, of the local Komsomol and Soviet executive committee, factory managers, scientific personnel, teachers, and professors were arrested; thousands were executed; among them, the leading economist and Politburo member, Vosnesenkii, the secretary to the Central Committee, Kusnetsov, and the chairman of the Council of Ministers of the Russian Soviet Republic, Rodionov.[8]

Even the security service, Stalin's main pillar of the terror, was not spared. Under the supervision of Stalin's chief henchman, Lavrenti Beria, it was split into three parts: the Ministry of Internal Affairs under Kruglov; the Ministry of State Security headed by Abakumov; and the special section for Stalin's personal safety, directed by General Vlasik. Soon Abakumov was arrested, Vlasik was accused of being a British spy, and even Beria fell from grace. He was banished from Stalin's presence, and in the so-called Migrelian case many of his creatures were arrested in a clear preliminary to his impending liquidation.[9]

For the aging dictator, everyone was suspect. He distrusted his own, steadily decimated circle of accomplices, so how much more did he distrust his foreign agents in the satellite countries? There were spies among them, he must have been certain of that. At home, the transformation of the USSR into a superpower made the staging of public show trials politically unwise, since the attention of the entire world was now riveted on what took place in Soviet internal affairs, hitherto ignored by the outside world. The shows in the Soviet Union had to be performed behind the scenes; the postwar purges in the USSR, therefore, were restricted to covert liquidations, secret mass murders, unmentioned and unmentionable. In the satellite countries, no such restraints existed. There, the road was open for the show trials.

*   *   *

Stalin's paranoia about enemies infiltrating into the top ranks of communist parties found a convenient validation in Tito's rebellion. It had its roots in the fact that Yugoslavia was the only East European country to have achieved its liberation and its socialist revolution by dint of its own efforts and not through the triumphs of the Red Army.[10]

From 1944 until June 1948, Soviet-Yugoslav relations were dominated by Stalin's attempts to turn Yugoslavia into a subservient client state, and Tito's resistance against this. Tito was, if anything, a more fervent Stalinist than were all of the other satellite party leaders. In his external and internal policies, he followed faithfully the line dictated by Moscow, accepted like a true believer the general validity of the Soviet model and the primacy of the Soviet Union. In the Information Bureau of the Communist Parties, the Cominform, a tool to force conformity upon the parties of the Soviet bloc, Yugoslavia was in the forefront of the attacks on all deviations from the one and only Soviet doctrine. The transformation of Yugoslavia into a socialist society patterned on the Soviet example was the most radical in all the people's democracies.

Tensions between the Soviet Union and Yugoslavia did not arise from alleged doctrinal differences, but from their incompatible conceptions of state and party relations. The ideological dispute was a later, artificial creation that was developed at the beginning of 1948. Stiffening Yugoslav resistance to Soviet attempts to penetrate the economy and the army, and its intention to subordinate the Yugoslav party to the control of Soviet security organs, forced Stalin to abandon the policy of covert infiltration and start an open attack to subjugate or, if necessary, eliminate Tito. Tito's growing authority in the people's democracies and his attempt to create a socialist federation of the nations of the Danubian basin and the Balkans posed an immediate threat to Stalin's satellite system. The showdown became inevitable.

It began in the spring of 1948 with a series of letters addressed to the Central Committee of the Yugoslav Communist Party in which Stalin accused Tito of deviating from the correct Marxist-Leninist line by adopting a policy favoring the petit bourgeoisie and the wealthy peasants, or kulaks, and by displaying an unfriendly attitude toward Soviet representatives, even hurling the charge of Trotzkyism, the deadliest invective of Stalinist vocabulary.[11] When the Yugoslavs refused to repent, Stalin tried to divide the party and thus weaken Tito's control, but this was foiled by the arrest of the two pro-Soviet Central Committee members, Žujović and Hebrang. To force a capitulation, Stalin convened a special meeting of the Cominform. In its resolution, published on May 28, 1948, the Soviet party and its satellites condemned Tito's anti-Marxist, anti-Soviet policy and expelled Yugoslavia from the Cominform. The resolution closed with an invitation to the "healthy elements" within the party to topple Tito and rejoin the Soviet camp.[12]

The break was complete, but Tito still could not be coerced into submission. He became, for Stalin, the "enemy number one." Titoism replaced Trotzkyism as the incarnation of evil. It filled the empty shell of the catchwork "spy"; the phantom threat to Stalin's autocratic rule over party, country, and empire was given a new, concrete content. Stalin's villain having been found, the show trials could begin immediately.

CHAPTER 2
PRELUDE IN ALBANIA

The postwar Stalinist show trials began on May 12, 1949, with the secret proceedings against the fallen Albanian Minister of the Interior Koci Xoxe. At the same time, however, his execution belongs to the prehistory of the East European purges; it signaled the bloody climax in the Soviet-Yugoslav conflict. He was not a made-up "Titoist," but rather a Titoist without quotation marks, Yugoslavia's trusted man in the Albanian communist party.

In its basic structure the Xoxe trial is a postwar copy of the old-fashioned, classical Stalinist purges of the thirties, transferred to a Balkan country. Factional power struggles and political differences were "solved" not only with the physical liquidation of the loser, but also with his political murder, the assassination of his character. The ideological platform he represented was falsified into espionage, treason, and sabotage; his past, his personal life was dragged in the mud; and the lie became truth by his extorted self-incriminating "confession." In this respect, Xoxe's fate did not differ from that of Bukharin and the other victims of the Trotzkyist trials in the Soviet Union. He was opposed to Stalin's man in Albania, and he lost.

The Xoxe trial belongs clearly to the classical type, and it was with some hesitation that it was included in this book, the more so as a rather lengthy account of Albania's internal and external problems seemed to be unavoidable in order to understand it. But the Albanian trial is, at the same time, a bridge between the old and the new purges, linked by the specific anti-Tito content of the lies and distortions. It was the starting shot for the beginning of the new phase of show trials, the exception that proved the rule.

* * *

The Albanians had always been and still remain an exceptional case. They are a brotherless people, descendants of a proto-Germanic clan and of the Illyrs; their language is related to no other. Since 3000 years ago, when they penetrated into the Balkan Peninsula, their history has been a constant struggle for independence and a fight against any foreign influence or domination, be it Roman, Turk, Italian, German, or Slav.[1]

The isolated new nation, carved out in 1912 from the disintegrated Turkish empire, entered the twentieth century as Europe's poorest and most backward country. Under the dictatorship of King Zogu, Albania became first a satellite, then, after Zogu fled the country in 1939, a colony of Italy, and was finally occupied by the German army. Yet only the upper classes went along with the changes; the people withdrew, as always, from the foreign influences. It required the war's penetration into the ravines to mobilize the farmers and shepherds into active resistance against the fascist occupying powers. The communist-led National Army of Liberation succeeded in liberating the entire country from the occupants in the fall of 1944, without the help of a single Red Army soldier or Yugoslav partisan. The way was clear for seizing power.

* * *

The 3,000-year-old defense mechanism of a tiny foreign body worked also under communist rule. It is the irony of history that the Albanian communist party was founded by the Yugoslavs. The few scattered groups were engaged in bitter fractional struggles, and several attempts by the Comintern to unite them were unsuccessful. Albania remained the only European country without a communist party until late in World War II.

After the German occupation of Yugoslavia, Tito dispatched two high party functionaries—Milovan Popović and Dušan Mugoša—to Tirana, and in November of 1941 they finally succeeded in uniting the factions into the Albanian Communist Party. The two Yugoslavs nominated the members of the provisional central committee with the teacher Enver Hoxha and the plumber Koci Xoxe at the top. They stayed in the country as "advisers" until the end of the war; the Albanian party became, in fact, a branch of the Yugoslav party, and Albania became a satellite of Yugoslavia.[2]

From the establishment of communist authority to Tito's break with Stalin, Albania mirrored Yugoslavia step for step. It ceded to his protector the province of Kosovo, heavily populated by Albanians; accepted a new constitution that was virtually identical to Yugoslavia's; ordered the nationalization of industry and the collectivization of agriculture, again based on the Yugoslav model; in the schools, the study of the Serb language became mandatory; and the young technical and administrative staff received their higher education in Yugoslavia. Foreign policy was identical, too. Under Tito's pressure, Albania followed an extremely anti-Western course, expelling the British and American missions. The isolation from the West seemed to be a good means for Yugoslavia to strengthen its authority over its satellite, undisturbed by foreign influence.[3]

Already during the war, the Yugoslavs pushed for the creation of an internal security organ to purge the party of "deviators" and "Trotskyites." The first victim was Anastas Lulo, head of the party's youth organization. Under pressure from the Yugoslavs, he was condemned as a "leftist deviator" and shot. Next came Lazar Fundo, one of the founding members of the communist movement. He returned from the Soviet exile a disappointed man; however, he joined the communist partisans. In the summer of 1944, he was arrested by his comrades and beaten to death before the horrified eyes of the British military mission. The "sin" of Mustafa Gjinishi, member of the provisional Politburo, was his deal with the bourgeois opposition groups to form a united front against the fascists. The Yugoslav advisor forced the Albanian party to cancel the agreement and Gjinishi was executed as a traitor.[4]

Parallel to securing its political influence, Yugoslavia tried to control the Albanian economy. Tito was certainly far more generous to his East European vassal than Stalin was, for entire factories were transferred from Yugoslavia to Albania under very favorable conditions. The advantages for the most under-developed country were undeniable. In contrast to the Soviet Union, Yugoslavia did not wish to plunder its satellite; it had other purposes for Albania. The Friendship Treaty of 1946 clearly indicated the trend: The economic plans of both countries were to be coordinated and a customs union established. In the summer of 1948, the process of merging both economic systems was well advanced, and Albania's membership in the Yugoslav Socialist Federal Republic appeared imminent.[5]

* * *

In view of the deep nationalistic tradition of Albania, it was not to be expected that the Yugoslav hegemony efforts would remain without opposition. Two factions in the party began to crystallize in November 1944. On one side were the moderates, the so-called intellectuals, under the leadership of Sejfulla Maleshova, Nako Spiru and Mehmet Shehu; on the other side were the so-called workers, led by Koci Xoxe, minister of the interior and head of the "Sigurimi," the security service controlled by the Yugoslav secret police UDB. Enver Hoxha, secretary general of the communist party, wavered between the two factions.

In November, the dispute dealt only indirectly with Yugoslavia's domineering position; the difference of opinion concerned mainly the pace of the socialist transformation, but Xoxe sensed the danger signals and, in February of 1946, with the help of Enver Hoxha, pushed the moderates aside, Maleshova was expelled from the Politburo and the Central Committee, and his clique was labeled as opportunists and anti-Yugoslavs.[6]

Hoxha now began to fear the growing power of Xoxe, who, with the open support of Tito, threatened his top position in leadership of the Albanian party. Early in 1946 he tried to find help in Moscow and asked for an audience with Stalin, but Stalin declined. Up to then, the Soviet Union had taken little interest in the Albanian problems; it entrusted the country to Yugoslavia.

A year later, in January 1947, according to Milovan Djilas in his book *Conversations with Stalin*, the Soviet dictator was even more cynical: "We have no special interests in Albania. We agree that Yugoslavia should swallow up Albania." His infamous advice to Djilas was clearly meant to be provocative at a time when the Yugoslav-Soviet conflict was beginning to unfold. Stalin attempted to aggravate the power struggle between Xoxe, Tito's protégé, and Enver Hoxha, the independent secretary-general.[7]

Hoxha sensed the upcoming storm and seized the offensive. In the spring of 1947, he began to object to the unequal conditions in the Yugoslav-Albanian economic treaty and reproached the Yugoslav advisors for deliberately wanting to slow down the country's development. The relations between the two countries reached a crisis point in April 1947, when an Albanian economic delegation, headed by Nako Spiru, proceeded to Belgrade demanding increased help and the signing of a new treaty. The Yugoslavs declined to negotiate as long as Albania was not willing to accept the coordination of the economic plans. Hoxha instructed Spiru to resist the pressure; he thought that a common Five-Year Plan would condemn Albania to the status of a backward agrarian country and raw material supplier, forever chained to Yugoslavia.[8]

In the face of the resistance, the Yugoslavs pushed Xoxe to seize the counteroffensive. In May 1947, he ordered nine anti-Yugoslavian members of the people's congress to be arrested—among them Maleshova. They were tried by the Xoxe-controlled people's court and sentenced to long prison sentences for "subversive activities." In June, Tito followed up with a sharp letter to the Albanian party. He blamed Enver Hoxha for creating an anti-Yugoslav mood and leading Albanian politics in an anti-Yugoslav direction.

The Tito letter had, however, the opposite effect: It strengthened resistance against Yugoslav domination. The Politburo rejected the charge as an inadmissible interference into the internal affairs of the Albanian party. Only Xoxe and Pandi Kristo, head of the powerful control commission, dissented.

Enver Hoxha again requested permission from Moscow to send a delegation to the Soviet Union, and this time Stalin agreed. Hoxha personally led the delegation, together with Nako Spiru. In July 1947, a trade agreement was signed. The fact that Moscow did not inform Yugoslavia of the negotiations and pledged Albania the assistance refused by the Yugoslavs was a warning sign to Tito that Stalin no longer stood behind his Albanian policies.[9]

Tito's answer was not long in coming. In November 1947, he sent a new letter to the Albanian Central Committee and this time selected the planning chief Nako Spiru as being responsible for the "misunderstandings," saying his "treacherous behavior poisons the atmosphere between the two brotherly Parties." A Central Committee meeting was convened to discuss Tito's letter. Xoxe accused an indignant Spiru of "subersive, nationalistic activity." The next morning, Spiru was found dead in his apartment. The first version reported an accident while cleaning his revolver; the second official report spoke of suicide, committed out of remorse; finally, after the ultimate break with Tito and Spiru's posthumous rehabilitation, it was said that he was murdered by Xoxe's security police, the version that probably corresponds to the facts.[10]

Stalin could no longer ignore the Albanian problem; it became for him a test of strength in the developing conflict with Tito. At the beginning of 1948, an unusually high number of ''specialists'' from Moscow streamed into Tirana, and the personnel at the Soviet embassy increased dramatically. At the same time, Yugoslavia decided to send, without consulting Moscow and in spite of Soviet protests, two army divisions to Albania, ostensibly to protect the country against an eventual Greek invasion.[11] Tito felt he could no longer delay the final decision in his plan of a Yugoslavian-Albanian union, and he instructed Xoxe to convene a full session of the Central Committee. The Eighth Plenum conferred under the threat of Tito's armies and brought a last victory for Xoxe in March. Enver Hoxha could only keep his post as secretary-general after offering a humiliating self-criticism; a number of his supporters were expelled from the Central Committee. Moscow-educated Mehmet Shehu, head of the general staff and opponent of the Yugoslavian orientation, was relieved of his post, and the Central Committee accepted Xoxe's motion to approve the merger of Albania's economy and army with Yugoslavia.[12]

Events now followed in rapid succession. In the middle of June, upon instruction of the Soviet ambassador, Hoxha ordered the closing of the Yugoslav Bureau of Information, and on July 1, 1948, four days after the Cominform resolution about ''Tito and his clique,'' he abrogated the trade agreements with Yugoslavia and ordered the immediate expulsion of all Yugoslav specialists and advisors.

With complete political and economic support from the Soviet Union, Hoxha now turned against his rival. Xoxe tried to prevent the unavoidable, offered self-criticism, affirmed his loyalty to the Soviet Union and the Cominform resolution, and ordered the secret service to track down and arrest Titoists. It was to no avail. The Central Committee revoked the resolutions of the Eighth Plenum, rehabilitated all leading communists purged by Xoxe, decided to relieve Xoxe of his post as minister of the interior, and replaced him with his former victim, Mehmet Shehu. Xoxe's supporters were quickly removed, their places in the secret service filled by Shehu's confidants and agents of the MVD, the Soviet secret police. On October 31, Xoxe was relieved of all party and government positions. On November 22, after a unanimous decision of the party congress, he was expelled from the communist party and arrested, together with his associate Pandi Kristo and dozens of others.[13]

* * *

With the Soviet ''advisers'' in charge of the Sigurimi, the character of the purge changed radically. Up to that time, show trials were unknown in the East European countries, even in Yugoslavia's subsatellite Albania. In the splintered Albanian communist movement, fraught with faction struggles, the archaic, vendetta-like tradition of a mountain people settled accounts with opponents in an especially brutal way, as the already-mentioned murders of Lulo, Fundo, and

Gjinishi prove. The purges in the Hoxha-Xoxe power struggle for the party leadership led to the imprisonment of opponents—not on trumped-up charges and with extorted false "confessions," but as actual exponents of the anti-Yugoslav faction. Nako Spiru's murder only proved the backwardness of Xoxe's secret police: They had not yet mastered the technique of murder through show trials, so they committed a common murder.

The purge of Xoxe had to be different; it had to fit into the general scenario prepared shortly before by Stalin and Beria. It was not enough to liquidate him— the Titoist Xoxe had to be made into a "Titoist" in quotation marks. He had to be shown not as head of the Yugoslav orientation in opposition to Hoxha's independent line, but as a common criminal, a traitor of his country, a tool of the imperialists. And above all, Xoxe should not be the main accused, but rather Tito, being "unmasked" through his Albanian ally as the arch-villain—the overall top agent of Western intelligence—an imperialist himself.

Koci Xoxe only partly fitted in Moscow's scenario of exposing Tito as the leader of a far-reaching East European anti-Soviet conspiracy in the service of the imperialist powers. He was Tito's man in Albania, a genuine Titoist; on the other hand, Enver Hoxha was also suspect. Quotation marks suited him even better, for his struggle for independence from foreign domination exhibited an ominous similarity to the roots of the Yugoslav-Soviet conflict. Furthermore, Albania had the big disadvantage of being far from the Soviet Union, surrounded by two neighbors hostile to Moscow, Yugoslavia, and Greece. Finally, Albania's insignificance and isolation had to be considered. The underdeveloped nation with a population of 1.2 million was a tiny dot on the European map, with no diplomatic relations to the Western world and almost no political or economic ties to any socialist state except Yugoslavia. There could hardly be any less suitable place to be chosen as a starting point in the Stalinist search for "Titoist subversion centers."

The Sigurimi, under the guidance of the MVD "teachers," did, however, as good a job as possible under the given circumstances. From the end of November 1948, Xoxe and his group were tortured day and night; it took the interrogators five months to break their resistance. By March 1949, the MVD could report to Stalin that the first incriminating "confessions" were signed. At the end of that month, Enver Hoxha was invited to Moscow to receive instructions on how to prepare the show trial along the prearranged lines.[14]

The trial of "Koci Xoxe and his gang" began on May 12, 1949, behind closed doors, surrounded by strict secrecy.[15] According to the indictment, the defendant conspired with Tito in the overthrow of the Albanian government, the murder of Enver Hoxha and other party leaders, the liquidation of Albania as a sovereign state, and its incorporation in Yugoslavia to form, on instructions of the Anglo-American imperialists, a united anti-Soviet bastion in the Balkans. Xoxe "admitted" that in the 1930s, he had been recruited by the monarchist police by King Zogu as an informer, and during the war, by the English and American intelligence agencies. The head of the British military mission in Albania divulged to him, in 1943, that Tito was their secret agent, and on the instruction of the British Secret Intelligence Service, he held numerous conspiratorial talks with the Macedonian Politburo member and imperialist spy Svetozar Vukmanović-Tempo. In those talks, it has been agreed that, after seizing power in both countries, Xoxe should steer the policy of the Albanian party in the direction to absorb Albania into Yugoslavia as its seventh federal republic.

With the help of the Politburo member Pandi Kristo, head of the Control Commission, he nominated his associates into leading positions and instructed Vargo Mitrojorji, chief of the State Security police, to arrest anti-Titoists. The task of Nosty Kerentyi, another Politburo member in charge of the State Planning Committee, had been to sabotage the economy and prepare its integration into the Yugoslav system. When, in the spring of 1948, the Soviet Central Committee began to criticize the Trotzkyist policy of the Yugoslav party, Tito instructed Xoxe to implement immediately the prearranged plans, and only the watchfulness of Enver Hoxha prevented, with the fraternal help of Stalin, the murder of the Albania party leader and the occupation of the country by Yugoslavia.

On July 8, 1949, a brief communique published in the press announced the verdict of the people's court: Xoxe was sentenced to death, Pandi Kristo received a sentence of twenty years of hard labor; and Nosty Kerentyi, Vargo Mitrojorji, Deputy Interior Minister Vaske Koletzki, and Central Committee propaganda head Huri Nota were sentenced to long prison terms. Xoxe was hanged a few days later.

Numerous smaller secret trials, in which hundreds of genuine and alleged Titoists were liquidated, accompanied the main trial, followed by a second "consolidating" purge with Politburo member Abedin Shehu as a central victim. Within a year, the whole Yugoslav wing of the Albanian party was in prison or in concentration camps, and the nationalist wing of Enver Hoxha fully in control.[16] The Soviet advisors did not know it yet, but they had helped another brand of "anti-Tito-Titoism" into power, which turned against them more than a decade later.[17]

* * *

"I just have to move my little finger and Tito is finished," Stalin boasted at the height of the Soviet-Yugoslav conflict. The Xoxe trial in Tirana was a substitute for the failed revenge in Belgrade. It served three purposes. First, it was meant as a warning to all potential insubordinates in the satellite countries: Anyone who tries to break away from Moscow or only to loosen their subservience or develop independent concepts will be dealt with similarly. Second, it attempted to brand anyone who displayed differences of opinion as a common criminal and/or an agent of imperialism, to distort tactical differences as betrayal, sabotage, and espionage. The third, immediate and preponderant purpose was to "unmask" Tito with the help of false, extorted confessions; Tito had to be proven not only a deviator from the single correct Moscow line, not only objectively a helper's helper of the anti-Soviet forces, but also subjectively a traitor, a conscious, old-time agent of the imperialists.

The Xoxe trial achieved its first goal to full extent; Tito's associates had to pay the price of death, imprisonment, and/or disgrace for their sympathies. The second and third points remained incomplete. Due to Albania's peripheral importance to the Soviet empire in Eastern Europe, a public show trial could not serve a useful purpose, and the secret proceedings, though a brutal, unmistakable warning for the satellite party leaders, deprived it of much of its broad propaganda value. Albania's geographical and political isolation led to a situation where no threads could be woven to other potential Titos—it had to remain a blind alley with no outlets to the East European satellites.

On May 18, 1949, six days after the opening of the Xoxe trial, the first arrests in Hungary were set in motion, and Xoxe was not yet hanged when in Bulgaria the purge began. The Rajk and Kostov trials were destined to complete the task. They constitute the real starting points of the East European show trials, with Hungary leading the way.

CHAPTER 3
THE KOSTOV TRIAL IN BULGARIA

Once the show trials in Yugoslavia's subsatellite, Albania, were ended, logic required that the next nation to undergo Stalin's postwar purge be Bulgaria—its Communist party being the one with the closest ties to Tito.

A federation uniting the two south Slav peoples of Yugoslavia and Bulgaria had long been a dream of liberals, socialists, and communists.[1] When the communists took over the governments of both nations, it appeared that a Balkan federation might at last become a reality. Not only would they be brought together under the dual banners of proletarian internationalism and Slav brotherhood, but such a solution would also solve a regional problem of long standing: what to do about the Macedonians. This Slav people with a separate culture and language had been divided between Bulgaria and Serbia at the end of the Second Balkan War, in 1913. Since that time, they had been a constant irritant, inflaming relations between the two nations. Both Tito and Georgi Dimitrov, the grand old man of Bulgarian communism, were enthusiastic promoters of such a federation, and Stalin also favored the plan at the end of World War II.[2] The reasons were twofold: The plan suited his own pan-Slav propaganda, and a union of communist Yugoslavia and communist Bulgaria seemed to him to offer a strong bulwark against British influence in the Balkans.

To this end, the Yugoslavs began negotiating with the Bulgarians in November 1944, when Edvard Kardelj, Tito's closest collaborator, traveled to Sofia for discussions with the new communist government, installed there just a few weeks previously. He proposed an immediate union of Bulgarian Macedonia with the Federal Macedonian Republic of Yugoslavia and the establishment in Belgrade of a committee of representatives of both countries to work out a system under which Bulgaria would become the seventh republic of a new federal socialist South Slav union. Understandably, the Bulgarians backed away from the plan, fearing that the Yugoslavs would swallow them up, and suggested instead a federation in which both nations would be on equal footing. Stalin backed the Yugoslavs, and the Bulgarians prepared to send a delegation to Belgrade to establish a joint regency council with Tito in the role of prime minister of the federation. Two hours before its scheduled departure time, the Soviets ordered the delegation to remain in Sofia; Great Britain had learned of the project and, together with the United States, intervened to halt the negotiations. In January 1945, Tito sent Moša Pijade to Moscow, where Stalin explained to him and Anton Yugov, the Bulgarian minister of the interior, the international implications of such a federation and ordered them to slow down the process of unification.[3]

But the plan for a Balkan federation had only been slowed, not halted. In June 1947, Dimitrov told the London *Daily Mail* that ". . . in accordance with the will of the Bulgarian people, I seek the conclusion of a treaty of friendship and mutual help with Yugoslavia which, naturally, will lead to economic, cultural and universal cooperation between the two countries." The treaty he envisioned was reached in July at a meeting between Tito and Dimitrov in Belgrade and signed on August 2. In a secret clause, published only after the Stalin-Tito rift, both countries agreed to establish a common nation under the name of the Union of the South Slav People's Republic. At the ratification ceremony in Sofia in November 1947, Tito was quite open about his eventual aims: "The cooperation between our two countries will be so general and so close that a federation will be a mere formality. We will create a great and strong South Slav union, for which no thunderstorm will be dangerous."

Tito and Dimitrov went beyond even this purpose in discussing their long-range goals. On January 17, 1948, Dimitrov told a press conference that "When the problem ripens, our people in Romania, Bulgaria, Yugoslavia, Albania, Czechoslovakia, Poland, Hungary and, perhaps, Greece, will themselves make the decisions. It is they who will decide whether or not it will be a federation or a confederation and when and how it will occur."

Stalin was furious. He read into Dimitrov's statement the nucleus of a Titoist strategy to build a socialist bloc independent of the Soviet Union, a challenge to his authority and to his determination that only he could make decisions involving the future of the communist world. On January 29, *Pravda* published a sharp disclaimer. "We do not share Comrade Dimitrov's opinion. On the contrary, we think that these countries don't need a problematic and forced federation or confederation . . ." On February 10, Stalin summoned the top Yugoslav and Bulgarian leaders to Moscow. Tito prudently remained at home and sent Kardelj and Djilas, but Dimitrov could not avoid attending in person. Stalin and Molotov attacked him sharply for planning a customs union with Romania and for not consulting the Soviet leaders beforehand and ordered him to halt immediately all plans for an East European federation. Stalin despised Dimitrov, but feared Tito. Suddenly, he instructed Yugoslavia and Bulgaria to unite without delay—a plan he had hitherto opposed, but now thought advisable in order to dilute Tito's strength and prestige. The once-defiant Dimitrov, now humiliated by his master, abjectly admitted his "errors" and promised to follow the "correct" line. Karelj and Djilas returned to Belgrade, where a Central Committee meeting of the communist party rejected the Soviet ultimatum for an immediate federation with

Bulgaria. The Soviet Union responded with a refusal to conclude a new trade agreement with Yugoslavia. Stalin decided that his rift with Tito could no longer be bridged.[4]

* * *

Stalin knew how to respond to the unfolding Yugoslav challenge: Nip it in the bud. He set out to liquidate anyone who might lead a rebellion against the policy of absolute primacy of Soviet policy. The possibility of a federated bloc extending from Poland in the northeast to Bulgaria in the southeast, as Dimitrov had described it, operating under Tito's leadership and responsive to the demands of its citizens, had to be countered by the elimination of any and all potentially independent leaders in the satellite parties. For this purpose, he reverted to a proven method, that of the show trials whose victims could be used to denounce the enemy—in this case, Tito. In May 1948, when the correspondence between the Soviet and Yugoslav parties indicated that Tito was not prepared to budge from his position, Stalin ordered Beria, minister of internal affairs and chief of the MVD, to ferret out "Tito's men" in the satellite countries and to prepare show trials for them.

Yugoslavia's subsatellite, Albania, offered few problems: Koci Xoxe was an obvious victim-designate. In each of the other countries, however, the leadership was faithful to Stalin. This did not faze Beria; if there were no "Titoists" already available, he was prepared to fabricate them.

As early as May 1948, the search for a "Bulgarian Tito" began in Sofia. The most likely candidate for the honor was Georgi Dimitrov, then sixty-three years old. Dimitrov, personally attached to Tito, might have had his personal doubts about Stalin, but he was no carbon copy of the Yugoslav leader. His nerve had been broken during long years as secretary-general of the Comintern in Moscow, where he functioned mainly as a figurehead of the international Communist movement under the constant surveillance of the secret police. There, he followed slavishly the intricate twists and turns of Stalin's policies, and observed with horror the bloody purges in the ranks of the Comintern. He saw, with his own eyes, the lethal consequences of any deviating thought and of even the slightest indication of displeasure in Stalin's expression. He was also well aware that his bodyguard and brother-in-law, Vulko Chervenkov, had been recruited by the secret police to spy on him.[5]

However, it would have been unthinkable for Stalin and Beria to put Dimitrov in the dock as a "Titoist conspirator" because the man was a hero of the entire antifascist world for his defiance of Goering in the Nazi courtroom during the Reichstag fire trial of 1933. He had the status of a demigod in Bulgaria and the respect of communists everywhere. So Stalin chose a much less obvious and more elegant way to dispose of him. In January 1949, Dimitrov disappeared from Sofia. Rumors said that he met Soviet Deputy Premier Andrei Vyshinsky at the airport and boarded the airplane to discuss some foreign policy matters, and that the door was locked behind him. There was silence on his fate until April, when a brief communique in the Bulgarian press informed the country that Dimitrov was ill and undergoing medical treatment in the Soviet Union. On July 2, 1949, he died in Moscow and was buried in a mausoleum in Sofia, embalmed by the same man who had preserved the corpse of Lenin.[6]

The remaining Bulgarian potential purge victims considered by Beria and Stalin were Vassil Kolarov, Anton Yugov, and Traicho Kostov. Kolarov was Dimitrov's most intimate friend. They participated together in the unsuccessful 1923 uprising and fled together to Moscow, where Kolarov occupied top positions in the Comintern as the leading member of its executive committee and head of its Balkan secretariat. After World War II, at the age of sixty-eight, he returned to Bulgaria as a member of the Politburo, deputy prime minister, and later, foreign minister. He was old, prematurely senile, suffering from disease of the heart and the liver, and was also a Muscovite. All in all, he did not seem to be a promising candidate for the leading role in a show trial.

The choice was thus narrowed to the two "home communists," Yugov and Kostov. Both had long histories as leaders of the anti-Nazi underground movement. In the communist-dominated Fatherland Front government, Yugov was appointed minister of the interior, and his state security police, organized and directed by Soviet advisers, launched a ferocious hunt for real and alleged "enemies of the people," a bloodbath unparalleled elsewhere in the satellite countries. It was estimated that as many as 100,000 people were killed during the first four years of his reign. He was hated and feared through Bulgaria, and his fall would have been a popular move among the masses.

The final choice was made easy for Beria by his eventual victim, Kostov, at first glance an unlikely candidate since he was known to be a faithful Stalinist who opposed Tito from the beginning and unquestioningly followed Soviet directives.[7] His principal responsibility was the Bulgarian economy. In the course of the tripartite conference, held in Moscow in February 1948, which discussed the possibility of a Yugoslav-Bulgarian federation, he complained to Stalin about some stipulations in the Soviet-Bulgarian technical assistance agreement, which he felt were unfavorable to his country. Stalin got angry at Kostov for criticizing the Soviet Union and diverting the discussion from the differences in foreign policy to, as he said, "minor matters of economic details."[8]

Stalin did not forget. When he ordered Beria to eliminate "Titoists" three months later, he mentioned Kostov's critical complaint. Beria asked for Kostov's file, thick with intelligence reports from his brother-in-law Chervenko and other MVD agents who had infiltrated the Bulgarian party. He found a previous "anti-Soviet sabotage act" that had occurred when Kostov discovered that the Soviet Union was purchasing Bulgarian tobacco and attar of roses and undercutting the Bulgarians on the world market. To stop this practice, Kostov, in the fall of

1947, ordered that the Law for Safeguarding State Secrets, which forbade divulging confidential economic information to foreign countries, be applied to the Soviet Union in the same way it was applied to other foreign states.[9]

For Beria, this completed the case. There was only one minor problem. Kostov was known to be the principal opponent within the Bulgarian party to Tito's plan for a South Slav union. He feared that under the plan, Yugoslavia would be the dominating partner. Dimitrov tried to dispel his mistrust, but failed. Kostov was one of the Bulgarian delegates to the Bucharest Cominform meeting of July 1948, at which Tito was excommunicated from the Soviet bloc. Until his arrest and even on the stand at his trial, Kostov continued to attack Tito, repeating faithfully the Soviet charges against the Yugoslav leader.

The mistrust was mutual. Tito disliked Kostov, and in a speech in April 1949, he delivered a shameful denunciation of his Bulgarian comrade just two months before Kostov's arrest. "Kostov was arrested during the reign of King Boris together with a number of other Communists. Although he was one of the main leaders of the party, his life alone was spared. Why?" Tito answered his own question. "Today we have proof that among some Communist parties, certain capitalist states infiltrated their own agents."[10]

Kostov's anti-Tito attitudes were, however, no serious obstacle to Beria, who knew very well how to transform a Stalinist into a "Titoist agent." The script, prepared in Moscow, provided the outlines of future show trials. Kostov was to "confess" to a Titoist plot which aspired to restore capitalism to a federated south Slav system and to "unmask" Tito as an imperialist agent. Beria left to Chervenkov and his MDV advisers the problem of working out the details, together with a list of prospective members of Kostov's "spy ring." The details and the names were sent to Beria, who reviewed, wrote, and approved them. In May 1949 all was ready, but the Bulgarian Fatherland Front elections delayed matters to the point where an impatient Stalin summoned Chervenkov to the Kremlin and gave him orders to proceed immediately with the liquidation of Kostov and his "gang."

* * *

Traicho Kostov, born in 1897, had been a high school teacher in Radomir. Together with Georgi Dimitrov, he was one of the founders of the Bulgarian communist party and, since 1924, a member of its Central Committee. In that year, he was arrested by the police and tortured so cruelly that, fearing he might betray his comrades, he threw himself out of a fourth floor window of police headquarters. He broke both his legs and, for the rest of his life, was a hunchback. After being released in 1929, he worked for two years in Moscow as an official of the Comintern's Balkan Secretariat. Back in Bulgaria, he became a member of the party's Politburo and organized the partisan struggle against the Nazis during World War II. In 1942 he was arrested again, together with five other prominent party leaders. The five were condemned to death and he alone received a life sentence, the circumstance referred to by Tito. Two years later, he was freed from prison by the partisans and was elected secretary-general, the highest post in the party, a position he handed over to Dimitrov when the latter returned from the Soviet Union. Kostov remained the second most powerful individual in Bulgaria, next to Dimitrov, whose successor he was assumed to be. In December 1948, the same month that Dimitrov left or was forced to leave for the Soviet Union, Kostov disappeared from public view.

By that time, the MVD and the Bulgarian security police were busy preparing the show trial. Political conditions were also being established for the change in Bulgarian leadership. Chervenkov was suddenly elevated to the position of act- ing secretary-general of the party, replacing Dimitrov. Kolarov became prime minister, and an inner cabinet was formed consisting of those two and Yugov, whose Ministry of the Interior and security apparatus were firmly in the hands of Soviet advisors and agents. Kolarov, seventy-two years old, had been reduced to a figurehead, a mouthpiece for Chervenkov, now the sole master of the party.

In a series of secret Central Committee meetings that began in January 1949, Kostov was sharply attacked for his "nationalistic deviations" and pressured to offer an "unsparing self-criticisms." It was not, however, his humiliation but his blood that they were after.[11] On March 26 and 27, at a Central Committee plenum, Kostov was condemned for anti-Soviet attitudes and for applying Bul- garia's laws forbidding the transmission of state secrets to the Soviet Union. In a unanimously approved resolution, he was accused of fostering a nationalistic line, of violating the principle of collective leadership, of fanning a fractional struggle within the party, of intriguing against Dimitrov, and of sowing distrust between the Bulgarian and Soviet communist parties. It was decided to remove him from the Politburo and to dismiss him from his posts of deputy prime minister and president of the State Economic Council.[12]

Kostov remained, however, a member of the Central Committee and in April was appointed director of the National Library, an obvious insult. He tried to fight back. He appealed to the Politburo and wrote to Stalin in a desperate effort to refute the charges of anti-Soviet activities, but his letters were never answered. At the end of May 1949, with preparations for the show trial completed, Cher- venkov went to Moscow to discuss them with Stalin and Beria for their final approval. The ill Dimitrov was never even consulted.[13]

On June 11, a showdown meeting of the Central Committee was held at which Kolarov said, "A number of new and very grave elements in the anti-party activity of Kostov have been revealed." He was accused of having disrupted the collectivization of agriculture, of plotting against Dimitrov, of undermining the unity of the party, and by refusing to acknowledge some of his errors, of having sought to conceal the grave harm he caused to the party and to Soviet-Bulgarian relations.

"There can be no doubt about the kinship linking Traicho Kostov's errors with treacherous Titoism," said Kolarov. "He has become a banner of international reaction, the miserable remnants of the defeated monarcho-fascist clique and all the reactionaries unite under him. Today his name is synonymous with everything hostile to our Party."

Not surprisingly, the Central Committee decided unanimously to strip Kostov from all of his party and state positions and to expel him from the party.

Kostov did not take part in the meeting; he had been arrested the previous night. This was not made known until July 20, when a brief communique of the Ministry of the Interior announced that he was being detained on charges of economic sabotage and espionage for imperialist powers.[14]

*　*　*

On the night of his arrest, Kostov was taken to the headquarters of the State Security police and placed inside a special, hermetically sealed cell with one window located at the top of a wall. Through this window, a firehose poured ice-cold water. Kostov was threatened with drowning unless he agreed to confess to his spying activities.[15] Thus began a four-month period during which ceaseless interrogations were interrupted only for barbarous tortures conducted by Yugov's security police, guided by Soviet MVD advisers. Only at the beginning of October did they succeed in breaking his will and obtaining his signature to a first, preliminary "confession."

Together with Kostov, about 200 persons were arrested, most of them high functionaries in the party and government who had had contacts with Kostov, official dealings with the Yugoslavs, or who were involved in the Bulgarian-Soviet trade negotiations. They, too, were tortured until they agreed to confess to their assigned roles in the imaginary Titoist conspiracy. From among these, the stage managers of the show trial selected ten of the most docile and willing prisoners and, after breaking Kostov's resistance, began to teach them their lines for the public trial. They had to learn by heart the testimony incriminating themselves and their fellow accused and they rehearsed it under the supervision of Soviet advisers.[16] All of them except Kostov were promised light sentences and readmission to the party in some distant future if they followed their scripts.

Early in November, the final drafts of the indictments were submitted first to Beria and then to the special investigating commission of the Bulgarian Central Committee, headed by Chervenkov. These were published on November 28 and the show trial was ready to begin.

*　*　*

The trial began on December 7, 1949, and concluded on December 14. It took place in the Central Home of the People's Army Hall in Sofia. Militiamen surrounded the building, keeping the public away from the courtroom, which was packed with secret policemen and selected delegations from factories and collective farms. The proceedings were broadcast by radio.[17]

In addition to Kostov, there were ten principal defendants, the most prominent of who was Ivan Stefanov, the minister of finance. In the 1920s he lived in exile, first in Berlin and Paris, and then in the Soviet Union. He had the misfortune of being related to an important Bulgarian communist, Khristian Rakovsky, who was purged in the trial of Bukharin in 1938. Stefanov returned to Bulgaria in 1929 and became a member of the party's Central Committee.

The remaining Central Committee members who stood trial with Kostov included Nikola Pavlov, deputy minister of construction, and Vassil Ivanovsky, head of the propaganda section. Five of the accused held important positions in economic areas. They were Nicola Nachev, assistant president of the Economic Council; Boris Andronov Khristov, trade attache in Moscow; Tsoniu Stefanov Tzonchev, governor of the national bank; Ivan Slavov Gevrenov, section head in the Ministry of Industry; and Ivan Georgiev Tutev, department chief in the Ministry of Foreign Trade. The two remaining defendants held a special place in the trial. Ilya Ivanon Bayaltsaliev, secretary of the Union of Construction Workers, spent the war years as political commissar with the Bulgarian partisans fighting the Germans and worked closely with Tito's Yugoslav partisans. Blagoy Ivanov Hadji-Panzov, a Macedonian, served in 1947 as counselor at the Yugoslav embassy in Sofia. After the Stalin-Tito break, he defected to Bulgaria and, under the supervision of the MVD and the Soviet ambassador in Sofia, was used for propaganda purposes to expose Tito as a tool of the imperialists.

In the show trial, facts and persons were turned upside down. The anti-Tito defector Hadji-Panzov became an agent of the Titoists. Dimitrov was described as a foe instead of a friend of Tito. Devoted, fanatical communists were politically transposed into informers for the facist police and spies for the imperialists. Above all, the "confessions" were used to "prove" that Yugoslav leaders— Tito, Kardelj, Djilas, Ranković and others—were nothing less than anglo-American stooges, the principal tools in a plot to overthrow the Bulgarian people's democracy and alienate it from the Soviet Union.

The scenario of the Kostov trial was a somewhat narrowed-down version of the Rajk trial in Hungary that had been staged three months previously. It focused on the two south Slav nations in contrast with the more general scope of the Hungarian trial with its broad ramifications for all of the satellite countries. First, the reputation of Kostov was demolished. He was turned into a Trotzkyist, "left sectarian" traitor who, as early as 1930, collaborated with the Comintern leaders Béla Kún and Valecki, murdered in the prewar Soviet purges. In 1942, the indictment read, Kostov was enrolled in the service of the Bulgarian monarchist police. In 1944, he was recruited by the British diplomats Colonel Bailey and General Oxley, and afterwards by the U.S. Ambassador Donald Reed Heath, as an agent of those nations' intelligence services. Later, the role of spymaster was given over by the Americans to the Yugoslavs, who instructed Kostov to plot for the annexation of Bulgaria as the seventh federal republic of a Titoist south Slav union; to sabotage the economic and political relations between the Soviet Union and Bulgaria; and to eliminate or, if necessary, to murder Dimitrov. The particulars of this "conspiracy" paralleled almost exactly their counterparts in the Rajk trial in Hungary; only the names were different—a crude confirmation of their common authorship in Moscow.

The narrower parameters in the Bulgarian trial and its restriction to a joint Titoist-imperialist conspiracy against Bulgaria can be explained by the different historical backgrounds of the two countries. Between the two world wars, the Bulgarian communists had much less contact with the West than did their Hungarian, Polish, Czechoslovak, or German comrades. For Bulgarian party members, when threatened by arrest and execution for clandestine activities or for participation in the International Brigade in Spain, the center of exile was not England or France but the nearby Soviet Union, where they could easily understand the language and join an already strong Bulgarian leadership in the Comintern. There was no Bulgarian government-in-exile in London during the war, nor was there an exile organization in Switzerland. Bulgarians did not join the French resistance movement, but that of the neighboring partisans.

The personality of Dimitrov also led to important procedural differences in the Kostov trial as compared to that in Hungary and those that followed. His friendship with Tito and his endorsement of a Balkan federation delayed the preparations for the Bulgarian trial until he was removed to Moscow and confined to a hospital. Until his death, Dimitrov refused all pressures from Chervenkov and Beria to implicate Kostov, his closest collaborator for thirty years. He knew he would die soon of his illness and he had nothing to lose by refusing to play along with Kostov's enemies. The Kostov trial, which should have taken place before that of Rajk, had to be postponed and remained a dead end, leading to no further developments in the satellite empire.

The most striking difference, however, was Kostov's retraction of his "confession" during his trial.

"Citizen Judges! I plead guilty to having had an incorrect attitude toward the Soviet Union, expressed in the methods of bargaining I employed in our commercial dealings with the USSR, by concealing certain prices arranged with the capitalist countries, and by applying the State Secret Laws to Soviet representatives. . . . These make me guilty of a nationalist deviation which merits a severe punishment," he began his testimony.

He went on to speak harshly of himself for showing a "liberal attitude" regarding anti-Soviet remarks made in his presence and for unjustly criticizing Dimitrov. Even these "confessions" of Kostov's were an obvious departure from the previously memorized text that had already been distributed to the court, and the nervous president of the tribunal tried to lead him back to the original lines.

"Kostov, in the indictment which you just heard, you were accused of crimes committed in April and May of 1942 in the service of the fascist police. What explanation can you give me on this matter?''

The reply came as a bombshell.

''I can tell you. I do not plead guilty to having capitulated before the fascist police, or to having been recruited as an agent in the Intelligence Service, nor to conspiratorial activities in collaboration with Tito and his clique. . . . I retract my statements made during the interrogation.''

As Kostov went on denying the charges, the president of the tribunal ordered the guards to remove him from the courtroom and instructed the court to proceed with the reading of Kostov's ''confessions'' made under torture during the interrogations.

On December 14, 1949, when the accused were called upon to deliver their final words, Kostov again refused to play the game according to the MVD's script.

''I consider it as a duty to my conscience to declare before this court and through it to Bulgarian public opinion, that I was never in the service of British intelligence, never participated in the conspiratorial and criminal plans of Tito and his clique, that I always acted as a communist, always respected and esteemed the Soviet Union . . .'' Again, Kostov was seized by the guards and removed from the courtroom.

But his retraction remained an exception. The trial continued smoothly with the ''confessions'' of all the other defendants; the statement of the fifty-one ''witnesses,'' some of whom were convicted fascist criminals and some tortured and broken communists dragged out of the state security cells awaiting their own show trial. The speeches of the defense attorneys, chosen and coached by the security services, repeated the charges made by the prosecution and Kostov's attorney, a Dr. Lubin Dukmedjiev, did not even mention the fact that his client had retracted his ''written confession.''

The court's verdict had been decided upon by Stalin, Beria, and Chervenkov before the trial began. All of the defendants were found guilty. Kostov was sentenced to death; Stefanov and Pavlov to life sentences; Nachev, Tsoniu Tzonchev, Slavov, Georgiev, and Hadji-Panzov received fifteen-year terms; Andonov and Atanasov 12 years; and Bayaltsaliev, eight years of close confinement.

In his death cell the day after the verdict, Kostov was visited by Chervenkov, who assured him that the Bulgarian and Soviet leaders were aware of his innocence and appealed to his conscience as a communist to take back his retraction, promising to spare his life. Kostov agreed and addressed a plea for clemency to the presidium of the National Assembly: ''. . . I plead guilty to the accusations . . . and fully confirm the depositions written in my own hand during the inquiry. . . . I regret sincerely my conduct before the court which was the result of extremely exicted nerves and the pathologic self-love of an intellectual. . . . I beg you to revoke the death sentence and to commute it to close confinement for life."

The next day, on December 16, on the order of Chervenkov, Kostov's petition was rejected and he was hanged.

* * *

The eleven initial victims were only the visible tip of the iceberg. A long series of secret trials followed involving about two hundred communist defendants, from leading party and government officials down to insignificant "co-conspirators" in the Macedonian and Yugoslav-Bulgarian organizations. Arrested and tried as "fascist police informers, imperialist spies and Titoist agents" were, among others, two members of the Politburo, Professor Petko Kunin, minister of industry, and Georgi Ganev, director of State Security; the organization secretary of the Central Committee, Ivan Maslarov; two department heads in the State Security, colonels Stefan Bogdanov and Nikola Zadgorsky; the head of army intelligence, Peter Vranchev; the minister of electrification, Lyubomir Bozhilov; the minister of railways, posts and telegraph, Stefan Tonchev; and five deputy ministers in the departments of foreign affairs, transport and internal trade.[18]

Chervenkov planned to follow the Kostov trial with another major courtroom drama in which the two leading "home communists," Dobri Terpeshev and Anton Yugov, would have been the stars in the dock. Terpeshev was the wartime commander of the Bulgarian partisan units, a member of the Central Committee and the Politburo, and at the time of the preparations for the Kostov trial was made vice premier. Yugov, the interior minister, Beria's tool in the security apparatus, was responsible not only for the liquidation of anticommunists, but took a significant role in the preparations for the Kostov trial, in the selection of those to be arrested and in the interrogation and even the torture of the victims.

At the Central Committee meeting on January 6, 1950, Chervenkov attacked both Terpeshev and Yugov for the "lack of vigilance" and their blindness toward the anti-Soviet, treacherous activities of Kostov and his gang. By tolerating the conspirators in their midst, Chervenkov said, they became objectively associated in Kostov's guilt. The speech had the ominous ring of a prelude to a new purge with trumped-up charges. But at this point, Stalin intervened. He wanted show trials, but only on his own terms. Thus the protecting arm of Stalin saved Yugov and Terpeshev and they got off after performing "self-criticism." Terpeshev was removed from the Politburo and both lost their jobs as deputy premiers and were demoted to lesser positions in the government.[19]

With the conclusion of the Kostov trial, the Bulgarian purges had accomplished their objectives. The scene of the show trials now moved from south to central and eastern Europe, from Albania and Bulgaria to Hungary, Czechoslovakia, East Germany, and Poland.

CHAPTER 4
THE FIELD CONNECTION

The Rajk trial in Hungary was the first pure postwar show trial in Eastern Europe. It served as a model for all the satellite countries. Representatives of the security services of Poland, Czechoslovakia, and East Germany came to Budapest to study its organization and procedure.

It was in Budapest that the legend of Noel Field was first created—the master spy from the United States who, during the war, recruited communists in exile for the U.S. espionage network and who ended up serving as liaison between the imperialists and Tito in order to undermine the east European communist parties. The fiction of Noel Field resulted in death and imprisonment for hundreds of communists in Hungary, Bulgaria, Romania, Poland, Czechoslovakia, and East Germany. Additional thousands of people fell victim to the charge of being friends, acquaintances, or fellow workers with people who knew Field.[1] The Field fiction provided the initial impetus for the Prague show trials and its ominous shadows spread over those in Warsaw and East Berlin. The name of Field was used when an attempt was made to put a noose around the neck of Gomułka and in preparing the gallows for the leading East German communists Paul Merker and Franz Dahlem.

In the latter cases, however, the executioners had run out of time. The death sentences in the Slánský trial were announced on November 27, 1952. Four months later, on March 5, 1953, Stalin died, and in December his chief hangman, Beria, was executed as a British spy. From the Soviet Union, preoccupied with the struggle for succession, came the orders for Ulbricht in the German Democratic Republic and for Bierut in Poland to halt the proceedings. The Field avalanche, started in Budapest, was slowed and later completely halted, and with it the succession of murderous postwar show trials.

* * *

The story of Noel Haviland Field is part of one of the most exciting, darkest, and hopeless periods of world history.[2] He was born in London, on January 23, 1904, the son of Dr. Herbert Haviland Field, scion of a respected Quaker family in the United States and a man with an international reputation as a biologist.

Field spent his childhood and youth in Zurich, where his father directed an international scientific bibliographic institute. During World War I, Dr. Field, faithful to the Quaker tradition, headed an organization that sent food to the hungry people of Europe. After the armistice, President Wilson appointed him a member of a U.S. committee charged with the preparation of the peace treaty. Neither peace nor work in the service of the persecuted were abstract ideas for the young Noel Field. They were the examples he saw in his own home, a part of the very air he breathed.

In 1921, following the death of his father, the family resettled in the United States, where Noel studied political science at Harvard. Obtaining his Ph.D. in 1926, he went to work for the State Department where, in the West European division, he was primarily occupied with matters concerning the League of Nations. One year later, he married his childhood girlfriend from Zurich, Herta Vieser. To the end, she shared his turbulent and tragic fate.

Field's subsequent office career was uneventful. He was promoted in 1930 to the post of senior economic advisor to the Western European Affairs Division. In 1936, he was transferred to Geneva as a delegate in the disarmament division of the Secretariat of the League of Nations. Two years later, Field was sent to Spain with a League of Nations committee to oversee the repatriation of foreign participants in the civil war. Disillusioned with the league because of its inability to prevent the defeat of the Spanish republic and the aggression of Hitler, he resigned in 1940, ending his career in the service of the United States government.

At the end of 1940, Noel and Herta Field took over joint direction of the Marseilles office of the Unitarian Service Committee (USC) and two years later, after the Germans had occupied Vichy, France, he became the USC's European director with an office in Geneva, Switzerland. The Unitarian Church has a centuries-old tradition of assistance to the poor, the oppressed, and the disenfranchised and the organization performed exemplary work in war-torn Europe. After their experiences with an impotent State Department and a bureaucratic League of Nations, the Fields felt that at last they had an opportunity, within the modest limits of the USC, to be of effective help to the victims of Nazism; they could allay hunger, find new homes for refugees and save people from the concentration camps, the brutalities of the Gestapo and the execution squads of Germany and its allies.

The war exhausted the slim financial resources of the USC and, in 1947, the office in Geneva was closed. The Fields were offered positions in Boston, but they declined in the hope of remaining in Europe. They counted on the many antifascists they had aided in times of trouble, many of whom had attained prominent political positions in central and East European countries, to find Noel a post at a university or research center. The communists were willing to help, but at the same time they were evasive and cautious in their dealings with him.

The Soviet occupation authorities, who had the final word on the Fields' request, would not even talk with him.

In his search for meaningful work, Field traveled from East Berlin to Prague, and from there to Warsaw. For a while, he looked around in Paris and finally, on May 5, 1949, he returned to Prague. On May 11, he simply disappeared from the Palace Hotel. Friends who came to inquire about him were told at the reception desk that no such person was registered there. His wife, Herta, who was in Geneva at the time, flew to Prague at the end of July to find out what had happened to him. She also stayed at the Palace Hotel. On August 26, she, too, disappeared without a trace.

Two weeks before her disappearance, Herta met Noel's younger brother, Hermann, in Prague. He, too, was searching for his brother. Unsuccessful, he proceeded to Warsaw, but there too he ran against complete silence. He prepared to return to Prague. He took a taxi to the airport, passed through customs and passport control, and vanished. The plane arrived in Prague, but nobody saw him leave the terminal. His name never appeared on the passenger manifest.

Hermann Field was a successful architect, uninvolved in world politics until the partition of Czechoslovakia in 1938. At the time he lived in London and, through the offices of his wife, Kate, who was working for British Trust, a small liberal aid organization, he was sent to Cracow, Poland, to organize an escape route for antifascists in danger of their lives. The route led from Czechoslovakia through Poland to London. When Hitler invaded Poland, Hermann Field's short excursion into active politics ended, not to be resumed until ten years later when history again overtook him and he disappeared through the dark trapdoor on Stalin's stage.

During the Spanish Civil War, Noel and Herta Field became friendly with a family named Glaser. He was a German medical doctor working in a hospital attached to the International Brigade. When the Brigade retreated during the final collapse of the Loyalist forces, their daughter, Erica, seventeen years old, fell ill and was separated from her parents. The Fields located her in one of the receiving camps along the French-Spanish border and brought her with them to Switzerland, treating her as if she was their own child.

In Switzerland, Erica joined the antifascist movement, participating in the activities of the German emigré group and, through it, coming to know members of a similar Hungarian group. When the war ended, she moved to the U.S. zone of Germany and got a job with the knowledge and consent of the communist party in the Office of Strategic Services (OSS), the forerunner of the CIA. Two years later, she left the OSS and openly joined the German communist party, working as secretary for the communist representatives in the Hesse Regional Parliament and helping edit the party journal.

Within a few months, she fell in love with Robert Wallach, a U.S. Army captain. When her superiors in the party objected to the relationship, Erica severed her connection with the party and the young couple moved to Paris from where, at the end of 1947, she was refused admission to the United States because of her communist past. She heard in Paris of the disappearance of her foster parents and of Hermann Field, and on August 26, 1950, traveled to East Berlin on the chance that, through old friends from Switzerland, she might learn of their fate. On leaving party headquarters in the eastern sector of the city, without having obtained any answers to her questions, she was arrested on the streets. She, too, vanished.

Now let us return to Noel Field, "agent of the American espionage organization, who smuggled his spies into the top ranks of the Communist parties in order to topple the socialist system in the service of the imperialists and Tito," as was stated during the East European show trials. Who, in fact, was Noel Field? He was, without a doubt, a sensitive, honest idealist—a good man, to use this regrettably unfashionable term. Peace, truth, a sense of responsibility, and a willingness to help others were not, for him, empty slogans to be used to further his career; they were the very purpose of his life. All who knew him are agreed on this description of his character—friends and enemies alike.

In evaluating his political role, however, opinions vary. Was Field a communist? Without a doubt, he was, and it is immaterial whether or not he was formally a member of the party. Certainly no one could have doubted his political loyalties after the collapse of the Spanish republic and the victory of Franco. As USC director in Switzerland, he considered the aiding of antifascist, mostly communist refugees to be a primary responsibility, alongside the task of cooperating with anti-Hitler underground movements.

Was Field an agent, and if so, for whom? Might he have been a double agent in the service of both the Soviet and U.S. intelligence systems? Flora Lewis, the New York *Times* columnist, has written a book about Field, *The Red Pawn*. She studied innumerable documents, interviewed every acquaintance of the Fields she could locate and came to the conclusion that, by 1935, Field had been enlisted in the Soviet Secret Service while he was living in the United States. She believes that from time to time, he furnished them with reports from the State Department. However, some of her sources are rather suspect. She bases her allegations on the confessions of J. B. Matthews, who was one of the least reliable witnesses before the House Un-American Activities Committee. Another of her sources was Hede Massing, who for many years served as a courier for one of the Soviet spy organizations and who, at the time of the McCarthy era, tried to atone for past sins by providing lengthy and made-up lists of alleged Soviet spies. Another "proof" offered by Lewis is the fact that the Fields and Alger Hisses were close friends.

The truth might be less sinister. In the 1930s, Field belonged to circles in which young government employees were looking with increasing sympathy to the Soviet Union as the only power willing and able to prevent the threatened outbreak of another world war, following the fascist victory in Spain. Nearly all of these "premature antifascists," as they were called after the McCarthy era, were named on the lists of professional informers like Matthews, Massing or Whittaker Chambers. It was quite natural that the name of Field would also appear on them.

During the war, a number of Soviet espionage agents were active in neutral Switzerland primarily, of course, in pursuit of military intelligence. The most successful network was led by a Hungarian emigré communist Sándor Radó, who after the war was called to Moscow and arrested. He was released only at the end of the 1950s. The Russians were not interested in Field, who had been aiding emigré communists. Had they asked him to provide information about fascists, Field would have aided them in good conscience, but the role of enlisted agent was totally foreign to his character.[3]

His attitude regarding the U.S. intelligence services was similar. From the time of his service with the State Department, Field knew Allen Dulles, who during the war headed the European operations of the OSS, within the framework of the embassy in Berne. The two men renewed their acquaintance in Switzerland, but the supposition that Field was an OSS agent existed only in the warped minds of Stalin's propagandists.

*　　*　　*

Noel Field and the other victims of Stalin's crimes had long since been rehabilitated and the crimes themselves exposed when, in 1974, a British journalist, Stewart Steven, authored a book, *Operation Splinter Factor*. With it, there developed a new Field legend, that Field had been a tool at the hands of Dulles and that the postwar terror was a deliberate provocation engineered by the Central Intelligence Agency.[4]

Steven's story begins factually enough with a 1929 meeting in Washington between Field and Dulles, when both men were preparing position papers for the London Conferences on Naval Disarmament. Fourteen years later, they met again in Switzerland and agreed to collaborate to their mutual advantage. Dulles, then the head of the OSS, used Field and his intimate connections with left-wing and communist groups in Switzerland, German-occupied Europe, and even Germany itself, to gather valuable, otherwise inaccessible political intelligence. Field used Dulles as a source of money and connections to finance the communist underground and to help antifascist refugees in the camps. Both were authorized by their superiors to continue the collaboration, Dulles with Washington and Field—through Swiss and German exile intermediaries—with the communist movement. Neither was squeamish in choosing allies for the common goal of victory over Hitler and his satellites.

Steven calls attention to two instances of joint action, both in December 1944. The Hungarian communist group in Switzerland, headed by Tibor Szőnyi, decided to return to partially liberated Hungary. Field contacted Dulles, who agreed to furnish money, U.S. and Yugoslav uniforms, and letters of recommendation so that they could be smuggled through France, Italy, and Yugoslavia to Hungary. The other joint operation involved parachuting German antifascists into Germany to organize resistance against the disintegrating Nazi administration. The persons in the group included communists suggested by Field.

At this point, Steven's report moves away from historical fact and introduces half-truths and distortions. He claims that Dulles felt he had been duped by Field, who was not a simple humanitarian but a devious communist, betraying his trust and embarrassing him severely in Washington by tricking him into actions that placed communists in power in Germany, Hungary, and Czechoslovakia. Dulles, according to Steven, did not forget this and vowed revenge.

The opportunity to settle accounts, wrote Steven, came in 1949. Dulles was now the head of the CIA, and he conceived a plan, code-named Splinter Factor, that would drive a wedge between Moscow and its satellites, foment a split inside the communist parties in Eastern Europe between nationalists or liberals and orthodoxes. The national communists, so Dulles is said to have argued, were even more dangerous to the cause of Western democracy than were the hard-line Stalinists; if the liberals were to gain a foothold in eastern Europe, then communism could be perceived in France and Italy as a tolerable, even respectable force that might be elected to the control of either or both governments.

Consequently, according to Steven, Dulles decided that the liberals must be compromised and the Stalinists provoked to such repression and terror that the masses would revolt and the giant monolith be splintered. To do this, he had to invent fictitious U.S. spies within the communist parties to trigger the terror. For this, Noel Field was an ideally situated tool. He had to be denounced to Moscow as a top U.S. spy who infiltrated his agents into high positions in party and government. This would, of course, accomplish the secondary goal of destroying Field and avenging his war-time affront to Dulles.

In Steven's scenario, the role of informer was given to Jozef Światło, a deputy director in the Polish secret police. In his account, Światło contacted the British Secret Intelligence Service (SIS) in 1948 and told them that he wanted to defect to the West. The British were skeptical and the SIS handed the case over to the CIA. Dulles, said Steven, was delighted. He sent word to Światło to postpone his defection and directed him to denounce top party leaders as U.S. agents, uncover a major Titoist-Trotzkyist conspiracy, financed and organized by the United States all over Eastern Europe, and expose Noel Field as the vital link between the traitors and the imperialists.

Światło took this information to Lavrenti Beria, head of the Soviet secret police, the MVD, who submitted it immediately to Stalin himself. He, in turn, found the report so frightening that he ordered the destruction of Field and the nest of vipers he controlled. He then ordered General Fyodor Byelkin, head of the southeast European section of the MVD, to purge the satellite parties of all spies and Titoists.

Steven claims that Światło remained the mover of Operation Splinter Factor. He denounced to Byelkin, Tibor Szőnyi, and László Rajk as Field's Hungarian stooges. After they were arrested in Budapest, he pressured Mátyás Rákosi, secretary-general of the Hungarian communist party, to implicate the Czechoslovak party leaders in the conspiracy. Światło furnished damaging information to the East German security organs about a "Fieldist network" and personally conducted the arrest and interrogation in Poland, first of Hermann Field, then of the "Fieldists" and "Titoists" like General Marian Spychalski and Wladisław Gomułka.

It is simply astonishing that a trained and experienced journalist like Stewart Steven could give credence to such a story. Particularly questionable is his political sophistication. There is a degree of naiveté in statements like "The peoples of eastern Europe welcomed the Red Army as liberators," or "The British secret service agents helped incite anti-Semitic demonstrations" in Poland; there is an uncritical acceptance of false assumptions about political differences between the Muscovites and the "home communists." He repeats insinuations of a possible "double game" and he offers denunciatory hints of treason, as in his sentence, "Men given high government and Party posts as respected communists had, in fact, been introduced into the prewar illegal communist parties as agents and provocateurs; others had become agents of the (fascist) secret police after arrest and perhaps torture." Many more examples could be cited in which facts were distorted and Stalinist falsifications accepted at face value.[5]

Unproven also is the key to his central thesis, that Jozef Światło was a double agent, who from 1948 until his defection to the West in December 1953, carried out Operation Splinter Factor for his spymaster, Allen Dulles.[6] No one, except of course the Polish government, has publicly accused Światło of having been a U.S. agent. He was the most ruthless investigator and torturer of the Polish secret police, but he remained totally under the control of the Soviet MVD and his superior, Colonel Anatol Fejgin. Given the rigid hierarchy of the security organs, his alleged direct contacts with Beria would hardly have been possible. His ultimate defection was for a much simpler reason than that stated by Steven. With Beria already executed in the Soviet Union and the head of Hungarian security, Gábor Péter, under arrest, Krushchev had begun to pressure the satellite parties to review the show trials and investigate the possible involvement of the secret police in "breaches of Socialist legality." Światło preferred not to wait for the outcome and chose instead a secure and materially profitable life in the United States.

Steven's book is politically significant because it was the first, and is still the only, attempt to describe and explain the period of the East European show trials.

That is also why it is politically dangerous and damaging. It was a bestseller in Britain and the United States, and was translated into German and French. His version of the show trials was adopted by several subsequent students of the time who wrote books on Dulles and the CIA. The principal reason for its success was that the subject of dirty tricks on the part of the CIA was of much interest at the time his book appeared and to have produced a mass slaughter of communists in Eastern Europe seemed, to many, to be the ultimate dirty trick. His thesis of U.S. responsibility appealed to some leftists who found in it a politically suitable interpretation of the never-fully-explained show trials. The book also had the immense advantage of being a well-written spy book with real actors and real events.

Stewart Steven's book is dangerous precisely because of its enticing mixture of fact and fiction. Undoubtedly, there was a CIA disinformation campaign as is practiced all the time by intelligence agencies; there might even have been one named Operation Splinter Factor, and it is even conceivable that Światło might have been used in it.[7] Efforts to drive a wedge between the Soviet Union and its satellites, to divide the Muscovites from the "home communists" are nothing new. Steven cites a number of examples of these: the 1949 stories planted in U.S. and British newspapers about an expected defection of the foreign minister of Czechoslovakia, Vladimir Clementis, and a speech by Secretary of State John Foster Dulles, brother of Allen, mentioning a covert operation to penetrate the ruling circles of the satellites, cited with great relish by the Hungarian prosecutor as a "proof" of the guilt in the Rajk trial.

But the notion that the crude maneuvers of Splinter Factor enabled the CIA to dupe Stalin by arousing his suspicions against the future victims of his purge and thus triggering the bloodbath of the show trials, is utterly naive and demonstrates a complete misunderstanding of the decisive forces behind the purge. Steven's fantasy, the alleged motive of revenge on the part of Dulles, an experienced intelligence chief, should have been sufficient to alert the critically minded reader to suspect the value of Steven's hypothesis. The fictitious whisper of Światło into Beria's ear about a Field conspiracy might have happened, in reality, the other way around. Perhaps, years later, past or active members of the communist security services whispered the theory into the ears of a gullible Stewart Steven, to exonerate themselves for the crimes they committed, to shift part of the blame for the trumped-up charges onto the CIA and to obscure further a shameful era of the communist underworld, the history of which they still want to keep in the dark.

CHAPTER 5

THE ROAD TO THE RAJK TRIAL

From its very inception, the trial of László Rajk in Hungary was destined to serve as a model for those East European purges that followed it. The trial in the Budapest courtroom required much more thorough preparations than did its predecessor in Albania or the simultaneously staged trial in Bulgaria, which was relegated to the status of a sideshow because of internal constraints.

For want of authentic source material, it is very difficult to establish an exact chronology of events, but the information that is available to us, however fragmentary in nature, does offer exceptional insight into the origins of and the secret preparations for the postwar Stalinist purges throughout the satellite states.

The suggestion of Stewart Steven, that the Rajk trial resulted from a cunning provocation on the part of the CIA, discussed in the chapter on the Field legends, is not only implausible but suspect as well.[1] Some former officials of the Hungarian State Security Agency (AVH) who participated in the events offer another version of its origin.[2] According to them, the Hungarian ambassador in Switzerland sent, in the summer of 1948, a confidential report to Budapest, detailing information given to him by a Hungarian emigrant. According to this informant, Tibor Szőnyi, during the war, maintained an espionage contact with Allen Dulles, head of the American OSS office in Bern. The intermediary was Noel Field. The AVH gave this information to the Soviet MVD. The Soviets were skeptical at first, but Mátyás Rákosi, secretary-general of the Hungarian party, pressured Beria to investigate. The MVD arrested Field in Prague and handed him over to the Hungarians, who in turn arrested Szőnyi. The "confessions" extorted from Szőnyi led to the arrest of Rajk and the other victims of the show trial.[3]

This version is equally misleading, but it does contain a fraction of the truth. János Kádár, who is now secretary-general of the party, has given another variant of this version.

However, before describing it, it is necessary to examine the power structure of the Hungarian communist party in 1948. Kádár, a member of the Central Committee and the Politburo, was a bit of window dressing; without any real power, he was placed on both bodies as a symbolic gesture so that the party could demonstrate that at least one member was a genuine worker. The inner circle consisted of Mátyás Rákosi, Ernő Gerő, Mihály Farkas, Jozsef Révai and László

Rajk. The first four came from Moscow, had been functionaries of the Comintern, and with the possible exception of Révai, the cultural "pope" of Hungarian Stalinism, were also trusted agents of the Soviet State Security. Rajk, however, was treated as an outsider by the Muscovites, who accepted him with deep misgivings only because they needed at least one Hungarian native in the inner sanctum. Ultimate power rested with the troika of Rákosi, Gerő, and Farkas, all of whom were confidants of Stalin.

Now let us examine the Kádár version of the origins of the purge. In his recent biography of Kádár, László Gyurkó gives an account of a Sunday in August 1948.

Rákosi invited Kádár to his home. At his arrival, he found Gerő, Farkas and Révai already there. He was surprised at the absence of Rajk, who also belonged to the top Party leadership. . .

'It soon became clear why he was missing,' says Kádár. 'Farkas reported on an intelligence report from the State Security office according to which Rajk was suspected of being an agent for the American espionage organization.'

'At first the words stuck in my throat, I was so stunned,' says Kádár. 'I could only say that that must be completely impossible.'

'Farkas explained that the information came from reliable agents in Switzerland.' Kádár protested. Gerő and Révai kept silent. The rather taciturn Rákosi closed the meeting by saying that in view of such a serious suspicion, even if not proven beyond doubt, Rajk could not remain head of the Interior Ministry, he should be transferred to the Foreign Ministry and Kádár should take over at the Ministry of the Interior.

'I immediately understood,' says Kádár, 'that Rákosi and his group had decided the question without me. It also became clear why Rákosi summoned me later than he did the others. Révai was very pale. So was I, I think.'[4]

Regardless of Kádár's embellishment of his role, the account is revealing. The confidential information from Switzerland is probably the same mentioned in the AVH version. The principal difference is that in one version it is Szőnyi, and in the other it is Rajk who is denounced as an American agent. This can be explained if we assume that only the name of Szőnyi had been revealed to the AVH officers and that of Rajk to Kádár, or perhaps there were two separate "Swiss Reports." But there can be no doubt that the letter from Berne was inspired, to say the least, by the MVD. This kind of proof by the use of disinformation is nothing new in intelligence circles. The most familiar example was perhaps the 1937 charge against Soviet Marshal Tukhachevsky. On Stalin's order, a former czarist general, Skoblin, a double agent living in Paris, passed on to Hitler's security organs a document, concocted by the NKVD, about an alleged conspiracy involving the Soviet marshal and the German general staff. Heydrich, the German security chief, enlarged the document into a thick file and used Czechoslovak President Beneš as an intermediary to transmit it back to

Stalin. A few weeks later, Tukhachevsky was arrested and executed.[5] Another, more recent example of such forgeries was a letter composed by the MVD and addressed to Slánský in which an alleged American agent offered him aid in escaping from imminent arrest. The letter was "fortunately" intercepted by the Security Service in time to arrest Slánský.[6]

* * *

The "Swiss letters," however, were not the true beginning of the purge process; its conception started long before that. At the Cominform session of July 1948 in Bucharest, Andrei Zhdanov, speaking for the Soviet Union, stunned the delegates by revealing that the MVD had proof in its possession about Tito's conspiratorial attempts to subvert the people's democracies in the service of the imperialist espionage agencies. It was unmistakably the announcement of the ongoing preparations for a new purge, this against the "Titoists" in the satellite countries. Stalin's order to Beria, chief of Soviet security, to begin organizing the purges, must have been issued in May 1948 after his critical Central Committee letters had proven unable to force Tito back into line and after the failed efforts by the Soviet ambassador and the MVD resident in Belgrade to have Tito replaced by more pliant allies such as Hebrang and Žujović. The show trials were intended, therefore, to unmask Tito and all potential Titos within the leadership of the satellite countries and to expose them as anti-Soviet traitors in communist disguise, imperialist agents bent on restoring capitalism.

A neglected aspect of the history of the purges has been the special significance of the subjective factor in the preparation of the trials. The contention that the party leaders in the satellite countries were nothing more than puppets, following slavishly every move of their wire-pullers in the Kremlin, was even in the darkest Stalinist period only conditionally true. They were all devoted Stalinists, enthusiastically carrying out the general strategies and tactics dictated by Moscow, as was proven by the nearly simultaneous liquidation of the bourgeois democratic parties, the mergers of the Social Democratic and communist parties, the inauguration of economic planning programs, the nationalization of industry and the banks, and the collectivization of agriculture.

However, when it came to liquidating comrades in arms, longstanding friends known to be innocent of the charges against them, differences emerged due to human character and the past party experiences of the individual Stalinist leaders. The general conception of a Titoist plot was readily accepted, as were the general suspect categories of former refugees returning from Western exile; "internationalist" veterans of the Spanish Civil War; Trotzkyists; leaders of the home underground; "cosmopolitans," a euphemism for Jews; in sum, all of the leading party functionaries who did not return to their countries from the Soviet Union and who had not been recruited, or at least approved, by the Soviet security services.

Difficulties for Beria began to occur at the stage of preparation where generalities had to be translated into specifics. These had to be worked out, not only with his own MVD and the local security organs it controlled, but also with local party leaders. In Romania Gheorghiu-Dej tried, with some success, to outsmart Beria and use the purges for his own personal ends. In Poland, Bierut searched for ways to sabotage the orders from Moscow for more and more purges, in fear for his own life. His colleague in Czechoslovakia, Gottwald, tried at the outset to thwart everything but a cursorily dutiful purge and had to be pressured into obedience. Dimitrov, in Bulgaria, stuck for so long to his friendship with Tito that he first had to be removed before show trials could be prepared. In Berlin, there were difficulties of quite another kind; there, it was not the personality of Ulbricht, but the East-West division of Germany that obstructed the course of the purge.

Hungary, however, offered Stalin and Beria ideal conditions; that is one of the reasons why the Budapest trial could be used as a model for the other satellite nations. The servility of Rákosi was well known and often tested. Gerő and Farkas, the two other members of the innermost triumvirate, were both MVD agents.[7] There were no factional differences, no democratic traditions to be overcome, no questions of divided loyalties or rivalries for power.

Rákosi considered himself to be the Stalin of Hungary. He was intelligent and cunning, but completely subservient to his master, easily kept on a leash held by Moscow. Gerő was far more talented, a good economist, and a hard policeman, as proven by his ruthless liquidation of Trotzkyists during the Spanish Civil War in the service of the Comintern. Farkas, the least intelligent of the trio, headed in the Central Committee the departments of the army, police, and security. He was a mean, cruel apparatchik; his conceit and his vindictive personality made him a willing tool of the MVD.

In the early summer of 1948, Rákosi was summoned to Moscow to receive his orders from Beria for the preparation of a show trial. They agreed on the choices for the leading cast: László Rajk as the principal victim and head of the fabricated conspiracy; Tibor Szőnyi as the link with the imperialists; Lazar Brankov as the link with Tito.[8]

Rajk was born in 1908 and joined the underground Hungarian communist party during his student years. After being expelled from Budapest University for "subversive activities," he became a construction worker and head of the communist faction in his union. During the Spanish Civil War, he fought in the ranks of the International Brigade and was named party secretary of the Rákosi battalion. After the defeat of the Republicans, he fled to France and spent three years in internment camps. In 1941, he managed to return to Hungary. As secretary of the Central Committee of the communist party, he was one of the leaders of the communist underground, organized the antifascist resistance against the Germans and their Hungarian puppets. Three years later, he was arrested and handed over to the Gestapo. After he was liberated from a prison near Munich, he returned in May 1945 to Hungary, was elected to the Central Committee and the Politburo and, in 1946, occupied the key power position of Interior Minister.

Rajk was a genuine Stalinist, sincerely devoted to the Soviet Union. As minister of the Interior, he smashed one bourgeois opposition party after another, determining which leader should be arrested and which exiled, organized the trial against Cardinal Mindszenty and, with it, destroyed the power of the Catholic church in Hungary.

Rajk was an ideal target for Stalin. He fitted not one, but two categories of purge victim, having been a "internationalist" in Spain and a home communist. He was a born leader, handsome, tall, without any doubt the most popular person in the party, a status that came about in part because, of the entire top party leadership, he was the only non-Jew. To Farkas, he represented a dangerous opponent in his drive to attain absolute power over the tools of repression.

After his return from Moscow, Farkas, together with Rákosi and Gerő, launched a cunning campaign against Rajk.[9] First, at a meeting of the Politburo, he accused him of having dissolved the party organization within the Ministry of the Interior. Rajk had to indulge in self-criticism, the quasireligious mea culpa of Stalinist liturgy, and was forced to restore the party organization in the ministry. At the beginning of July 1948, a second attack developed when Gerő asked why Rajk had organized a special police force, equipped with the latest weaponry and answerable only to himself. Perhaps he was planning an armed uprising, Gerő inquired. Rajk defended himself indignantly; the special force was established with the full knowledge and approval of the Soviet military command. In August, the forged "Swiss letter" was leaked to some members of the Politburo, followed in September by Rajk's removal from the Ministry of the Interior and his shift to the insignificant Ministry for Foreign Affairs. The Security Service had, in the meantime, been detached from the Ministry of the Interior and made into an autonomous agency, directly responsible to the Security Commission of the Central Committee.

Rákosi did not yet want to alert his victim to the presence of imminent danger. Rajk remained a member of the Central Committee and the Politburo and, at the beginning of 1949, he was even nominated general secretary of the National People's Front. In April, his name was fourth on the list of candidates for the parliamentary "elections" and on May 16, he sat together with the Muscovites in the forefront of the dais to celebrate the election victory. On May 29, he was invited for lunch to the Rákosis. On the next day, he was arrested.[10]

* * *

The list of "conspirators" prepared by Rákosi and his clique included initially friends and colleagues of Rajk in the Ministry of the Interior and the police; his comrades in arms in Spain; and his friends in the Hungarian underground. The Security Commission reviewed the list carefully, adding some friends of friends and deleting some who had close contacts with the security services or with the MVD.

To the category of "Rajkists" was added that of the left Social Democrats who collaborated with the communists, but who retained a critical attitude toward the Soviet Union; they were considered "Trotzkyists" and had to be liquidated. The most prominent among these was Pál Justus. He had belonged to the extreme left wing of the party since the late 1920s, was arrested in 1932 and forced to emigrate to France. In 1936, he returned to Hungary, where he was one of the initiators of a united antifascist front with the underground communist party. After liberation, he became the leading theorist of the Social Democrats and an advocate for the fusion of the two workers' parties. The communists rewarded him with a seat on the Central Committee of the now-united party. Justus fitted well within Stalin's list of suspect categories. He was not only a "Trotzkyist" but an emigrant to the West with close Western connections, an intellectual, and a Jew.

High officers of the prewar Hungarian army formed a special category. Most of them, in the last phase of the war, joined the underground resistance led by the communists or were taken prisoner on the eastern front and re-educated by the political commissars in antifascist schools. After liberation, they formed the nucleus of the new army and were placed by the Soviets in positions of command. The most prominent among them was Lieutenant-General György Pálffy. At the outset of the war, he joined the outlawed communist party, organizing the military resistance of the underground. In 1945, he became head of the counterespionage department in the Ministry of Defense. Soon friction arose between military intelligence and the AVH, the security police, and the forthcoming show trial gave AVH Chief Péter his long-awaited opportunity to rid himself of his rival.

Tibor Szőnyi fitted in for other reasons. As head of the Central Cadre Department, he had been responsible for nominating communists to leading party and government posts. The MVD was alerted to him because of his wartime contacts with Noel Field and cast him in the role of the chief Hungarian contact with the United States intelligence services. He was sixteen years old when, as a high school student, he joined the communists and had to escape from Hungary to Austria after the suppression of the revolution of 1919. In Vienna, he studied medicine and returned home with a doctorate in psychiatry. He held a high position in the underground party, but soon, to avoid arrest, he had to leave again. When he was back in Vienna, the Comintern assigned him the task of maintaining contact between the party in Hungary and the Hungarian communist groups in Western countries. When the Germans entered Vienna in 1938, he fled to Zurich and organized first the Austrian, then the Hungarian groups. In March

1945, he returned to Hungary and two years later, was elected to the Central Committee as head of party personnel. For Rákosi and the AVH, Szőnyi promised to be a gold mine, since he furnished, through his wartime contacts to Noel Field, the hitherto missing American connection. With him, into the net, came all of the members of his former Swiss exile group.

As an additional bonus, the Stalinist stage managers unearthed the ideological crime of "Browderism" to accuse Szőnyi with it. Earl Browder, the general secretary of the Communist Party of the United States, declared in December 1943 that after the Teheran conference of Stalin, Roosevelt, and Churchill, the way was open for a peaceful coexistence. Collaboration between capitalism and communism in a democratic post-war world was now possible. His "Teheran Theses" were reprinted and disseminated by the Swiss CP and became in 1944 an authoritative text of theoretical instruction for all the exile groups in Switzerland, and also for the Hungarian group led by Szőnyi.

In April 1945 Jacques Duclos, head of the French CP, denounced in an article inspired by Stalin, Browder's "political platform of class peace" as a "dangerous opportunist illusion," a "deviation from the correct Marxist analysis." Subsequently, Browder was dismissed from his position and expelled from the CPUSA. Four years later, this heresy was used as a pretext to stamp Szőnyi as a "deviationist", a worthy candidate for the show trial.

Lazar Brankov, the "Tito connection," joined the Yugoslav communists as a young man and fought with them in the partisan's war of liberation. In 1945, Tito appointed him chief of the Yugoslav Military Mission in Hungary and later, councillor of his embassy in Budapest, where he functioned as director of the UDB, the Yugoslav intelligence agency. After the break between Tito and Stalin, he was pressured by the Soviet and Hungarian security agencies to denounce Tito and thus he became a valuable tool to be used in the anti-Tito campaign. A couple of months later, the Soviet stage managers decided to turn his role around and use him in the show trial as an agent of Tito.

Rákosi submitted the new and enlarged list of victims to Beria and received orders for the next steps to be taken. Within the AVH, a secret special branch had been formed under Péter and his two closest aides, Colonels Ernö Szücs and Gyula Décsi. Its task was to adjust the general guidelines from Moscow to suit Hungarian conditions and to outline the contours of the imaginary connections linking so disparate a group of individuals as Rajk, Szőnyi, Pálffy, Justus, and Brankov. The special branch was responsible both to Rákosi and to MVD General Byelkin, head of the Soviet Security Services for southeastern Europe.

Byelkin dispatched two of his associates, MVD Generals Likhachov and Makarov, to Budapest as chief advisers to the special branch in preparing and organizing the show trial. The team of Soviet "advisers" soon swelled to twelve, and reached forty at the peak of the purges.

On Beria's instructions, the arrests were delayed until the final stage directions from Moscow were carried out. In March 1949, Jindřich Veselý, the director of the Czechoslovak security forces, received an order from Byelkin to lure Noel Field from Geneva to Prague. Veselý sent a letter to Field inviting him to discuss a possible teaching position at a Czech university. Field arrived in Prague on May 5, at the same time as AVH Colonel Szücs from Budapest. Szücs asked his Czech counterpart to arrest Field and to hand him over to Hungarian security. Veselý hesitated, but Byelkin intervened and on May 11 and Field was arrested.[11] The next day, he was taken to Budapest and jailed in the cellar of a secret cottage occupied by the MVD.

On May 17, AVH General Péter called a conference of leading security officials. There he unveiled a monstrous conspiracy involving the Western imperialists and their hireling, Tito. The identity of the plotters and spies, camouflaged as high party functionaries, was known, he told the officials, and arrests would begin on the following night. The task of the AVH, he told them, was now to uncover, with the aid of their Soviet advisers, the details of the plot and to bring the guilty to confess their abominable crimes.

On the night of May 18, Tibor Szőnyi and the first members of his "Swiss group" were arrested. The machinery of terror had been set into motion.

Personal Notes I: May 1949

It was a joy to be a communist, to serve the cause of humanity, to be present at the birth of a better future. After all the horrors of the Second World War, at last the world seemed to be taking on a semblance of order. And what a beautiful order it promised to be. The ruins left by the war were already disappearing, the process of rebuilding the nation was well under way, and the first Five-Year Plan had begun. We were building a socialist Hungary under the banner of the communist party.

To me, the party was not an abstraction, it was a vital and consuming part of my life. I was happy and secure, proud that the party—and through it, the nation—could use my talents. My dream of becoming a journalist had come true. I was on the editorial staff of an economic journal. My German was excellent and I worked as the Budapest correspondent of the prestigious Swiss newspaper *Neue Zürcher Zeitung* and the Austrian daily *Neues Österreich*. I spoke English and French with some fluency, so the party assigned me the task of assisting the Budapest correspondents of the London *Times* and the French news agency, *Agence France Presse,* in covering Hungarian political developments. I saw no conflict of interest in working for bourgeois newspapers; on the contrary, I felt I was making an important contribution to the cause in counterbalancing the malicious propaganda of the enemy by reportage that I thought to be factual and objective. Anyway, there was nothing to hide in our beautiful new socialist Hungary, or at least nothing really important. If excesses happened, they were the inevitable, if regrettable results of a revolutionary process, injustices that afflicted a few so that there might be a greater justice for all. You can't make an omelette without breaking eggs.

Only one warning voice kept breaking into my peace of mind. My wife, Marta, told me time and again that things in Hungary were not going as well as I imagined. Her coworkers at the research institute were angry, she told me. The communists, they said, are enslaving the country. They have banned the free expression of opinion, they have banned unbiased research, people occupy leading scientific positions with no more qualification than having the party's membership book in their pocket.

I laughed it off. The institute, I said, is a hotbed of prewar reactionaries who preach the slanders of yesterday in order to sabotage the future. Don't listen to them, I warned her, any more than to the gossips who sit in the next chair at the hairdresser. There may be some mistakes, I conceded, but they are a part of the process of growing up. Socialism will overcome them in due time. Ah, it was a joy to be a communist and to have answers to satisfy all doubts.

I was not alone in the innocence and purity of my faith. I shared my vision with all of my friends. Those colleagues who might have had a more critical point of view kept such things to themselves in my presence. We, after all, were the select few, keepers of the truth, speaking, thinking and acting on behalf of the masses. We wore our blinders proudly, totally isolated from reality.

It was a joy to carry the red flag in the endless May Day parade through the streets of Budapest. Red flags fluttered out of the windows of the city. Rákosi, Rajk, and the other party leaders seemed to smile down upon me from the festively decorated stands in Hero's Square. I still, to this day, remember how I raised my fist in comradely greeting as I marched past 60 Andrassy Street, headquarters of the State Security Office, with its banner atop the entrance proudly proclaiming "Long Live the AVH, Hard Fist of the Proletarian Dictatorship!"

It was a joy to participate in the huge rally on May 16, celebrating our victory in the parliamentary elections. The opposition parties were already smashed, the Social Democrats having been swallowed alive, as it were, by the communists. It was a new kind of an election, one in which there was no choice offered the voters, the candidates on the list of the People's Front having all been nominated by the party. The result could have only been a near-unanimous vote and the party's announcement of a 95.6 percent victory was, for me, the sure sign of how much the people trusted us.

The principal speaker at the celebration damned the traitor Tito and praised the wise leadership of the great Stalin and of his best Hungarian pupil, comrade Rákosi. "Long live free, independent, democratic Hungary," he concluded.

The speaker was László Rajk, recently named to the position of secretary-general of the People's Front.

Even I, the true believer, had some difficulty understanding and explaining the excommunication of Marshal Tito. He had turned against Stalin and, without doubt, those who separated themselves from the Soviet Union harmed the cause of socialism. But Tito's sudden transformation from idol to "chained dog of the imperialists" confused me. It must be a propaganda ploy with unfathomable purposes, I thought. But I knew that the party was always correct. Stalin knows what he is doing and why he is doing it.

In May, the *Neue Zürcher Zeitung* began to serialize *Darkness at Noon,* the novel about the Soviet prewar purges, written by Arthur Koestler. I did not believe one word of the novel, considered it a dirty slander, and soon stopped reading the installments.

*   *   *

On the evening of May 19, 1949, Kati Földi, my friend's wife, called me in hysterics. During the previous night, a group of men had broken into their apartment, handcuffed Iván, and taken him away. She had no idea who they were, what they wanted, where they had taken him, what it was all about. I consoled her. He will return tomorrow, it must be a mistake.

I didn't realize it then, but on that evening, the beautiful, clear, reasonable world in which I lived began to shatter into pieces. It was, for me, the first indication of the catastrophe to come.

CHAPTER 6

PREPARATIONS FOR THE MODEL TRIAL

When Szőnyi was dragged, handcuffed and blindfolded, into the secret MVD cottage on the outskirts of Budapest, he was met by an illustrious group of people. They included the chief of the AVH, Gábor Péter, his deputy, Colonel Szücs, the Soviet General Fyodor Byelkin, and Byelkin's interpreter.[1]

Its mixed Hungarian-Soviet composition existed in appearance only. Péter was recruited by the NKVD in the wartime Hungarian communist underground, and Szücs received Soviet citizenship and was trained by the Soviet security services during his lengthy stay in Moscow. From its inception and first arrests to its final sentences and executions, the Hungarian purge was a purely Soviet affair, and the MVD controlled its every aspect.

Szőnyi was a good choice as the initial victim of the purge. His wartime connections with Noel Field aroused the suspicions of his captors. They also caused him to feel inner, personal doubts about some of his actions when, during his first interrogation, Field was brought out of an adjoining room and told the Hungarian to his face about his contacts with Allen Dulles, director of the OSS office in Switzerland. If Field had been an American agent, then he, Szőnyi, was certainly lacking in vigilance; he might even have been used by Field and the United States intelligence services.

The result was that even before the beatings began, Szőnyi was filled with self-doubt, even before the rubber truncheons were brought into play and he was forced to crawl on the floor, confessing his contacts with Dulles who, in fact, he had never met.[2] The beatings were not intended, however, to extort false confessions from him—there was time enough for that later—but rather to prove to him that he was no longer a member of the Central Committee, no longer a party comrade, but now nothing more than a common criminal, a spy, and a traitor, at the absolute mercy of the Hungarian and Soviet security services.

Because of the wide web of his associations and friendships established during many years of undercover work on behalf of the Hungarian communist party and the underground movement in Switzerland and elsewhere, Szőnyi was an ideal net into which to entrap "enemies" infiltrated into the party. He was forced to write long lists of names of individuals, the members of his "Swiss group," and the names of all communists who, after the war, returned from the West and were assigned by the Cadre Department to responsible posts in the party and government. The lists were transformed into arrest warrants signed by Farkas. During the next few weeks, the cellars of the AVH headquarters on Andrássy Street were filled with "Westerners" who soon became, under torture, confessed "members of the Szőnyi gang." Their associations during their Western exiles became "spy connections" with the American intelligence or the French Deuxième Bureau or the British Intelligence Service, depending upon in which country they had spent the war years. Their place of work in Hungary furnished their "spy material," their position in the hierarchy determined their future role in the still vague outlines of the "conspiracy to topple the People's Democracy." They were forced to write endless autobiographies, to list their friends and coworkers. The names, in turn, were submitted to the Security Committee, which selected from among them those that fitted comfortably into one or another suspect category. New arrest warrants were issued and the process began again.

The wider and wider concentric circles drawn around Szőnyi and Field soon became a side issue. On the subject of Szőnyi's guilt, his active participation in the "conspiracy," the matter was settled early on in the proceedings. After only one week of beatings, Szőnyi accepted the "logic" of his interrogators, that the chain that led from him through Field to Dulles was, in a political sense, identical to having a direct contact with American intelligence and that receiving financial support from them, whatever the pretext, was basically no different from being on their payroll. When, eight days after his arrest, Szőnyi was confronted with Béla Szász, a returnee from Argentina, he was already psychologically a broken man.[3] A week later, he was confronted with another arrested comrade and by that time he was a human wreck, his head shrunken into a deathlike skull, his eyes darting from side to side with the terror of a wounded and trapped animal, his feet so swollen they could hardly bear the weight of his bent body. The preliminary phase was over and it was time to begin the tortures that would lead to his confession "unmasking" Rajk as an American spy and head of a "Titoist plot."

It had been relatively simple to force Szőnyi to sign incriminating documents in which his contacts with Field were transformed into spy missions. With Rajk, however, he had had hardly any dealings. The two men knew each other only casually. Their contacts came about when Szőnyi was director of the Cadre Department and Rajk would occasionally ask him to find a job for an old comrade from the International Brigade. Here, there were no latent guilt feelings that Szőnyi's interrogators could manipulate in order to convince him that there was some logic to his accusers' distortions. Szőnyi was simply incapable of confessing to having "recruited" Rajk into the American espionage network on Field's orders. No brutal or sophisticated physical torture could bring him to incriminate Rajk, not even the arrest of his wife, in her seventh month of pregnancy.

The Soviet and Hungarian examiners were soon forced to drop this line of interrogation. It would have been convenient for them to have been able to pursue it, but its failure resulted in no irremedial harm to their case. If Szőnyi would not play the role of "spymaster," they could find another candidate. Szőnyi and Field had done their useful tasks; they could be granted a respite. The focus of the interrogations now shifted to Rajk, who had been arrested twelve days after Szőnyi, and with him, from the United States to the Yugoslav connection.

With Rajk, the interrogators did not have the advantage of manipulatable latent guilt feelings. Naked physical and psychological torture had to be applied in order to turn him into a fascist police informer, a spy of the Deuxième Bureau, and an agent of the Gestapo. Here, there was no sophisticated application of subtle psychological techniques, but endless brutality to force confession that he was Tito's agent who plotted to seize power with a military coup, to murder Rákosi, Gerő, and Farkas and to restore capitalism to Hungary. The interrupted search for a spymaster was ended; the new chain of command went from the imperialists through Tito to Rajk.

Parallel to the interrogation of Rajk, there began the tortures of Lieutenant General György Pálffy and the defected Yugoslav diplomat, Lazar Brankov. Their roles had been assigned to them long before in Moscow and Budapest, Pálffy to be the coup's military commander and Brankov the liaison between Tito and Rajk.

This prefabricated scenario required a sizeable cast of characters. Rajk, Szőnyi, Brankov, and Pálffy must not be isolated traitors but the heads of a band of conspirators; otherwise, the concocted stories would not be believable. The AVH headquarters were hurriedly enlarged, with neighboring buildings taken over and new subterranean isolation cells constructed to accommodate the flow of new arrivals. These included the veterans from Spain, underground fighters of the resistance, high-ranking officers of the army and police, leading officials of the Ministries of Interior and Defense, and any government or party functionaries who, before the Cominform split, had any dealings with Yugoslavia, as well as all the representatives of the Hungarian-Yugoslav Society.

The inherent dynamics of the Stalinist purge required that the proceedings be carried out at a constantly accelerating rate. The expanding circles drawn around Rajk and Pálffy provided more and more victims, including not only those who were originally scheduled to be arrested, but also many whose names were unintentionally dropped by the victims already being interrogated. These were added to the liquidation lists on the slightest pretext.

At this stage of the purge, with names being added daily to this list of those to be arrested, the Soviet stage managers and their Hungarian underlings had to decide how to fit this number of "plotters," now about three hundred communists, into the grand conceptual framework of the predetermined plot. It was a difficult and time-consuming task. Thousands of statements had to be read in order to determine the future direction of the investigation. There were staging problems to be dealt with and roles to be assigned, such as how to fit in the left-wing socialists, headed by Pál Justus or how to find a properly effective stage role for András Szalai, deputy to Szőnyi in the Cadre Department. Should he be cast with Szőnyi as an American spy or with Rajk as a Yugoslav agent?

The starting point was always the autobiography of the arrested person, his own account of his political life. Only then could the interrogators begin a political reinterpretation of that life, achieved with rubber truncheons, rifle butts, electric shocks, sleeplessness, hunger, and cold—a mixture of the most advanced and archaically barbaric methods of physical and psychological tortures. The interrogators suggested "reinterpretations" of previous arrests for underground communists' activities so that they became informer services for the fascist police. Personal or professional contacts with the co-accused became plotting with and spying for the agents of imperialism. Step by step, each version was transformed by torture into a new and uglier one until every moment of the accused's life was reinterpreted into an abominable crime.

The duration of this brutal transformation of the defendants from faithful communists to traitors varied from individual to individual, according to the character and the moral and physical strength of the accused. But by the end of the ordeal, nearly all "confessed." The few exceptions did not pose any great difficulty to the organizers of the purge. They were not put on trial, but simply disappeared in one of the many secret camps of the AVH. The thugs, torturers, and technicians received strict instructions to be careful, to make sure the accused remained alive, but some mishaps did take place and victims were inadvertently beaten to death or died of heart attacks before they could be brought to trial. The poet and writer Endre Havas, a fighter in the French resistance movement, had been the Hungarian cultural attaché in Paris after the war. He was recalled "for consultations" and taken straight to AVH headquarters, where his tortures drove him to insanity. He was of no further use, so he was placed in an isolation cell, where his cries of "Help me, Stalin!" were a constant source of humor to his jailers. It was regarded as special fun to kick him when they found him lying in his own feces. One day, they gave him one kick too many and Havas died of his beatings.

* * *

Did the accusers actually believe in the guilt of their victims? The principal initiators of the purge, Stalin, Beria, and the Hungarian troika of Rákosi, Gerő, and Farkas certainly did not, having concocted the charges themselves out of whole cloth. The evidence of this was seen in the mission of János Kádár, to be discussed later in this chapter, who visited with Rajk shortly before his trial began and assured him that the inner party circle was well aware of his innocence.

It cannot be established how far down the party and security hierarchies the truth was openly divulged. It might well have been that at the beginning, even the head of the AVH, Péter and his Soviet advisers were not completely initiated into the real nature of the purge. The interrogators were initially convinced of the guilt of their victims, but very early in the proceedings they must have become aware of the vast gap between fact and fiction. As unavoidable human relationships began to develop between interrogators and victims, more and more interrogators had to be removed from their cases, since they began to voice disbelief in the correctness of the proceedings. Colonel László Angyal, one of Rajk's interrogators, committed suicide; he could not bear the pressure of torturing a comrade he was convinced was innocent.[4] On the orders of the Soviet advisers, investigating teams were rotated to prevent interrogators from getting too soft. At a later stage of the investigations, a relatively small number of AVH officers remained on the case, thoroughly cynical tools of the Soviets, understanding perfectly well, without being told in so many words, that their task was not to find the truth, but to prove a politically necessary lie. Only the professional thugs who performed the brutal tasks of beating and torture, and the prison guards in the cellars who opened and closed the cell doors, believed in the guilt of the victims.

* * *

The second and final phase of the interrogations began in the middle of August 1949, three months after the initial arrests. By that time, all of the victims scheduled for the main show trial had made partial confessions. Why they confessed is well-known from the memoirs of the survivors. The murdered cannot bear witness. András Szalai, captured by the fascist police, was beaten half to death by them, but never betrayed his party or his comrades. In the cells of the AVH, he signed statements admitting to having been a police informer who delivered his comrades to the fascist gallows. Colonel László Marschall risked his life for the party in the Spanish Civil War and with the French Maquis; now he confessed to having been an imperialist spy and a traitor. A tin pot circulated through the prison with his message scratched upon it: "Long Live the Party!" These were just two examples from among the dozens of exemplary communists who were executed.

What made this possible? The tortures inflicted upon them by their own comrades, unlike those they suffered at the hands of the fascist enemy, destroyed not only their bodies but their entire lives. Their moral resistance collapsed; they felt guilty because their party told them they were guilty, and the party was always right. Abandoned by the party, isolated, helplessly delivered to an incomprehensible, thuggish, pitiless netherworld, they were, step by step, programmed into becoming lifeless automata, puppets in the hands of others, transformed by a hellish alchemy into becoming their own accusers, the accomplices of their executioners.

In the middle of August, there came a pause in the activities in the AVH cellars. All of the statements were translated into Russian and examined by a mixed team of Soviet and Hungarian security officials. New directives were issued, aimed at coordinating the individual confessions with the general plan for the show trial. It also had to be decided which of the victims would be used in the main public trial and how to dispose of the remaining prisoners—to try them later in secret proceedings or make them disappear in secret labor camps. The principal task of the AVH now became to construct from the loosely connected, often contradictory mosaic stones of the individual preliminary statements a coherent story linking them all together. Each of the accused had to be assigned a specific role, creating a total picture and incriminating both themselves and their accused comrades.

This new phase required new methods. Tortures, which had been used to their maximum effectiveness, could now be abandoned. The new relationship between interrogator and victim was not to be based on terror and violence, but on common interests. We know you were good communists, the accused were told. You made some mistakes, of course, but who doesn't? It is unfortunate that those mistakes, in their political contexts, are of use to the enemy, but now the party needs your help in unmasking Tito and the imperialists. We no longer threaten you with the noose, we offer you promises. If you change your statement to a version that is politically useful, the party will show you its appreciation. It will demonstrate mercy. To the outside world, you will be treated like a common criminal, but the verdict of the court will be a mere formality. After a couple of years, you will be set free and allowed to build a new life for yourself.

The most important aim of this phase was to convince Rajk to collaborate with the stage managers of the show trial. The task was entrusted to János Kádár, the new minister of the Interior. Kádár was an old friend of Rajk and, only six months before, had been the godfather of the Rajks' newborn child. Now he visited Rajk in his cell at the AVH headquarters and asked his former comrade to end his resistance and serve the party with testimony proving unequivocably to the entire world Tito's role as an agent of the imperialists. Comrade Rákosi, Kádár assured Rajk, knew the truth, as did the members of the Politburo. They did not doubt his innocence, but asked him to make a supreme sacrifice for the party. Even if he was sentenced to death, Kádár told Rajk, it would be for the sake of appearances only, and his life would be spared; the sentence would not be carried out. He would be brought, together with his family, to the Soviet Union and be given a new name and a new future. Some day, Rajk was promised, he would be once again a member of the party in good standing.

It is possible that Kádár even believed what he was telling Rajk, but it is hardly probable that Rajk believed it. Life, for him, no longer had any meaning. He gave his consent as a final proof of his fanatical loyalty to the party. (The conversation between the two men was taped, and Rákosi played the tape at a meeting of the Central Committee in 1956, shortly before the beginning of the Hungarian revolution. His purpose was to shift responsibility for the Rajk trial from himself onto the shoulders of Kádár, his rival for power).[5]

A similar tactic was used with the other prisoners. It was not Kádár, but the top AVH leadership—Péter, Szücs, Décsi, and Károlyi—who lured them into the trap. Suddenly, the tortures ceased, the food improved, the prisoners were taken for short, solitary night walks and allowed to breathe fresh air for the first time in months. The interrogators appealed to their prisoners, with cynical complicity, for their cooperation in unmasking Tito and the imperialists. All received the same promises: They would not be executed, a political trial allowed for political verdicts, pseudo-sentences for the sake of public opinion, but they would be freed in a few years regardless of the formal decisions of a court that was, after all, controlled by the AVH. The interrogators cited the example of the Soviet leader Karl Radek who, for his full cooperation with the interrogation, received a mild sentence of only ten years in the main Trotzkyist trial in Moscow and then had been hidden away in a cottage in the Urals. The prisoners might have been less sanguine about the promises, had they known that the "cottage" was, in reality, a labor camp in the Arctics where Radek was subsequently beaten to death.

But the victims believed the promises. Tortured into unthinking clumps of bleeding flesh only a few days before, they now eagerly embraced the possibility offered of demonstrating their devotion to the party. Thankfully, they chose the road set before them that would lead them out of hell. If the party could transform good communists into abominable criminals, it could also return to them their lives and the meanings of those lives. At that point, in their statements, they had become the dregs of society, their fates were sealed. The only choice appeared to be between the hangman and the certainty of rotting away in a prison cellar. Now, miraculously, a new choice was offered them. At the price of a few more charges, a few additional incriminations, their lives would be placed in the hands of the party.

They signed everything. The cellar cells were transformed into livable rooms. Gourmet food appeared three times daily from the excellent AVH kitchen. Cigarettes and books were distributed and the prisoners were permitted to write their first letters since their arrests. At night, the wardens wore felt slippers so as not to awaken their charges. Doctors appeared to heal the wounds of torture and to distribute vitamins and medicines. In sunlit rooms upstairs, interrogators and victims worked together in friendly collaboration, setting up the carefully coordinated final statements.

In the final days of August, every defendant of the main show trial received a typewritten copy of his confession, the questions to be posed by the president of the people's court, and the answers to those questions. Each had to learn them by heart. Then came rehearsals, supervised by the Soviet stage managers, in which the interrogator played the role of chairman of the tribunal and also that of stage director, giving instructions to the defendant when to raise and lower his voice, how to stand and which facial expressions to use. The rehearsals were repeated until everything went perfectly.

Then came the turn of the judiciary. The state prosecutor's office and its president, Gyula Alapi, the members of the people's court and its chairman, Péter Jankó,[6] became puppets under the control of Rákosi and the security agency. The indictment was signed by Alapi, but was drawn up by Rákosi, edited by the legal experts of the Soviet and Hungarian secret police, and submitted to Stalin and Beria. Only after their approval was the final indictment handed to Alapi shortly before the beginning of the trial. A few days before the trial began, the state prosecutor summoned Jankó and the four carefully screened people's judges to his office and handed them the script of the trial, complete with their questions and the well-rehearsed answers of the defendants. They were given strict orders not to deviate from the text. In the unexpected event that one of the defendants would speak out of turn, the chairman had orders to interrupt the proceedings and adjourn the trial for that day.

Rákosi instructed the minister of justice to submit a list of reliable attorneys for the defense. The list was screened by the AVH and eight of the most trustworthy and obsequious were selected. The texts of their speeches were written by the AVH legal experts and they were introduced to their "clients" just minutes before the start of the trial, in the presence of the same AVH officers who had prepared the defendants.

A no-less-cynical travesty of justice took place with the witnesses. There were no witnesses for the defense, only those for the prosecution—twenty in all. They were without exception detainees of the AVH, prepared for the trial as were the defendants, made to rehearse their texts over and over again in the cellars. Five among them were former police or justice officials in the prewar regime who were in prison for having committed genuine crimes. Dragged out of their prisons or internment camps, they gave their AVH interrogators far less trouble than did the defendants. With a few beatings and a lot of promises, it was possible to persuade them to refresh their memories and testify to the requested lies. After the trial, they were all sentenced, in secret trials, to new and longer prison sentences for having persecuted and tortured communists during the fascist era.

The remaining fifteen "witnesses" were selected by the AVH from among the ranks of the codefendants, scheduled for later trials. Having already signed statements listing their own abominable crimes, they could be fully trusted, in this nightmarish netherworld, to help pull the rope tighter around the necks of their more prominent friends and comrades. They were promised that the party would honor their services, but in subsequent trials all of them were sentenced to life in prison with the exception of three: Endre Szebenyi, deputy minister of the Interior, András Villányi, deputy minister of Trade, and Dezső Németh, chief of staff of the border guard and military attaché in Moscow, who were sentenced to death and executed.[7]

On September 16, 1949, a Friday morning, in the Great Hall of the central building of the Iron and Metal Worker's Union, the curtain rose on the show trial of "Lászlo Rajk and his accomplices."

Personal Notes II: July–August 1949

I had been expecting them, more or less, when they finally came for me at one in the morning on July 6, 1949. For weeks, my friends had been disappearing, one by one—dragged from their beds at night until it seemed that the entire "Swiss group" had vanished. To hear the knock on my door meant that, at last, I would find out what was happening. It was almost with a sense of relief that I awoke and rose to let them in.

It had been less than a month before, on June 16, that the Hungarian public first had a hint that anything was wrong. On that day, under the heading "Resolution of the Central Committee and the Central Control Commission of the Hungarian Worker's Party," there appeared in the party newspaper *Szabad Nép* a one-sentence paragraph. It read: "The Central Committee has expelled Lászlo Rajk and Tibor Szőnyi from the ranks of the party as spies for imperialist powers and Trotzkyist agents." Three days later, another brief notice was published, this one from the Ministry of the Interior. "The state security organs have arrested László Rajk, Tibor Szőnyi, Pál Justus and 17 accomplices for espionage activities in the service of foreign powers. No workers or poor peasants are among the arrested."

I was dumbfounded. I did not know Rajk personally, but Szőnyi had been a friend since I first joined the small group of Hungarian communists living in Switzerland during the war. And Földi, Kálmán, Vági, and Demeter and his wife had also disappeared, all of them close friends and comrades from those years in exile. I would stake my life on their devotion and dedication to the party. By no means could they possibly be considered traitors.

Now it was my turn. But surely they sent for me only to ask for information, to help clear up the misunderstanding that was apparently taking place. I went with them feeling no fear. Good communists need not worry about the AVH, our State Security office whose hard fist struck only at the enemies of our people's democracy.

There were four of them. They showed me their identity cards and ordered me to dress. I was calm and sure of myself. There was a bowl filled with cherries in the living room.

"Comrades, help yourselves while I dress," I told them. They looked at me in astonishment. My wife, Marta, white and shivering, told me to take a pullover with me.

"What for?" I answered. "It is warm, and tomorrow I will be home."

I took 70 filler from my purse, the exact amount I would need for a return ticket on the street car, kissed my wife and daughter, and left, accompanied by two of the AVH men. It was a beautiful summer night under a sky full of stars. Their automobile, a large American model with drawn curtains, was parked at the next corner.

Two AVH men remained in the apartment. Five and a half years later, when I next saw my wife and child, I learned that the proceedings there were not so cheerful. They pulled down all the shutters, turned on the lights, and began tearing the apartment apart. Mattresses were thrown from the beds, letters and papers were stuffed into their suitcases, my two-year-old daughter was dragged from her room while they searched every corner of it, and even my Montblanc pen would have disappeared had Marta not snatched it from the hand of an AVH man. Marta, to be sure, had always had doubts about the nobility of communism and the justice dispensed by its iron fist. Even in Switzerland, my comrades had warned me: "She is a petite bourgeoise." I knew better.

*   *   *

The "Swiss group," of which I was a member, consisted of Hungarian students at the universities of Zurich and Geneva who were caught in that country at the beginning of the Second World War. There were, perhaps, a dozen of us— young, idealistic, the children of good middle-class families. The world in which we lived was black and white, clear and transparent, thanks to the Marxist-Leninist theory we had absorbed in our studies. We were absolutely certain that after Hitler's downfall, a classless, socialist society would rise on the ruins of fascist Hungary. Stalin, to us, was a kindly *atyushka,* father of the oppressed and downtrodden, who kissed children and patted heads, the personification of humanism, the guarantor of a just future for all of mankind.

The neutrality and isolation of Switzerland, a calm, ordered oasis in the midst of bleeding, war-ravaged Europe, was partly responsible for our remaining in a state of political innocence. The Swiss communist party was banned at the end of 1940, and the police severely persecuted even the slightest political activity on our part, in deference to the wishes of the nation's powerful German neighbor. Nonetheless, the neutrality of the Swiss kept us relatively safe; we knew that if we were discovered, no concentration camps awaited us, but at worst internment in a Swiss labor camp. So, for us, party work did not mean joining an underground movement in which a false step or a careless word meant torture and execution, but rather studying Marx, Engels, Lenin, and Stalin, and where even conspiratorial, illegal activity acquired the quality of an exciting game of hide and seek. Our lack of contact with the brutal world around us meant that we lived in a kind of cocoon, in an atmosphere that enabled us to believe in all kinds of dogmas, abstractions, and unrealistic notions, while at the same time it generated within us a sense of arrogance, of having been chosen, by our very avoidance of the slaughter taking place elsewhere, to be a reserve army of world revolution, to emerge when the time came and help to bring about that revolution in our native Hungary.

The "Swiss group" originated in a series of loose contacts among leftist students united by a common hatred of fascism and war, but it quickly solidified into close friendship. We began with endless discussions and much reading of theory, but with every new victory of Hitler's armies, every expansion of terror in Europe, our impatience grew. Discussions were not enough; we had to do something, to become personally involved in the struggle against Hitler. How could we help? To whom could we turn?

We need not have worried; those who needed us found us soon enough. First, there came Ferenc Vági. Though only a few years older than we were, he was no starry-eyed beginner in the movement. In 1936, he joined a communist student group in Hungary, was arrested, expelled from the university, and exiled to Switzerland. There, continuing his studies, he joined the communist party and was arrested for publishing an illegal newspaper. Having spent more than a year in Witzwil Prison, an infamous Swiss detention center for antifascists, he became in our eyes a hero, a martyr for the cause.

With even greater awe did we look up to András Kálmán, a medical doctor who had joined, as a student, the Hungarian communist party, fought in Spain with the International Brigade, and made his way to Switzerland after the collapse of the Republican government. His warm, caring personality and charming, boyish smile effectively counterbalanced the cold, ascetic, sharp intellect of Vági. Together, they became our teachers and models.

Tibor Szőnyi was, for us, a demigod, a legend from the early days of the brief revolution of Béla Kun. He had held important posts in the party and in the Comintern and evaded, at the last moment, the German occupation of Czechoslovakia. When, in the summer of 1942, the Swiss party instructed him to abandon his top position in the Austrian exile organization and put together a Hungarian communist group, we found our leader. He formed us into a disciplined, active organization, turning us from mere sympathizers and fellow-travelers into dedicated communists.

We began to organize the Hungarians residing in Switzerland, we published an underground newspaper to keep them informed of conditions in our homeland, and we tried to rally them around a broad democratic national front under our guidance.

In retrospect, our efforts, no matter how vital and heroic they seemed to us, had little influence on the course of events. Our most important contribution was a postwar one. We provided the Hungarian communist party and the young People's Democracy with a handful of dedicated, idealistic functionaries. After four brief years, the grateful party arrested us all and hanged two of our leaders, Szőnyi and Vági. The third, András Kálmán, sentenced to life imprisonment, committed suicide in his cell at the end of 1952, when they intended to drag him into a new show trial—this time on charges of Zionism.

* * *

My development from the son of a wealthy merchant to a communist was not so large a leap as it may now seem. Being Jewish helped, of course. To the slaps, kicks, curses and other abuses that I received regularly in school, on the streets, and in the playgrounds from anti-Semitic children and teachers, the logical as well as the emotional response had to be leftist. Genes may also have played a role. In my family, there were musicians, scientists, liberal writers, and even socialist journalists. Having been raised during the 1930s in a home whose atmosphere was one of tolerance and sensitivity, it was only natural that I reacted vehemently both to my personal injustices and to those being endured by millions of hungry peasants and workers in my semifeudal, semifascist country, as well as to a world being slowly devoured by the rapacious barbarism of Nazi Germany. The only unyielding opposition to Hitler and his Hungarian allies came from the Left. Socialism, it seemed to me, offered the only alternative to an unjust society, to anti-Semitism, poverty, oppression, and war. At fourteen, I went out into the streets to demonstrate with leftist students. At fifteen, I dreamed of fighting with the International Brigade, and I could hardly wait to reach the age of sixteen so as to join the youth organization of the Social Democratic party. I distributed their leaflets, wrote their forbidden slogans on walls, and on May 1 marched with the party button on my lapel, its picture of a worker holding high a red hammer. Had I known then that my father, grandmother, and all my aunts, uncles, and cousins would perish in Nazi concentration camps or be shot and their bodies disappear in the Danube, my leftist beginnings would have been even more radical.

Hungary's anti-Semitic laws prohibited me from attending a university in that country, so my family sent me to Switzerland to continue my studies. With Kautsky's *Basic Principles of Marxism* buried deep in my luggage, I left for Zurich in July 1939.

There I began writing reports for the social democratic newspaper in Hungary, but after a few months, the editors asked me to have more understanding for the need of the party to survive and to write in a less radical tone. By that time, however, I was past moderation. In the Swiss Socialist Youth, much more radical than their Hungarian counterparts, I met Mira Munkh, a psychologist who had been expelled by the German communist party as a Trotzkyist. In her seminars, a new road began to open for me, an alternative to the reformism and opportunism of the social democrats and the dogmatism of the sectarian communists.

But once I met Vági in the coffee shop of the University of Zurich, that road was quickly blocked. Night after night we discussed Trotzky, Lenin, and the correct interpretation of Marxism. Vági was a brilliant debater with a deep knowledge of history and philosophy, and it did not take him long to convert me to communism. I still remember a discussion between us on the Trotzkyist trials in the Soviet Union. Do not look at the details, he insisted, but consider them in their total political context. Some of the accusations may have been false, he conceded, and gave as an example the statement of Piatakov, who confessed to having met Trotzky on December 12, 1935, in Oslo in order to join forces in a conspiracy against Stalin and the Soviet system. It has since been shown, said Vági, that on that day neither Trotzky nor Piatakov could have been in Oslo. The trial, he pointed out, did not hinge upon a single meeting, but on the objective role of Trotzkyism. With the liquidation of Stalin toward which both men were working, there would have been an end to socialism and Soviet power, thus bringing about the triumph of reaction and fascism. It is the historical truth and not the correctness of some incidental details that is essential; the trials were necessary and just, Vági said. What might Vági have thought about such matters nine years later while he stood under the gallows. . . .

*   *   *

The car halted at a side entrance of the State Security headquarters in Andrássy Street. I was handed over to a uniformed AVH man and was led through twisting corridors into a large room.

"Sit down, face the wall, and don't open your mouth," he ordered.

I was indignant. Can't they distinguish between a comrade and a fascist criminal? But then it seemed understandable; how could this corporal know about such things?

I sat there for hours, unmoving, unthinking. Gradually, the room grew lighter; sunshine pierced through the dirty, barred windows. It was ten o'clock before I was ordered to stand, place my hands behind my back, and follow an AVH man to an interrogation room on an upper floor. Behind the desk sat a man in civilian clothing whom I discovered later was a lieutenant. He looked at me.

"You know why you are here."

"Yes, you want some information about my friends."

He did not ask me to sit. How impolite, I thought.

"We don't want any information about your friends. They are all criminals. They told us everything about their criminal activities as well as yours. You can only save your own neck if you make a full confession."

"Confession of what?"

He answered brusquely that it was the AVH that was asking the questions and that my duty was to supply honest answers. If I would expose my role and those of my accomplices, the party would show leniency and perhaps forgive me.

"Sit down. Here are pencils and paper. Write an unsparing, self-critical resume of your life, all your activities, your contacts, from the beginning to the present."

He left the room. A soldier remained to watch me.

There followed the longest forty-eight hours of my life. I stared at the blank paper. What should I write? What did I do wrong? To what do they want me to confess? I began writing, trying not to spare myself, but the only incriminating element I could think of was my bourgeois background. When I completed my report, the sheets of paper were removed. I was handed a paper with written questions on it, mostly about my activities in Switzerland and my contacts with foreign journalists in Budapest after the war. Then there were new questions, new demands to elaborate on the answers already given. It was night again. Then dawn returned, and I was still writing.

Finally the lieutenant returned, freshly shaven and well-rested. He called me a hardened criminal who should understand that fairy tales were not what was wanted from me.

"Begin again from the beginning, and this time, write the truth."

It all started a second time, the report, the written questions that included long-forgotten details I had omitted. These gave me the impression that they actually knew everything about me and believed that I was trying to hide something from them.

At first, during the long ordeal, I was assailed by hunger, but as night returned, I forgot that I had had nothing to eat or drink and was overcome, instead, by a need to sleep. But as soon as my head began to nod, a guard would shake me awake. So it went for two days and two nights: questions, reports, new demands, new details. I wanted to cooperate and clear up misunderstandings, to unmask myself without pity, since this was what my party demanded of me. But what was there to unmask?

Late in the second afternoon, the process suddenly ended. I was escorted down to the basement, fingerprinted, photographed, made to empty my pockets and remove my tie and shoelaces. Then I was led to a tiny cell and the door was locked behind me. I looked around and saw moist stone walls illuminated by a small bulb, a bare wooden cot, and high above me a tiny opening leading only to darkness. Still I felt no fear. Soon, I knew, everything would be made clear, apologies would be offered, and I would return home. I devoured hungrily a pot of sticky, cold beans, lay down on the cot, and fell asleep instantly.

But not for long. In the middle of the night, I was awakened and returned to the interrogation room. There was the lieutenant, freshly shaven, well-rested. The cycle was repeated.

"You are a hardened criminal and a liar," he informed me. "Your accomplices have already confessed to their crimes. Your friend, Tibor Szőnyi, was the first. Or do you think that we arrest a member of the Central Committee without having proof that he is a spy?"

Again he left me with pencil and paper, and I racked my brain to recall even the most remote events. I forced myself to reply as fully as I could so that they would know they could trust me and allow me to return to my wife and child and to my party.

When, after another twenty-four hours, the ordeal ended and I was escorted back to my cell, I could not even bring myself to eat the cold beans in the tin bowl that was placed just outside my cell door.

For the next two days and nights, I expected that at any moment the door would be opened and I would be told that this was all an unfortunate mistake. Go home, comrade, they would tell me, we are sorry that we doubted for even a moment your loyalty to the party. But, of course, it did not happen. I slept a great deal; I wanted desperately to sleep, to dream of being at home, to imagine that this was all a nightmare, that the silent guard did not come to me every morning to lead me to a doorless toilet and washbowl and to place a tin bowl of lukewarm brownish liquid in my cell and later—in the evening—return with another filled with sticky beans.

On the third night, I could not sleep. Maybe, I thought in terror, they had forgotten me, I was being confined only because of some administrative error. By now, they must certainly have realized that I was innocent of whatever mysterious crimes they attributed to me. I banged on the steel door and demanded to see the interrogator. To my great relief, I was taken to him and asked him for permission to make a statement.

"Yes," he said, "it is time you made your confession." I told him that there must have been a mistake; all my adult life I had tried to be a good communist. He did not let me finish.

"That is why you wanted to see me?" he yelled at me. "You are an abominable criminal, Hodos, a shameless spy. Until now, we gave you time to confess, we did not touch you, we let you eat and sleep. But now your time is up. Believe me, we will break you. It may take a week or a month or a year. And if you still have not confessed, you will rot here forever. Think it over, Hodos."

And with that, he called the guard to take me back to my cell.

Now my treatment in the cellar changed drastically. During the day, I was not allowed to sit on my cot, only to walk endlessly back and forth in the cell. Moreover, they removed the threadbare blanket that had protected me even slightly from the bitter cold. Every quarter hour during the night, the guard would wake me by banging on the eyehole of my cell. Now my exhausted brain began to produce a new train of thoughts. Could it be possible, I asked myself, that I had unknowingly been involved in some crime? The lieutenant must be right on one point: The party would not have arrested Szőnyi without good reason; the party was always right. Maybe Szőnyi tried to lure me into some hostile action of which I was unaware. The thought seemed so absurd that I thought I might be losing my mind. But then, again, the party must have reason to suspect me for things of which I was unaware. The party, the AVH, must know.

After three more days, my nerves snapped. I hammered on the door. I was ready to confess.

I thought it over, I told the lieutenant. I must have committed some crime.

"Please help me find out where and when I have been used by the enemy."

"That is not how it is done," he replied. "You let me know you want to confess, but you still play the innocent. We know that you are a Trotzkyist, a spy. If you want us to help you, don't try to deceive us. I have no time for you. We have methods to make you talk, and when you do, you will talk so much we will hardly be able to stop you."

We have methods. . . . Very soon, I began to get acquainted with them. I was led into a different room. Instead of my lieutenant, there were two AVH men. They greeted me.

"So you have not yet confessed? You are a swine, you stink, that you can still walk on two legs is a mistake that we shall correct immediately."

One of them took his rubber truncheon, made me lie down on my stomach, feet up in the air. I counted twenty blows on my soles.

"That is only the beginning. Tonight you will not be able to sleep from the pain, but it will pass. Next time, you will not be able to walk for weeks, only crawl and whimper, like swine do."

The pain passed quickly, but I still did not know what they wanted of me, what crimes I was supposed to have committed. In the end, I knew they would have to let me free or beat me to death.

CHAPTER 7

THE RAJK TRIAL

Eight defendants stood before the people's court in Budapest: László Rajk, György Pálffy, Tibor Szőnyi, András Szalai, Béla Korondy, Pál Justus, Lazar Brankov, and Milan Ognjenovic. In his closing statement, the prosecutor spelled out the significance of the show trial.

"This trial is of international importance," he said. "In this courtroom, we pass judgment not only on the accused. . . . Not only Rajk and his associates are here in the dock, but with them sit their foreign masters, the imperialist instigators from Belgrade and Washington. . . . Rajk and his accomplices were the serfs and servants of foreign imperialists, but the special feature, the unique quality of their case lies in the fact that the clique of rulers in Yugoslavia, Tito and his band, have put the heroic people of that country under their yoke and usurped power, taking onto themselves the role of intermediaries, chief agents and storm troopers for the foreign imperialists.

"It is only just," continued the prosecutor, "that the Hungarian People's Court, in passing sentence upon Rajk and his gang, should also pass sentence in a moral and political sense, on the traitors of Yugoslavia, the criminal gang of Tito, Ranković, Kardelj, and Djilas. We have demonstrated their duplicity, their perfidy, their intrigues against democracy and socialism, their plans for and acts of assassination. This trial exposed the Titoites in their role of allies of the American imperialists and common agents of the imperialist intelligence organizations.

"It is clear from the evidence heard at this trial, that even during the war against Hitler, the American intelligence services were preparing for the fight against the forces of socialism and democracy. Behind Ranković, there stand the shadows of Field and Dulles. And as recently as the spring of 1948, Allan Dulles's brother, John Foster Dulles, announced the so-called 'Operation X,' a project for organizing underground movements in the people's democracies. The substance of that secret plan was summarized in the Swiss newspaper *Die Tat* on April 26 of this year: 'The west attempted first of all to penetrate into the cadres and elite of the ruling classes of those countries and it is said that they succeeded in doing so far beyond their hopes.' Well, the material of the whole trial is contained in this confession. Here the practical execution of the project of the

American imperialists called 'Operation X' was unveiled. The plot in Hungary, planned by Tito and his clique to be put into action by Rajk's spy ring cannot be understood out of context of the international plans of the American imperialists."[1]

* * *

The "confessions" of the defendants and the "evidence" of the witnesses had the sole purpose to squeeze flesh and blood into this phantom plot. First, the political past of the victims had to be dragged through the mud, their prestige had to be destroyed, their lifelong fight for the socialist revolution turned into a service for the fascist counterrevolution.

Rajk confessed to having been an informer since his early youth; at the university he had delivered his communist fellow students to the police and, as a union leader, he denounced his comrades. He went to Spain on the orders of the police to spy on the Hungarian volunteers in the International Brigade. After the Republican collapse, he furnished the Deuxième Bureau with confidential reports on communist internees in France and, while there, he was approached by Noel Field and asked to work for American intelligence. With the assistance of the Gestapo, he returned to Hungary and offered his services to the police to disrupt the underground resistance movement.

In the summer of 1945, after the liberation of Hungary, he was contacted by a Colonel Kovach of the American military mission in Budapest. "He ordered me to place myself at the disposal of the American intelligence service. If I refused, they threatened to tell the Communist Party leadership about my past role as agent and informer. Of course I agreed to do this. . . . Independently of the Americans, I had been in touch with the Yugoslav intelligence through Brankov, the head of their military mission and gave him information on the political situation, especially on state secrets. . . .

"In the summer of 1947, I spent my holidays in Yugoslavia. In Abbazia, I met with Ranković. He told me that he had come on direct orders from Tito to warn me that if I should not support Tito's policies, they would expose my connections with the fascist police and the American intelligence services. Ranković also told me that from now on, I would receive my instructions not from the Americans, but from the Yugoslavs . . ."[2]

In the same way, Szalai, one of the outstanding figures in the underground resistance, confessed to having been a police informer from the age of fifteen. "At the end of 1943, I was arrested. The prison commander suggested that I work for him. . . . In January, 1944, I told him that the political prisoners were planning to break out. He took countermeasures and the attempted jailbreak was suppressed. Not a single prisoner escaped, 54 were shot and ten more were courtmartialed and executed. That was my activity with the police."

What followed was predictable. "The Yugoslav espionage recruited me in

1946. A member of their military mission told me that he knew of my role in the prison and threatened to expose me if I did not carry out all of their wishes.''[3]

The procedure was repeated with all of the other defendants. Pálffy, organizer of the armed underground, confessed that his admiration for Mussolini, in his early youth, made it possible for him to commit military espionage and to plot a murderous uprising against the communist regime. Szőnyi admitted to having sold himself and his comrades in exile in Switzerland to Field and Dulles for a couple of hundred francs, and later to receiving instructions from his American paymasters to place his group of spies at the disposal of Rajk and the Yugoslavs. Justus told how, as a youngster, he delivered his communist and socialist comrades to the police and how later the French and subsequently the Yugoslav intelligence services blackmailed him and his Trotzkyist gang into attempting to overthrow the government.

The same tactic of transforming communists into fascists was applied to the Yugoslav leaders with the important difference that Tito and his comrades could not be placed in the dock and made to repeat extorted confessions. With them, the task of providing proof was given to Rajk and his "gang of plotters." Rajk explained that since 1939, when the French set up internment camps for those who fled the fascist victory in Spain, the Yugoslav fighters among them had been recruited by the Deuxième Bureau and the Gestapo. In the fall of 1946, he added, when the Americans told him that their espionage net in southeastern Europe was being handed over to the Yugoslavs, Ranković gave him irrefutable proof that not only those Yugoslavs who were recruited in France before the war, but also Tito, Ranković, and other high officials in the government were collaborating with the imperialists.

Even more concrete were the confessions of Brankov. "The hostile attitude of Tito, Kardelj, Djilas, and Ranković did not begin after the Cominform resolution, but much earlier," he said. "During the war, the imperialists succeeded in drawing them into their service. . . . It is evident that the Yugoslav plans to subvert the Balkans and central Europe were instigated by the British and American intelligence agencies and that Tito was merely their tool.''[4]

Szőnyi rounded off the picture. He confessed that in 1944, instructed by the Yugoslav emigré Miša Lompar, he had steered his Hungarian group in Switzerland in a chauvinistic, pro-American direction. "In this, the theory of Browder, then leader of the Communist Party of the USA, played an important part. Copies of Browder's books were distributed by Lompar and Field, both in Switzerland and in France, on behalf of the American secret service. It lead my group to the conclusion that after the war we had to take a political line within the Communist Party to range Hungary on the side of the United States."

In his last plea, Szőnyi closed the circle, the Yugoslav spy Lompar put him in touch with Allen Dulles, thus proving the early origins of the conspiracy. "The joint plan of the American imperialists and Tito against peace and freedom was not recently hatched,'' he said. "The architects, the organizers and the controllers are the American warmongers together with Tito and his gang who are entirely in agreement with them and play the same tune. These plans are the offspring of the marriage into which Tito entered with the imperialists back in 1944 . . .''[5]

*   *   *

We confine ourselves here to the main political scenario of the show trial. It would be superfluous to go into the details of the fabricated charges of conspiracy, espionage, and murder. The function of the trial was to "unmask" Tito who, as Rajk was forced to say in his final plea, "is following in the footsteps of Hitler." With the "exposure" of the Yugoslav leaders, this was accomplished; the fantastic stories of the individual crimes were only necessary for the pseudojuridical proceedings. The charges and the defendants were interchangeable, the essence remained the same: A joint American-Yugoslav plot existed to infiltrate the communist party with agents in order to overthrow the government with a military coup; to murder the beloved Hungarian leaders, Rákosi, Gerő, and Farkas; to restore capitalism; and to detach the country from the Soviet Union. Every one of the defendants confessed to the most atrocious crimes and accused all of the others while every witness corroborated the charges. The performance, transmitted throughout the country by radio, was flawless.

The only mishap, a slight one, occurred when Szőnyi failed to recognize a photograph of Allen Dulles. The only clue to the truth was detected by reading carefully the text of Rajk's final plea, in which he said, "I fully agree with most of the statements of the prosecutor; I don't mean the secondary and in any case unimportant details, but the substance."[6] This refutation of the charges, dressed in the form of a confession, the dismissal of details while acknowledging the political necessity of the substance was Rajk's only message to the outside world. It escaped the vigilance of the Soviet and Hungarian stage managers.

The trial lasted one week. The verdict, determined well in advance by Rákosi and Beria and ratified by Stalin, was announced on September 24. Rajk, Szőnyi, and Szalai were sentenced to death by hanging. Brankov and Justus received life imprisonment. Ognjenovic, an official of the Yugoslav minority organization, was given a nine-year sentence. The cases of Pálffy and police colonel Korondy, his alleged associate in the planned uprising, were transferred to the military tribunal, which ordered both men to be shot. The executions were carried out on October 15.[7]

*   *   *

The details, charges, and persons in the Rajk trail were deliberately kept interchangeable, since it was intended to serve, with certain local variations, as a blueprint for the subsequent show trials in Stalin's satellite empire. This function was clearly evident in the confessions. Pálffy declared that his Yugoslav masters and employers often told him about conspiratorial activities in all of the people's democracies, coordinated according to a common plan.

"I know of it," he said, "because they enumerated to me the countries involved in the plot to create a Balkan federation, made up of Hungary, Bulgaria, and Albania, with Yugoslavia as the leading power. I also was told about Poland which, under the American plan, was the next country after Hungary to be turned around."

The Soviet timetable, however, had been changed in the time between the memorizing of Pálffy's confession and his stating it in the trial. There had been some unexpected delays in the Gomułka case, so the prosecutor interrupted in order to update the script.

"Of course, Czechoslovakia cannot be left out between Hungary and Poland."

"Probably not."

"Don't you know about the Yugoslavs pursuing similar activities there?"

"I don't recall their mentioning Czechoslovakia specifically, but I have no doubt they would not leave that country out."[8]

Brankov confirmed the international dimensions of the joint Titoist-imperialist plan. "The gist of it was that Yugoslavia should become a central, leading state in the Balkans and in central Europe and should organize a bloc which would become a federation of bourgeois democratic republics with an orientation toward the West rather than toward the Soviet Union. . . . Ranković mentioned that such a plan existed in Romania, but it did not quite succeed there. He mentioned Patrascanu, then the Minister of Justice, who wanted to carry out Tito's plan in Romania, but the Central Committee of the Romanian party removed him in time and isolated him from the party. Ranković told me that work would have to be continued there.

"I recall the case of Gomułka in Poland. They attached great hopes to it and hoped Gomułka would carry out Tito's plans in Poland and they were awaiting developments. But as is known, Gomułka did not carry them out and admitted that it was a wrong policy. Once, Ranković even complained that they must start afresh in Poland. . . .

"There was also a case in Bulgaria. I cannot remember that anyone mentioned a specific person. The point was that there, too, they should do everything possible to carry out this plan. There was a very serious attempt made in Albania to overthrow the government but it was frustrated.

"I know that in Czechoslovakia, Yugoslav diplomats work very hard on similar espionage and wrecking activities. Ranković once told me that they worked much better in Czechoslovakia than in Hungary. . ."[9]

Szőnyi answered the prosecutor's question about groups that the Americans sent across the borders to carry out espionage activities.

"In connection with Czechoslovakia, I have definite knowledge that the American intelligence built a secret organization there. . . . With regard to other countries, I know such a group in Germany . . . and I know that in Poland, too, there were similar contacts. . . . In addition to that in all countries where, with Noel Field as intermediary, aid organizations of the Unitarian Service Committee were set up, these branches were, in reality, cover organizations for the American secret service."[10]

The name of Noel Field appeared in most of the confessions. His role, according to the prosecutor, was paramount in recruiting spies for American intelligence, in undermining the Hungarian communist party, and in forming a link between the Titoists and the imperialists. Field first recruited Rajk into the service of the Americans, he was the spymaster of Szőnyi, and according to Brankov, he was Tito's intermediary to Allen Dulles during the war. However, only his shadow was present in the courtroom; he did not appear at the trial, even as a witness. Field remained in his cell in the Soviet MVD cottage in Budapest and was later transferred to a cell specially prepared for him in the Budapest prison. There he remained completely isolated from all of the other prisoners. His only visitors were security officers from Czechoslovakia, Poland, and East Germany to interrogate him about their victims. He was held as a ghost, kept alive to serve as a starting point for the later copies of the Rajk trial scheduled to take place in the rest of Stalin's satellites.

*   *   *

When the public trial ended, only a small segment of the Rajk trial was concluded. General Byelkin left for his headquarters near Vienna, but the MVD advisers remained and prepared, together with their Hungarian helpers, the secret trials of hundreds of "Rajkists." They were divided into groups of about a dozen defendants each, prepared and coached in the same way as the victims of the main trial. From March 1950 to the end of that year, one group after another was tried behind closed doors: the Swiss, the French, the English, the Ministry of the Interior, the Trotzkyists, the soldiers, the policemen, the undergrounders, and the Spaniards. In most of the groups, one or two defendants were sentenced to death and executed. Those victims who, for one reason or another, did not fit into any group were tried individually or together with one or two similarly unfitting comrades. Hundreds of other Rajkists were deemed to be too unimportant or too unpredictable to be brought into court; they were sent without trial to secret internment camps of the AVH in Kistarcsa and Recsk, buried alive in complete isolation.

The secret trials served the same cynical purpose as the public show. While the trial of Rajk was staged to prove the guilt of the main defendants, to create forged historical facts of a Titoist-imperialist plot, the secret trials had to prove the public one, to furnish the confidential party archives the documentary evidence of a widespread conspiracy. There was no more political need for public trials, the disappearances were well known, the terror fully entrenched.

* * *

The single public and many secret trials ended the Rajk affair. The MVD generals Likhachev and Makarov left for Prague to speed up the sluggish beginning of the Slánský "conspiracy." In Hungary, the inherent laws of Stalinist terror required more and more victims. In the summer of 1950, a new purge engulfed the Social Democrats, both rightists and leftists, about 4,000 of them. The principal victims were Anna Kéthly, the prewar leader of the party; Árpád Szakasits, chairman of the United Worker's Party and head of state; justice minister and Central Committee member István Riesz; and György Marosán, Politburo member and closest fellow traveler of the communists. Another purge swept into prison the top ranks of the army, trained and educated in the prewar period. Between May 20 and July 24, 1950, eighteen generals had been arrested, seven of them executed; among them were Chief of Staff László Sólyom; Chief Inspector General László Kuthy; and the Generals Illy, Beleznay, and Pórffy. One of the murdered, General Kálmán Révay, director of the military academy, commanded eight months before his arrest the firing squad at the execution of his old friend and comrade Pálffy in the courtyard of the military prison on Conti Street.[11] In April 1951 came the turn of the home communists. These included János Kádár, removed ten months earlier as minister of Interior; Ferenc Donáth, deputy minister of agriculture; Gyula Kállai, former minister of foreign affairs, and Géza Losonczy, Sándor Haraszti, and Szilárd Ujhelyi, three top party functionaries and intellectuals. They were accused of antiparty activities committed during the war. After the dissolution of the Comintern, the underground leadership in Hungary decided in 1943 to dissolve the communist party and reestablish it under the name of Peace party. This decision inflicted great damage to the underground communist movement, according to the initial charges, and was responsible for the ineffective resistance against the German occupiers. Soon the charges were politically reinterpreted into an anti-Soviet, Trotzkyist plot first against the wartime Moscow leadership, then into a conspiracy to overthrow the Muscovite leaders of the party and to establish a nationalistic Titoist regime in Hungary. Kádár had the special honor to be tortured by AVH Colonel Vladimir Farkas, son of the troika member Mihály Farkas.

Kállai and Losonczy were condemned to death, their sentences later commuted to life imprisonment; the rest received long prison terms. Kadar's successor as minister of Interior, Sandor Zöld, learned that he was being selected for the next purge, and killed his wife, his mother-in-law, his two young children, and himself.[12]

By 1952, the AVH terror reached into every government office, every party branch, and every organization. This was too much, even for Colonel Ernö

Szücs, the deputy of AVH chief Péter. He decided to go to Moscow and make a confidential report directly to Stalin, stating that the dimensions of the purge had become uncontrollable and threatened to destroy the party. Soviet security officials promised to forward the report to Stalin. Back in Budapest, he was immediately arrested, interrogated by a joint Soviet-Hungarian team, and hanged as a spy. His brother, Miklós Szücs, had been in London during the war. After liberation, he was appointed councillor at the embassy in London. At the time of the Rajk trial, he was recalled to Budapest, arrested, and cast in the role of defendant in the English group. On the intervention of his brother, he was released, the only known release of an arrested victim. But following the "treacherous" Moscow trip of the AVH colonel, Miklós was rearrested and tortured to incriminate his brother as an agent of the British Secret Service. He was never brought to trial, but was beaten to death in an AVH prison.

At the end of 1952, emulating the Slánský trial in Czechoslovakia, a new purge was instituted to uncover Zionist agents. Dozens of Jewish communists in high posts were arrested. The campaign peaked with the arrest of Jewish doctors working in exclusive party and AVH hospitals and institutes, thus mirroring the "doctors' plot" in the Soviet Union. The Jewish troika of Rákosi, Gerő, and Farkas, slavish initiators of the new anti-Semitic purge in Hungary, remained untouchable, but the AVH chief Péter, also Jewish, was caught in his own terror net.

His arrest was demanded in December 1952 by Stalin personally. He called Rákosi on the direct line and told him that the Minister of State Security Abakumov and his gang had been arrested as Zionist agents. One of the gang was Fyodor Byelkin, the MVD general who organized in Hungary the Rajk trial. Byelkin confessed, so Stalin explained, that at that time he had recruited Gábor Péter in his espionage net in the service of the British and Zionist intelligence.

Péter was arrested on January 1, 1953. His former colleagues and their Soviet advisers began the torture to extract from him a confession of his crimes. His wife, Jolán Simon, was arrested with him, and her body broken on a wheel to make her incriminate her husband. When they found in his house a photograph picturing him together with Allen Dulles, whom he had met in 1945 during a party mission to Switzerland to negotiate the extradiction of war criminals, they added to the charges espionage for the Office of Strategic Services and the CIA.

Stalin's death and Beria's execution saved his life. The charges against Péter switched from Zionist spy to Beria's agent and having been an informer of the fascist police during his underground activities. At the beginning of 1954, when Khrushchev demanded an inquiry into the Stalinist purges, most of the concocted accusations were dropped, and on March 12, 1954, he was sentenced in a secret trial to life in prison for subverting socialist legality by extorting false confessions from innocent communists. Rákosi, Gerő, and Farkas, the real instigators of the show trials, were eager to throw the blame on their faithful underling. A number of his close collaborators in the AVH, among them his former deputy Gyula Décsi, at that time minister of justice, also received long prison terms.[13]

Gábor Péter, the last victim of the Stalinist purges, was finally purged on a justified charge, a symbol of the beginning and at the same time the end of a period. He served only seven years of his sentence, was pardoned in 1959 by one of his former victims, Kádár, and lives today in comfortable retirement in Budapest.

Personal Notes III: August 1949–March 1950

The next few weeks were so unreal that often, in the loneliness of my cell, I dug my fingernails into my wounded flesh to make sure that I was not going through an evil, crazy dream. Night after night, they hauled me up to the interrogation room. There was no vagueness any more. Evidently, my role had been determined and my lieutenant tried to explain it to me. All my friends had been imperialist agents, he told me again and again in a patient, even friendly tone, so how could I alone be innocent? I am a spy using the cover of a foreign correspondent. Didn't I know that all the Western journalists I worked for were agents of the intelligent services, all my newspaper articles were spy reports— parts of Szőnyi's treacherous network?

Because I remained skeptical, I had to be handed over to the bad guys, who tried to convince me with the help of rubber truncheons, slaps, kicks, and gymnastic exercises. Back at the interrogation room, my lieutenant asked me if I now remembered what Szőnyi's orders were, at what time, and how I was recruited. When I told him that Szőnyi did not have anything to do with my journalistic work, my contacts with foreign correspondents were cleared by Endre Rosta, head of the Central Press Department of the party, the triumphantly laughing lieutenant robbed me of even this last saving straw: "Rosta is a dirty Trotzkyist spy; he is downstairs in a neighboring cell and he confessed already how he used you as an agent." Rosta, who had spent three years in the fascist prison, an old communist with no "Swiss connections," even he is arrested? Might there be any truth, after all, to this unbelievable spider's net they are talking about?

I still refused to understand, and the cycle began all over again: the bad guys with their rubber truncheons, gymnastic exercises, and statements such as, "We don't need your confession," "No one will ever find out about you," and "You are nothing but a vermin whom the party will crush."

I spent weeks in the damp, cold basement cell with no blanket, my clothes in rags, the soles of my shoes worn out to a stinking, sticking, brownish-black mass covering my swollen feet. Every time I was escorted down to the eternal light of my cellar catacomb, I felt happy and relieved, but after a couple of hours, the deadly silence seemed to hurt more than all the fantastic accusations, all the beatings. I felt I was buried alive, there would be no return, and I yearned to be led upstairs to my lieutenant, to hear a human voice, to explain and to understand.

At last it happened. It must have been the middle of August when I sensed the changed.

"How are you, Hodos?" my lieutenant greeted me with a friendly smile.

"Is it not too cold in the cellar? Do you smoke?" And when he offered me a cigarette, I was sure they would let me free. But the moment passed quickly, as he continued: "Don't you think it is about time that you cooperate with us and help us to unmask the enemies of the party? You are but a speck in the vast conspiracy, and your espionage contacts with the foreign journalists are just a small side branch. Help us and we will help you."

I answered that I did not know that my contacts were spies.

"Don't try to be difficult again, Hodos. I told you they were agents, so now you know. Write a comprehensive protocol containing all the incriminating aspects of your activities, the extenuating aspects will come later in a separate protocol, don't worry. You were a party member long enough, you know the dialectics, that well-intentioned deeds, under certain conditions, can turn into the opposite. You must have confidence in the party, it can tell the difference between those who were deliberate enemies and those who were their victims."

Suddenly it became clear to me that the party knew at last: I had been a victim, misled by the enemies of the party. I could trust the AVH because it wanted only the dialectical truth from me. And I began to write.

I wrote that I had not been sufficiently vigilant in understanding the class enemy, that in my bourgeois blindness, I had not recognized Trotzkyists and foreign agents, and collaborated with imperialist spies disguised as Western journalists.

I was very proud of my unsparing self-criticism, confessing my mistake of walking guilelessly into the diabolical net spread by the agents of imperialist intelligence services. Why did I sign such a statement? Fear, of course, played a great role—fear of beatings, of madness, and above all, fear of hopelessly rotting forever in the cellar. No doubt, also, the well-known "Stockholm syndrome" contributed to it, the psychological mechanism of identification with the interrogator. But the decisive reason of my surrender was my conviction that the party must always be right. Up to that moment, I resisted—not because I was a hero or a tough fighter, but because I did not understand what they wanted from me. I fought to prove that they had made a mistake. Now my lieutenant seemed to offer a plausible explanation. My arrest was no mistake, I was a victim, not of the party, but of a cunning plot of internal and external enemies. I believed in it because I wanted desperately to believe, I wanted to put an end to my ordeal. I thought I had found, at last, the solution. I confessed to my guilt, but at the same time, I asserted my innocence.

I handed the papers to the lieutenant. He read them carefully and then said, "You are the most stubborn Trotzkyist I have ever met. You have just signed your own death sentence."

However, I know it now and they knew it immediately, that was the moment they broke me—I felt guilty for the first time since my arrest. I believed them that there was a crime committed against the party and that I had participated in it, by not being vigilant enough. In the real underworld of communist secret police, there was only a small step from subjective guilt to objective crime. You trusted spies, though you did not know that they were spies? Don't be such a ridiculous apolitical bourgeois: You helped the enemies of the party, so you are an enemy.

They must have known it, that from here on, it needed only a little kind comradely push to entrap me into their sick logic. X is a spy because we say so. What is a careless person who helps a spy? A tool of a spy—a spy himself—isn't he? You can sign it with good conscience, we know both sides of the truth. Now the party needs only the one side, but we won't forget the other.

I had crossed their line. They could now send their bad guys to others, to teach them how to feel guilty.

A few days later, I was moved from the cellar cell in Andrássy Street to the prison of Markó Street, the second floor of which had been taken over by the AVH. Here, there was a window to the sky, doves settled on the roof of the gray court building across the prison. My food improved, I received five cigarettes every day, and even books. Best of all, I was not alone any more, I had cell mates.

The first one was Colonel Géza Vietoris, a district chief of police. Before the war, he had been a printer in contact with the underground communist organization. In 1945, he was one of the founders of the political police until Gábor Péter took control of the apparatus. It was one of those instances where personal reasons contributed to the arrest; Péter simply could not stand him. At his arrest, two of his teeth were knocked out before he even left his house, and the savage beatings continued at the AVH headquarters.

With his body torn and bleeding, he signed a confession that he was a police informer and a go-between for Rajk and the fascist police. Then he asked for a cigarette; when he finished it, he retracted the confession. For weeks, the cycle was repeated: torture, confession, retraction. Finally, he was brought to Markó Street.

Vietoris was a tough man; the tortures didn't break his spirit. When he spoke to me of Rákosi, he only called him "that arsehead." The first time I heard it, I thought we would be struck by lightning. True, Comrade Rákosi is completely bald, but how could one be so blasphemous and talk in such a disrespectful way of the leader of our party! A few days later I got used to it, I even began to like it. Vietoris helped me quite a bit in regaining my sanity. I knew now that I was not the only innocent in this dirty political game, and I learned that lightning would not strike if I began to doubt the party, the AVH.

Six years later, I learned that the AVH never did dare to call him as a witness against Rajk for fear of a public retraction. He was sent without trial to a concentration camp and finally freed in 1954, when Rajk and the other murdered victims were posthumously rehabilitated and the survivors released from prison.

János Reisman, one of Hungary's finest photographers, was my second cellmate. He lived in Berlin until Hitler came to power, and then emigrated to the Soviet Union, where he had the incredibly good luck not to be purged in the trials of the 1930s. In 1939, he was expelled from the Soviet Union and spent the war years in Paris, working with the resistance.

After the war, he returned to Hungary where he was given a post in the cultural section of the embassy in Paris. An urgent telegram called him home, and when he arrived at the railway station in Budapest, he was arrested by the AVH. He was still tanned from the sun of a vacation on the French Riviera when they pushed him into my cell.

His interrogation was short, he told me. After the first blows, he gave up. He asked for a glass of cognac and when, to his greatest surprise, he got it, he began to spin a fantastic tale centering on his recruitment by the United States intelligence service. It was a poetic masterpiece of a confession, worthy of his artistic nature. When he described it to me, trembling, he said that since he was convinced we were going to be hanged no matter what we did, he had concocted a statement of such nonsense that hopefully, some day, someone reading it would understand the absurdity of the whole proceeding.

"It is the netherworld," he whispered, with deathly fear in his eyes. "I had seen it all in the Soviet Union. They could not let us out alive, we are witnesses to their crimes. They will dispose of us, with or without confession."

We met again later in the prison of Vác, after the secret trial of the French group. He had been sentenced to life imprisonment.

In February 1950 I was returned to Andrássy Street. This time the interrogator was someone I knew, a Lieutenant Ervin Faludi, whom I had met in a local party organization. The statements I had signed, he told me, were useless; I could not be sentenced on the basis of such ridiculous self-criticism.

"Then let me go home," I replied.

He laughed. "Don't be a child, Hodos. You are a political person. By now, you must have guessed the rules of the game. Your protocol has to fit into the overall picture. Here, I give you the 'Blue Book,' the script of the Rajk trial with the confessions of Szőnyi and some of your friends. Read it in the cell and you will see in what a horrendous conspiracy you got involved. The preparations for the trial of the Swiss group are complete; only your statement is missing. If we don't do it now, you will be tried anyhow, and thirteen witnesses will prove your guilt. You will never leave the prison alive.''

Then he sent the silent typist out of the room.

"Listen well, Hodos," he continued, and reverted to the familiar thou form of address; he actually winked at me with a cynical smile of complicity on his fat face.

"I know you were a devoted member of the party. You must understand that we have to reinterpret your statements, politicize the mistakes. I will help you to draw up properly the final protocol. If you collaborate, we will know that you are not an enemy.''

He and I would write the final protocol together and I would receive a short prison sentence: three years. He could assure me of that even before the trial. "You know that the court is in our hands, they do what we tell them to do." For the first six weeks, I would live in a villa, my wife could visit me, and then when the entire affair had been forgotten, I would work under an assumed name for one of the provincial newspapers until it would be possible to return to Budapest. By now, he pointed out with great reasonableness, I should realize that it was not me that the party was concerned about. After all, Rajk and Szőnyi had already been hanged and the Swiss group was now part of the history of the international labor movement. It was just my bad luck that I had been a member of the group, so the party had no choice.

I had become a particle of dust to be trodden into the ground by the party at any time, with no one to notice. I had been in the netherworld from which there was no escape—but now, everything would be cleared up. The party knew everything. Six weeks in a villa and it would be forgotten—a particle of dust that the party can once again turn into a human being.

I collaborated. I signed.

The protocol was five pages long. It described how Szőnyi had recruited me in Switzerland for the American intelligence service and how, following his instructions, I made contact in Hungary with such imperialist spies as O. Matter, economic editor of the *Neue Zürcher Zeitung,* listed as an agent of the OSS; Jacques Clergier of *Agence France Press,* an agent of the Deuxième Bureau; Peter Smolka, foreign affairs editor of the *Neues Österreich;* and Michael Burn, Budapest correspondent of the London *Times,* both agents of the British Intelligence Service who, under the guise of foreign reporting, smuggled out my spy reports on the political and economic situation in Hungary and passed them on to the U.S.

It was that easy.

I remained in the cellar for a few more days, this time, however, supplied with blanket, cigarettes, and books, until I was finally brought to the huge, elegant office of Colonel Márton Károlyi of the AVH. He pushed a typewritten document towards me.

"Here is your indictment, the questions you will be asked by the president of the people's court, and your answers. Memorize them word for word, so that there will be no slip-up during the trial. In three days, I will call you again and we will have a dress rehearsal."

I told him he could depend on me, provided that both he and the party were aware that not a single word in the indictment was consistent with the truth.

Károlyi laughed. "We know everything. The trial is just a circus, a formality, and soon you will return to your family."

I was transported back to the Markó Street prison. Suddenly, the food was excellent, even dessert was not missing, cigarettes as plentiful as I wanted, books as soon as I asked for them, the service was excellent, and the wardens were polite. I was visited by a doctor who asked if I had any complaints, and Lieutenant Faludi showed his concern by inquiring as to whether or not I had any wishes. To have it behind me and to go home as soon as possible, I said. He grinned encouragingly.

After two weeks of pampering, they walked into my cell early one morning, took my measurements, and returned an hour later with fresh underwear, a white shirt, and a dark suit. Dress quickly, was the instruction, they will call for you in ten minutes. It was March 16, 1950. The Swiss group once again reassembled and smiled sadly at each other in the prison corridor, on their way to the trial.

CHAPTER 8

THE UNLEASHED TERROR IN PRAGUE

The trial of László Rajk in Hungary actually began in Czechoslovakia with the arrest of Noel Field at the beginning of May 1949. The trial of Rudolf Slánský in Czechoslovakia got its start in Hungary with the torture of Gejza and Charlotte Pavlik at the end of May. One month later, the Pavliks were returned to Prague, from which they had originally been kidnapped, accompanied by their extorted confessions, which were conducted by the same Soviet advisers who organized the Rajk trial.[1]

There were, however, several important differences. The purge in Budapest, which began in May 1949, essentially came to an end in November 1950 when the last "plotters" were hanged or jailed. The Hungarian show trials that followed were not part of the imaginary Great Conspiracy but random, blind consequences of the larger terror set in motion by the Rajk trial, a pattern that followed the inherent laws of the Stalinist purges.

The Slánský affair, on the other hand, raged for five and a half years, the final trials taking place in November 1954, more than a year after the death of Stalin himself. In Hungary, the trials resulted in five lives taken publicly, another fifty in the secret followups, and hundreds of prison sentences. In Czechoslovakia's principal trial, eleven people were executed. More than one hundred perished subsequently and tens of thousands were jailed or deported. More than 136,000 Czechs, communists and noncommunists, were victims in one way or another of the terror; these out of a total national population of 14 million.

The explanation for these differences in scope lies in the different historical experiences of the two nations. Prewar Hungary was a semifascist agrarian country with an insignificant underground communist party, only a very few small, scattered groups living in exile in Western countries. In contrast, highly industrialized and democratic Czechoslovakia had, after Germany and France, the third largest communist party in Europe. Its volunteers had been prominent in the International Brigade during the Spanish Civil War, and most of its leaders and cadres had fled from Hitler to France and later to England, where they joined the Czech government in exile. Postwar Czechoslovakia included, therefore, the largest contingent of any East European state of Stalin's suspect categories, as Westerners, Spaniards, Trotzkyists, and other unreliable elements.

The Czech deviation from the Hungarian purge model did not differ only in size. In Hungary, the Soviets relied solely on three leaders, Rákosi, Gerő, and Farkas, to carry out their instructions. Members of the Politburo and of the Central Committee were relegated to the role of extras, nodding approval when and if required to. In Czechoslovakia, the surviving remnants of a democratic tradition, together with the length and breadth of the purge, necessitated a far wider circle of initiated and responsible executioners. In the leading role, there was cast Klement Gottwald, the Muscovite president of the republic. Just below him were a large number of party leaders who had parts to play in the drama. These included Gottwald's brother-in-law, Alexej Čepička; General Secretary Rudolf Slánský and his successor, Antonin Novotný; Prime Minister Zápotocký and his deputy, Široký; and the two ministers of State Security, Kopřiva and Bacilek, to name only the most important ones. All of them were aware of the use of torture during interrogations; all of them took part in creating the false charges; all of them participated in the selection of victims and dictated to the courts the nature of their sentences.

With their involvement in the purges, a relatively broad section of the party leadership became active accomplices of the Soviet purge managers. This explains why in Czechoslovakia, unlike elsewhere, Stalin's death and Beria's execution did not stop the Stalinist terror. The final show trials in Czechoslovakia were staged when all of the survivors of the Hungarian trials had already been set free and the verdicts declared null and void. In Prague, the purges did not involve only a handful of collaborators, but the entire upper echelon of party leaders, the terror continued so that every loose end might be buried in anticipation of the inevitable day of reckoning.

The Czechoslovak purge got off to a much slower start than did its Hungarian counterpart. Gottwald and the top-level party leadership hesitated for months before unleashing the terror against their comrades. For a while, they even put up resistance to the pressure exerted against them by the Soviets and the fraternal parties in the other satellite states. This reluctance is explained in part by the remnants of Czechoslovakia's prewar democratic traditions; Czechoslovakia became a satellite nation only in 1948, three years after that status was given to Hungary and the remaining nations of Eastern Europe. Even more important, it was the only satellite state not physically occupied by the Red Army. But the increasing pressure finally swept away the traditional values and moral considerations, and the resulting purge exploded with a ferocity unequalled in neighboring states.

The Czechoslovak show trials also differed significantly in substance from the Hungarian model. The Rajk trial centered exclusively on the anti-Tito/anti-imperialist campaign. In Czechoslovakia, however, Tito and the imperialists had to share the villain's role with bourgeois nationalism and Zionism. During its evolution, the purge became more and more permeated with a rabid anti-Semitism. The defendants of the principal trial were selected in such a way that eleven out of fourteen were Jews, and in every instance the indictment stressed their Jewish descent. The shift in emphasis came at the instruction of the Soviet advisers because Stalin had decided to export his own new-found emphasis on anti-Semitism to Czechoslovakia and to the rest of his satellite empire.

The immediate cause of Stalin's new campaign against the Jews was the rapid deterioration of Soviet-Israeli relations. During the initial postwar years, the Soviet Union supported the struggle of the Jewish people for national independence in Palestine, but after the establishment of the state of Israel, Stalin switched sides and became a champion of the Arab cause. The change was accompanied by a vicious anti-Semitic witch hunt at home, cloaked as a campaign against cosmopolitanism. Jewish cultural and political organizations were suppressed, their leaders arrested and murdered. This anti-Semitic terror reached its culmination in the "unmasking" of the Jewish doctors' plot, an alleged conspiracy to kill the Soviet leaders, and in the preparation of plans to deport the Soviet Jews to Birobidjan in the Far East. This was foiled only by the death of Stalin in March 1953. But while the Soviet leader was still alive, the unfolding Slánský trial offered him the opportunity to force his version of the "final solution of the Jewish problem" on his satellites.

This anti-Semitism also explains why Stalin gave permission to his Czech minions to liquidate party leaders who had spent the war in Moscow and returned to Prague after its end, the so-called Muscovites who in other countries had been immune to the purges. Suddenly, Jewish descent carried more weight as a determinant of life or death than prewar emigration to Moscow. A free hand was given to the Soviet advisers to arrest Bedřich Geminder, a trusted Comintern apparatchik, and Bedřich Reicin, former head of the Czechoslovak radio propaganda office in Moscow and political commissar of the Red Army's Czechoslovak brigade. The trap also snapped shut on some non-Jewish Muscovites such as Minister of Defense Ludvik Svoboda, commander of the Czechoslovak Army Corps in the USSR, and Marie Švermová, deputy general-secretary of the party.

The best known of the Jewish victims among the Muscovites was Rudolf Slánský. He had been a founding member of the communist party and soon became its second most powerful man. After Hitler dismembered Czechoslovakia, Slánský fled to Moscow and organized the partisan war in Slovakia. With the defeat of Germany, he was elected general secretary of the party. Slánský was Stalin's and Beria's trusted operative and played a prominent role in the initial stages of the purge, ferreting out from among his comrades enemies of the party and delivering them to the Soviet and Czechoslovak secret police. On Slánský's fiftieth birthday, Gottwald sent him a telegram that read: "Honored comrade! Together with our entire party I send you Bolshevik greetings and our heartiest congratulations. . . . You were always an effective fighter for the promulgation of the Bolshevik line against all opportunist saboteurs and traitors and for the forging of a Bolshevik party. . . . Our whole party, our working people salute you as their faithful son and warrior filled with love for the working classes and with loyalty to the Soviet Union and to the great Stalin.''[2]

The date on this hymn of praise was July 31, 1951. On that very same day, in the cellars of the Ruzyn prison in Prague, Soviet teachers (as the advisors were called by the Czech colleagues) were busy torturing their—and Slánský's— victims to extort from them incriminating false evidence against the faithful son and warrior.

* * *

Like its counterpart in Hungary, the Slánský affair began with the arrest of a Swiss group. On May 28, 1949, ten days after the first secret arrests in Hungary, the Hungarian AVH Colonel Ernö Szücs arrived in Prague and demanded the extradition of Gejza and Charlotte Pavlik who had been, according to the confession of Szönyi, members of a Trotzkyist group in Switzerland and agents of the American spy, Noel Field.[3]

Pavlik had fought in the Red Army during the Russian Revolution, took part in the Hungarian communist uprising of 1919, and became a functionary of the party in Czechslovakia. After the German occupation, he fled to Switzerland and, with the financial assistance of Field, organized there a Czechoslovak group in exile. He returned to his liberated country in 1945, first as director of the Prague office of Field's humanitarian Unitarian Service Committee and later as director of the state travel bureau.

Gottwald agreed to the extradition demand. In Budapest, Soviet and Hungarian security officers extorted from the Pavliks a full confession and the names of sixty prominent Czechoslovak communists who allegedly were participants in a Titoist-imperialist plot to subvert the people's democracies.[4] After four weeks of incessant torture, the Pavliks were handed back to Czechoslovak security. Pavlik immediately retracted the Budapest confessions as having been forced by torture. Gottwald and Slánský appointed a party commission, headed by cadre chief Kopřiva, security chief Veselý, and his deputy, Karel Šváb, to examine the charges. After consulting with the Soviet general Byelkin, the commission branded Pavlik's retraction as a provocation and recommended the immediate detention of his accomplices. Arrested were Rudolf Feigl, a high official in the Ministry of Information, and his common-law wife, Vlasta Veselá, who had served on a medical team with the International Brigade in Spain; Alice Kohnová, also a "Spaniard"; Karel Markus, section chief in the Ministry of Foreign Trade; Milan Reiman, department chief in the office of the prime minister; and six other communist functionaries[5]. Gottwald informed Byelkin that with the arrest of the "Field group," the purge of the U.S. spies who had infiltrated the party had been completed.

Months later, however, at the secret trial of the Field group, only twelve defendants stood in the dock. Reiman and Miss Veselá escaped by committing suicide in their prison cells. The rest were found guilty of espionage, treason, and conspiracy. Gejza Pavlik was sentenced to life imprisonment, the others received long prison terms.

The party commission also examined the cases of the remaining suspects on the Hungarian list of sixty names, most of them "Londoners" who had escaped from the German occupation to England, either through France, where they had the assistance of Noel Field, or through Poland, helped by Noel's brother Hermann, who worked for the rescue organization British Trust. They were subjected to long interrogations by party and security organs, shadowed and spied upon for months. In August 1949, the commission reported to Gottwald that no hard evidence could be found of any treacherous activity and it recommended that the suspects be kept under surveillance. That seemed to conclude the purge in Czechoslovakia.[6]

Stalin was furious. This apolitical legalism did not suit his plans. He considered the arrest of the relatively insignificant Field group to be a half-hearted exercise designed to placate him. It represented to him certain indication of the existence of traitors and saboteurs in the party leadership and he demanded the uncovering of the "Czechoslovak Rajk."

For Rákosi, in Hungary, the standstill in Prague could easily lead to catastrophe. Should no widespread conspiracy be uncovered within the Czechoslovak party, then the confessions of Rajk and his codefendants would lose their credibility. The entire horror story about the subversive activity of Tito and the imperialists operating against all of the people's democracies would be revealed as a sick fantasy.

Stalin used his Hungarian puppets to bring the Czechoslovaks to their senses. At the beginning of August 1949, AVH Colonel Szücs returned to Prague and suggested to his colleague, Karel Šváb, that in view of the slow process of the purge and the international implications of the alleged anti-Soviet plot, the investigations of party enemies should be taken over by the Soviet MVD. The Czechs agreed to consider the suggestion, but they did not act upon it. On September 3, Rákosi sent an urgent letter, writing that he was concerned about the state of affairs of Czechoslovakia.

"You have the names of the persons whom the prisoners here identified as Czechoslovak spies for western imperialism or who have given information to western espionage services. They are not yet arrested," he complained. Then he came to the heart of the matter.

"In two weeks, we shall begin the case of the first group accused in the Rajk trial. The indictment will be published in a week. In this connection, we come up against the difficulty that Czechoslovak names will appear by the dozens at the hearing, names which you also know. All these people are at liberty, they will protest vehemently about the things said in court and will try to undermine the credibility of the charges. . . ."[7]

On September 7, Gottwald dispatched Security Colonel Šváb to Budapest where both Rákosi and General Byelkin urged him to proceed with the arrests. As a next step, Stalin and Beria mobilized their Polish puppets to put pressure on Prague. The Polish head of state, Bolesław Bierut, asked Gottwald to send a trusted official for consultation. On September 12, Jindřich Veselý arrived in Warsaw. First Rozanski and Swiatło, officers of the Polish security office, informed him about the confessions of the Polish Field group incriminating some Czech communists, and then he was summoned to a meeting with the Polish minister of the Interior, Radkiewicz, Party Secretary-General Zambrowski, and Security Chief Berman. They urged him to take vigorous and immediate action against the Czech plotters and traitors.[8]

This coordinated Soviet, Hungarian, and Polish pressure achieved the desired results. At the end of September, Gottwald asked Stalin to send Soviet advisers to help Czech security organs at their task. In October, two MVD generals, Makarov and Likhachev, moved from Budapest to Prague, soon followed by a second team headed by General Boyarsky. In the final stages of the purge, the MVD teachers operated under the command of Soviet General Alexander Beschasnov.[9]

*   *   *

With the arrival of the Soviet advisers, the initial, hesitant phase of the purge came to an abrupt end. From then on, the mechanics of the Hungarian model were strictly implemented, and terror was given free reign. From September 1949 until the close of the year, a number of Londoners were arrested. The most prominent of these were Evžen Löbl, deputy minister of trade, and Vilem Nový, editor in chief of the central party newspaper, *Rudé Právo*.

The next year, the search for a Czechoslovak Rajk was intensified. The terror reached higher and higher into the ranks of the party and state hierarchy. The expanding concentric circles drawn around the leadership pitilessly devoured more and more comrades. The prisons of Pankrac, Kolodeje, Leopoldov, Ruzyn, and the infamous cottage on the outskirts of Prague were crowded with thousands of communists. The terror swallowed, among others, the two deputy ministers of foreign affairs, Vavro Hajdu and Artur London. The latter committed not only the crime of fighting in the International Brigade, but also of joining the French resistance, being jailed in the concentration camp of Mauthausen, and after liberation, recuperating from tuberculosis in a Swiss hospital at the expense of Noel Field's Unitarian Service Committee. The purge soon reached the diplomats Pavel Kavan, Karel Dufek, and Eduard Goldstrücker; then Otto Šling, head of the powerful party organization of Brno, and Josef Smrkovský, deputy minister of agriculture, both members of the Central Committee. Šling's arrest proved fatal to his collaborator, Marie Švermová, secretary at the Central Party office and member of the Presidium. For the Soviet advisers, she was extremely important, as she was the sister of Security Chief Šváb and a long-time, intimate friend of Gottwald and Slánský. Her arrest could lead them to the very top of the structure.

Not only were Westerners, Spaniards, and other suspect categories familiar from the Hungarian model caught up in the purge, but the terror broke through the barriers set in the original and created new categories of suspects. Under the label of "bourgeois nationalism," nearly the entire leadership of the Slovak communist party was arrested, among them Gustav Husák, Ladislav Novomeský, Josef Való, Ivan Horváth, and as the chief criminal, the minister of foreign affairs, Vladimir Clementis. Next came the turn of the military, Generals Bulander, Novák, Kopold, Hromadko; even Ludvik Svoboda, hero of the Soviet Union, was not spared, nor was his Muscovite companion Bedřich Reicin, chief of military intelligence and deputy minister of defense. The former Social Democrats were not separated from the central purge as they had been in Hungary. They formed a huge group of more than six hundred detainees headed by Mrs. Milada Horáková.

Even the persecutors of the persecuted were caught in their own terror net. The head of security, Osvald Závodský; the two deputy ministers of the Interior, Josef Pavel and Oskar Valeš, together with dozens of high officers of the security organs, culminating in the arrest of Karel Šváb, the once all-powerful chief of the secret police. In the eyes of the Soviet advisers, all of them were unreliable; Spaniards, Londoners, or Jews, they were suspected of sabotaging current and future investigations.

All of those mentioned here were arbitrarily selected from the mass of communist victims arrested during the years 1950–1951 to demonstrate the broad range of the purge.[10] Stalin, however, remained unsatiated; the great show trial had to be constantly postponed because none of the victims could fill the role of a Czechoslovak Rajk. The last list of potential stars for such a trial, which was submitted to him during this preparatory phase, including the names of Artur London, Clementis, Lőbl, Švermová, and Šling as the main defendants, but he rejected the lot as inadequate and unrepresentative. The search had to continue.

Late in the spring of 1951, Beria instructed the Soviet advisors to construct, parallel with the Titoist-Trotzkyite conspiracy, a Jewish-Zionist plot involving the top party leaders.[11] At that time, the investigations, arrests, and interrogations were completely in the hands of the MVD. Not only were the Czechoslovak security police, headed by Colonels Doubek, Kohoutek, and Kŏstal their willing tools, but also, Gottwald and the Minister of Security Kopřiva were reduced to mere accomplices who simply followed orders without question.

The intended victim was the party's general secretary, Rudolf Slánský. Without even informing the party, Soviet and Czech security officers began to interrogate detainees about Slánský and extorted incriminating evidence in order to prepare for his arrest. Only in August 1951 did the Soviets present Gottwald with false depositions accusing Slánský of antiparty activities. Gottwald decided to meet the Soviets halfway. At his suggestion, the Central Committee removed Slánský from his position on September 6 and demoted him to the powerless post of deputy prime minister. As a reason for this, Gottwald mentioned "grave mistakes of Comrade Slánský in his cadre policy."

Nothing could better illuminate the subservient relationship of the Czechoslovak communist party—and all of the other satellite parties—to the Soviet Union and its security organs than the fact that the alleged mistakes were compiled by the Soviet advisors Galkin and Yesikov from extorted confessions by Slánský's arrested comrades, translated into Czech by Security Colonel Doubek, and then handed over to Security Minister Kopřiva, who submitted them to Gottwald. They comprised the text of his speech condemning the general secretary of the party.[12]

In the prisons, the interrogations took a new turn. London, Šváb, Šling, and the other leading communist detainees were now tortured to obtain depositions accusing Slánský of more than mere antiparty activities; their protocols had to be rewritten to make of Slánský the central figure of the conspiracy. The subversive crimes to which they had already confessed had to appear to have been committed with Slánský's approval and at his instructions. At the beginning of November 1951, the Soviets presented Gottwald with a new memorandum containing evidence of Slánský's guilt as the head of a Zionist-imperialist plot, and demanded his arrest.

Gottwald hesitated for the last time. Slánský was an old friend, a comrade in arms since the formation of the party thirty years ago, and his most reliable supporter in the party leadership even in the pitiless purge of infiltrated enemies. If the Muscovite Slánský could be arrested, then he, Gottwald, might be the next victim. But Stalin would not tolerate any delay. When he was informed of Gottwald's reluctance, he dispatched Anastas Mikoyan on November 11 with a personal message requiring Slánský's immediate arrest.[13]

At the same time, the chief Soviet adviser, General Beschasnov, provided Gottwald with final proof, a letter forged by the MVD framing Slánský. In the letter, allegedly intercepted by the security organs and addressed to the "Great Crossing Sweeper," the CIA warned the recipient that he was in danger of meeting the same fate as Gomułka and offered assistance in crossing the frontier and a safe refuge in the West. The recipient, so Beschasnov argued, could only be Slánský. Gottwald knew that with this evidence, he no longer had a choice in the matter. He told Mikoyan that he was now convinced of the correctness of Stalin's demand, and on November 23, he ordered the arrest of Slánský. At long last, the Soviets had found their Czechoslovak Rajk.[14]

In the following days and weeks, the majority of the top Jewish party and state leaders still at liberty were arrested. These included Bedřich Geminder, head of the party's international department; Rudolf Margolius, head of the economic department of the president's office; Ludvik Frejka, head of the planning office; Otto Fischl, deputy minister of finance; and André Simone, chief foreign editor of *Rudé Právo*. Together with Slánský and the previously arrested Reicin, London, Löbl, Hajdu, and Šling, they would be the eleven Jewish defendants at the main trial. Of the eleven, eight were hanged.

The Soviet teachers and their Czech pupils were jubilant. When Colonel Kohoutek extorted from Lőbl the protocols incriminating Slánský, he comforted his victim.

"Don't be afraid, Lőbl. You won't play a leading role in the trial, you are now small potatoes. Now the cellars are crowded with ministers, members of the Politburo and the Central Committee. A mere deputy minister has no attraction anymore."[15]

Slánský was tortured with special barbarism. For two months he withstood the onslaught, and even the urgings of Karol Bacilek, the new minister of security, were of no avail when he came to Slánský's cell and promised to spare his life in return for a confession. But in the end, after a failed suicide attempt, his resistance was broken and he signed everything they asked of him.

The team of torturers worked for half a year to reformulate hundreds of statements so that Slánský might now become the center of the conspiracy, and to coordinate the new versions of the old confessions into a coherent, interconnected horror story.

In August 1952 the beating phase concluded, and in sunlit offices, dehumanized victims edited their own death sentences in friendly collusion with their suddenly understanding interrogators. It was the phase of fake complicity already described in the chapter on the Hungarian trials. The diet improved, concerned doctors healed tortured bodies, kind interrogators promised light sentences and rehearsed with their victims the memorized confessions.[16]

At the end of August, Beschasnov submitted to Gottwald the draft of the indictment. A special party commission, consisting of Gottwald's brother-in-law Čepička, Security Minister Bacilek, Minister of Information Kopecký, general secretary Novotný, and Minister of Justice Rais drew up the final text, which was then forwarded to and approved by Stalin. The commission appointed Josef Urválek to be chief prosecutor, selected the members of the court and the counsels for the defense, and handed out the script for the trial with its questions and answers.[17] The commission's task ended with the predetermination of the sentences to be meted out.

The Czechs even improved on the Hungarian model. In Budapest, only Rajk was visited in prison by Kádár with the false promise to spare his life if he would consent to the ultimate sacrifice of the show trial. In Prague, Bacilek summoned all of the defendants, appealed to their loyalty to the party, and promised them lenient sentences if they behaved correctly.[18] Another innovation was even more ghastly. The dress rehearsal of the trial, with the interrogators playing the role of the judges, was tape recorded to be used in the event, however improbable, that at the public performance, a defendant might retract his confession. The tape was played back, a couple of days before the trial, to an audience consisting of Gottwald and chosen members of the party leadership, an act of cynicism unparalleled even in the annals of Stalinist justice.[19]

CHAPTER 9
THE SLÁNSKÝ TRIAL

The "Trial of the Leadership of the Anti-State Conspiratorial Center led by Rudolf Slánský" began on November 20 and concluded on November 27, 1952. Each of its fourteen defendants was a high-ranking communist. They had fought on the battlefields of Spain and in World War II, they had served in the French resistance or with the partisans in the forests of Slovakia, and they had survived the terrors of Nazi prisons and concentration camps. Tried by their own comrades, their entire lives, devoted to the ideals of the revolutionary movement, were turned end over end. In the courtroom of the Pankrac prison, before a carefully selected audience, one defendant after another confessed to having been, from the days of their youth on, imperialist spies, police informers, Trotzkyist traitors, and agents of a Titoist-bourgeois-nationalist plot to overthrow the communist government of Czechoslovakia and murder its head of state, Klement Gottwald.

The particulars of their crimes are unimportant; they were, as in the Hungarian model, arbitrarily selected and incidental to the purpose and the course of the trial.[1] Every Western or Yugoslav contact these people had over the years was transformed into an espionage contact. The differences from the Hungarian scenario resulted from differences in historical background and present circumstances. London, the wartime seat of the Czech government-in-exile headed by President Eduard Beneš and Foreign Minister Hubert Ripka, was now reinterpreted as having been a training school for future spies and conspirators. The Londoners, Frejka, Clementis, Hadju, Lőbl, Šling, and Simone, became the tools of the "notorious Western agent, Beneš." The indictment describes them as "corrupt creatures of Beneš and Ripka, bought by foreign espionage agencies. After the war, they descended like locusts into the territory of liberated Czechoslovakia in order to act here in the interests of the Western imperialists."

This emphasis on the London connection explains why, in the Slánský trial, British intelligence played a much more prominent role than it had in the show trials of the other satellite countries. The role of the arch criminal was attributed to Konni Zilliacus, a leftist Labor member of parliament.

"The hideous plans of the imperialist arsonists placed a special emphasis on the liquidation of the democratic system in Czechoslovakia and entrusted this important task to their trusted pimp, the master of deceit and provocation, Konni Zilliacus, one of the most successful agents of the British Intelligence Service. . . . After establishing direct contact with Slánský, he supported and guided the subversive activities of the plotters with the purpose of detaching Czechoslovakia from the Soviet Union and from the camp of the people's democracies." Thus read the indictment, in a typically vulgar Stalinist formulation.

With Zilliacus, the Soviets intended to establish a second link between Western imperialist agents and Stalin's enemies in the satellite countries, the first being Noel Field.

"The aims of the ruling imperialist circles were directed not only at Czechoslovakia, but at all other democratic countries, as well. Therefore, Zilliacus specialized his activities to subvert the countries of Eastern Europe; he wore the mask of a Left-socialist in order to conceal his true intentions. . . . This is why, for instance, he maintained close contacts with Gomułka, the imperialist agent in Poland," read the indictment.

Noel Field continued in his role of master spy, but in Prague his function became secondary to that of his brother, Hermann Field, who in 1938 had helped hundreds of Czech political refugees escape through Cracow, Poland, to England.

"Hermann Field worked for the British Trust Fund, which was an important arm of the imperialist espionage movement," read the indictment.

"Under the guise of humanitarian aid, he recruited from among the refugees in Cracow a number of agents and turned them over, as did his brother Noel Field, to British and American espionage agencies. . . . In the selection of refugee agents, the Field brothers followed two criteria. First, they must belong to the political left, and second, they should be Jews."

Thus a connection was established between the old Trotzkyist-Titoist enemy and the new one, the Jews. Anti-Semitism occupied a central place in the Slánský trial; its manifestations appeared in every segment of the indictment. For example, one of the witnesses testified about Slánský's alleged contacts with a U.S. citizen named Granville—characteristically called in the indictment "the notorious American spy Geiringer-Granville, a representative of international Zionism"—as follows:

"Granville said that his main source of information was Slánský, the solid pillar of his spy net, the most intelligent Jew that he (Granville) ever knew." Another witness declared: "Slánský is the son of a wealthy Jewish family, the great hope of all of the Jews within the Communist Party."

In the indictment, the Jewish descent of the defendants was constantly stressed: "The Trotzkyist and Jewish-bourgeois nationalist Bedřich Geminder"; "André Simone, whose real name is Otto Katz, an international spy, Zionist and Trotzkyite"; "Hanuš Lomský, originally called Gabriel Lieben"; "Under the pretext of helping the Jewish emigration to Israel, Slánský assisted the illegal flight of a great number of capitalist elements who fraudulently smuggled out of the country large quantities of gold, silver, and jewelry.''

In Prague, Jew baiting became an integral part of the trial procedure.

''Slánský, Geminder, and the other plotters supported the subversive activities of Zionism, the trusted agent of the imperialists,'' the indictment continued. ''For the American imperialists the Zionist organizations offered an advanced base in their fight against the people's democracies and the Soviet Union.''

Israel itself soon became the target. ''The government of Ben-Gurion, the lackey of American imperialism, transformed Israel into an American possession and supports unconditionally the criminal plans of the American warmongers to turn Israel into a deployment zone against the USSR.''

In the Slánský trial, Israel is directly connected to the conspirators. At the end of 1951, the security police in Prague arrested Mordecai Oren, a left-socialist Israeli citizen who was traveling through Czechoslovakia on a semi-official mission to elicit sympathy for the Jewish state; at the trial he confessed to having been the contact man between Slánský and the Israeli espionage agency. The indictment offered other evidence as well. ''The American spies used Israeli diplomatic passports as a cover for their activities. The former Israeli ambassador to Czechoslovakia, Ehud Avriel, as well as embassy officials, Felix and Ben Shalom, established an espionage contact with Geminder and Fischl. . . . Israeli diplomats in the service of American intelligence committed, together with the plotters, acts of sabotage and wrecking which caused heavy damage to Czechoslovakia.''

Compared to the English-American imperialists and their Israeli lackeys, Titoism played a minor role in the Slánský trial. The indictment often refers to the ''Fascist-Tito clique'' and some of the defendants admitted to having served the Yugoslavs because, as Slánský said in his deposition, ''the anti-state conspiracy center followed a line similar to that of Tito.'' He confessed to a meeting with Moša Pijade, who gave him Tito's order to intensify the counterrevolutionary struggle in Czechoslovakia. In contrast to the Hungarian model, however, Yugoslavia was placed in the background and that component of the trial was given only lip service, being almost a postscript to an earlier period.

On November 27, 1952, the court pronounced its prearranged verdicts: life in prison for London, Löbl, and Hajdu; and death for Slánský, Geminder, Frejka, Frank, Clementis, Reicin, Šváb, Margolius, Fischl, Šling, and Simone. Six days later, on December 3, they were hanged.[2]

* * *

The Slánský trial did not end with the sentencing. Even its title, ''Anti-State Conspiratorial *Center*'' (italics mine) indicated the need for peripheral follow-up trials. Hundreds of high officials of the party and the state, officers of the security services and the military, together with hundreds of the witnesses who participated in the initial trial, were themselves brought into the dock in connection with the center. Thousands of unimportant communists were sentenced summarily to long terms in prison or sent to concentration camps on fictitious charges of espionage, sabotage, and bourgeois-nationalist or Zionist crimes. Many of them waited for two or three years in prison before their cases were decided upon. They signed new versions of their confessions in accordance with the latest changes in government policy. The adviser team headed by MVD General Beschasnov and his Czech helpers had its hands full sorting the victims into the proper groups and dictating their statements in preparation for new show trials.

In the midst of these proceedings, on March 5, 1953, there came the news of the death of Stalin. On April 4, the Jewish physicians arrested in connection with the alleged "doctors' plot" were released from their Moscow prison cells. An article in *Pravda* denounced the anti-Semitic aspect the trial was to have had. On June 26, Khrushchev ordered the arrest of Beria and during the following months the terror apparatus of the Soviet Ministry of the Interior and the Ministry of State Security was broken up and its leaders arrested. At the same time, the first group of survivors of Stalin's terror was released from prison and the Gulag camps. The year 1953 ended in the Soviet Union with the execution of Beria and a number of his associates including the former state Security Minister Abakumov and General Byelkin, who stage-managed the show trials in Eastern Europe. Others who were shot at the same time included Generals Makarov and Likhachev, the two main MVD advisers in the Rajk trial and in the Czech purges. Their executions marked the beginning of the long process of de-Stalinization in the Soviet Union, which included a condemnation of the show trials and the rehabilitation of some of their victims.

* * *

The Soviet thaw, however, did not penetrate into Czechoslovakia. Gottwald died on May 14, 1953, a few months after the death of his master in Moscow. Gottwald was not followed by a Czech version of the Soviet Union's Khrushchev. A committee led by Antonin Zápotocký, Gottwald's successor, and including Čepicka, Kopecký, and Bacilek, continued with the terror. They could not follow the pattern established in Moscow for the simple reason that had they done so, as entangled in the purge as they were, and responsible for the tortures of their comrades, they would have been in the dock themselves.

In the first follow-up trial that took place in May 1953, a number of diplomats and high officials of the Ministry of Foreign Affairs were sentenced to long terms in prison.[3] These included Eduard Goldstücker, former ambassador to Israel and Sweden; Karel Dufek, chargé d'Affaires in Turkey; and Pavel Kavan, counselor at the embassy in London. The diplomat group was followed, during the months from September 1953 to January 1954, by defendants in six secret trials of officials of the Ministry of the Interior, including the head of its security department, Osvald Závodský, a commander of the International Brigade in Spain, who was sentenced to death; the Deputy Minister Josef Pavel received twenty-five years of penal servitude; and eight others received long prison terms. In January 1954, there began six secret trials of army commanders with the generals Drnec, Drgač, and the Spaniards Hromadko and Antonin Svoboda at their head. In the same month, the fate of the high party officials left out of the main Slánský trial was settled. These included heads of the regional organizations; members of the Central Committee, most of them Jews; and the main defendant, Marie Švermová, for whom the prosecutor asked the death penalty, but who was sentenced to life imprisonment.

A short pause followed. It was used for the arrest of suspects hitherto missed by the security police and for rewriting the confessions of those already awaiting trial in accordance with new policy lines in the Soviet Union. In February 1954 the pace picked up again. First came the trial of the "Trotzkyist Grand Council," seven communist leaders of the second rank who were sentenced to a total of 103 years in prison; one of these, Oldřich Černý, died shortly after the trial because the prison doctor refused to treat him for illness.

Preparation for the major show trial of the Slovak communist leaders, arrested two to three years before, began immediately after the Slánský trial, but the extortion of false statements proceeded at an unexpectedly slow pace. Stalin's death strengthened the resistance of the prisoners, and many of them retracted their previous confessions. Developments within the Soviet Union tempered the brutality of the investigating team. The indictment had to be redrafted several times by Security Minister Bacilek until finally, in April, the trial was ready to commence. In this trial of the "Slovak bourgeois-nationalists," Gustav Husák was sentenced to life imprisonment and the others, among them three members of the Slovak Central Committee, to long prison terms. The shadows of Khrushchev's de-Stalinization program were beginning to be felt; for the first time a defendant, Husák, retracted his confession in court.[4]

* * *

In April 1954, with the highest ranked Czech and Slovak communist leaders deep inside their prison cellars, in neighboring Hungary, de-Stalinization was proceeding in a contradictory, hesitant, but irresistible manner. The ruling troika, Rákosi, Gerő, and Farkas, was compelled to accede, in helpless rage, to the demand by Khrushchev's man in Hungary, Imre Nagy, that a party commission conduct an inquiry into the show trials. The new Soviet leadership also tried to put pressure on the Czechoslovak rulers, but the only concession made was to release the former defense minister, Ludvik Svoboda, from prison. In July and August 1954, the show trials of the economists were held and the best known of the seven defendants, the deputy minister of agriculture and member of the Central Committee, Josef Smrkovský, was sentenced to life imprisonment.

The verdicts against the economists marked the end of the group show trials. In the following months, individual communists stood before their carefully coached judges. Dozens of alleged criminals who could not be fitted into a formal group were tried behind closed doors. The conclusion of these isolated purges came in November 1954 with the trial of Dr. Outrata, an economist who could not be tried with his fellows because of illness. His was the last show trial of the Czechoslovak Stalinist terror.

*   *   *

After Stalin's death and Beria's execution, a number of Soviet advisers were recalled to Moscow. Those who remained in Prague were paralyzed by the changes in the USSR and left the preparation and conduct of the trials to Karel Bacilek. The terror program of the Czech Security Minister was more and more hampered by events in the neighboring satellites and in the Soviet Union. In the latter, the new government's denuciation of the anti-Semitic tendencies was followed by a reassessment of its anti-Tito policies. In the spring of 1954, a special committee of the Soviet Communist Party acknowledged Yugoslavia as a socialist country, and in October, *Pravda* commemorated the tenth anniversary of Belgrade's liberation by praising the "blood fraternity of the peoples of socialist Yugoslavia and the Soviet Union." In Poland, the spring of 1954 saw the purge of the machinery of terror. Colonel Rozański, a notorious sadist of the State Security office, was arrested, and shortly after he was followed into jail by his commander, Anatol Fejgin. The next purge disposed of the Deputy Minister of Security Romkowski, and soon afterward his superior, Security Minister Radkiewicz, was arrested. In September, Gomułka was released from prison, and Hermann Field and the surviving prisoners of the Field group were set free.

The worst shock for the organizers of the Czech terror came from Hungary, the original model for the show trials. In March 1954, secret police chief Gábor Péter was sentenced to life in prison; in July, the "Trotzkyite-nationalist conspirators" Kádár and his comrades were fully rehabilitated; and the revision of the show trials was speeded up. In August and September, the survivors of the Rajk trial were released, and on October 3, the Central Committee of the Hungarian party declared the verdicts in the Rajk trial to be null and void, stating that the "sentences passed on the comrades were based on fraudulent indictments and false, extorted confessions." Finally, in November Noel and Herta Field were released and rehabilitated in full. Stalin's concept of "imperialist agents and Titoist traitors infiltrated into the ranks of the Communist parties" was declared in Budapest to be a "fabricated, illegal provocation."

The show trials in Czechoslovakia began in Hungary and there they ended— five years later. The sentencing of Dr. Outrata on November 2, 1954, was the final scene in the drama. The professor never saw the day of his rehabilitation; he died in 1955, the last innocent casualty of the Stalinist purges in Czechoslovakia.

Personal Notes IV: May 16, 1950

I remember only vaguely my trial. The gap in my memory comes, perhaps, from the self-delusive wish I had felt to have it over quickly, an unimportant, formal ritual at the end of which the promise is waiting: six weeks in a villa, and I can see my wife again, tell her not to worry, everything will soon be over. The trial seemed to me the door leading to freedom in the not-so-distant future; I had to pass through it quickly. Important was only what comes after it.

They escorted us, twelve men and two women, through the prison yard to the court building in Markó Street. In the waiting room, our handcuffs were removed. I looked around. It was similar to a plenary session of the Swiss party group in the old times, and the thought made me laugh. But then I remembered that Szőnyi was missing, and the laughter got stuck in my throat. Two other comrades were also missing; one of them, as I found out much later, was for some inscrutable reason not brought to trial but sent to an internment camp; the other one escaped arrest altogether, in gratitude for important services he had rendered in the past for the AVH.

In compensation, two non-Swiss were included. Endre Rosta, the espionage boss of my protocol, was probably attached to the group on my account, but also, perhaps, because he had a Swiss wife. György Aczél, a provincial party secretary, had definitely nothing to do with Switzerland. He had been a childhood friend of Demeter and his wife; as soon as he learned of their arrest, he rushed to Budapest and went to the Central Party building in the Akadémia Street to vouch for the innocence of his friends; he was referred to the AVH headquarters where a colonel listened with great interest to his explanations, rang for the guard, and had him escorted straight down to the cellar.

It was a relief to be among old friends. My new guardian angel and babysitter, Lieutenant Faludi, pulled me to the side. He would now introduce me to my defense counsel; he knows of nothing, he assured me, he has no inkling what a political trial means; He was not even allowed to read my indictment.

"We instructed him to ask you only the one question, what extenuating circumstances he should mention to the court. Tell him he should ask for consideration in view of your full confession," he said with a cynical, conspiratorial smile. The middle-aged gentleman he introduced me to (I didn't catch his name) was evidently well coached, but to my surprise, he asked me also, do I have children? He then told me that he might add my three-year-old daughter as a mercy factor. Otherwise, we both held to the script.

Then the defendants were led to the courtroom. The audience consisted of about two dozen civilians, AVH torturers and interrogators, probably one or two Soviet advisors among them, and the uniformed AVH guards with their commander, Major Gyula Princz, chief of the torturing squad. On the platform sat the four people's judges, headed by their chairman Péter Jankó. He read the indictment. We were all accused of high treason and of conspiracy to overthrow the government. Jankó enumerated the long list of our crimes: how we had been recruited in Switzerland by Szőnyi in the American espionage, how Field and Dulles helped us come back to Hungary with the instruction to occupy high positions in the party and in the government, how each of us had fulfilled the tasks given by our imperialist masters in the service of the conspiracy led by Rajk.

I listened, but the words did not really register, even the mention of my name did not shake me from the dazed indifference—retrospectively, I think they might have put a lot of tranquilizers in our breakfast coffee. I looked at my friends sitting in the benches, I tried to find a sign of encouragement in their faces, an ironic smile maybe, to show me that they too know that it is only a theater, politically necessary, but not to be taken seriously. There was no response; all thirteen stared fixedly straight ahead. Is the trial really the next to the last act of the show, followed by an early release, or is it maybe a trap that will swallow us? Maybe I should not recite docilely the memorized horror story, but retract my confession and tell the court the truth. . . .

This late, last flicker of human dignity and rebellion died very soon. The chairman finished the reading of the indictment and called the first defendant, Ferenc Vági, to the platform; the others had to leave the room.

In the meantime, the waiting room had been converted into a coffee shop. Small tables were set up, sandwiches were served, expresso poured in the cups, and sweet desserts passed around, friendly interrogators offered us cigarettes; only the white waiter's apron was missing from the elegant suits of the bustling AVH officers. I was bewildered. What will happen to us, I asked Lieutenant Faludi.

"Don't lose your head, Hodos, I told you what will happen," he said soothingly. "However, I have unpleasant news for you. Your verdict will not be three, but eight years of prison. We have to abide by certain juridical forms to save the credibility of the trial, and with your protocol, you couldn't get a lighter sentence. But don't worry, eight years or three, it is just the same. You will lodge an appeal and the higher court will reduce your sentence to the three years I promised. And also, after the verdict, you will remain under our protection. Do you want a certain friend as a roommate for the first few weeks? Yes? I will see to it that you are put together with G." (One promise he did keep, G. was my first cellmate. The other he kept only partially: I appealed the verdict, but it was increased to ten years.)

He succeeded, in any case, in reassuring me. I was the eleventh to be called, and when the chairman asked if I declared myself guilty, I replied without hesitation, "yes, I am guilty."

"Then tell the court when and how you were recruited into the spy gang of Szőnyi."

I recited the memorized text and gave the rehearsed answers to the prearranged questions. The only witness called was my spymaster, Rosta, who corroborated my confession. Everything went smoothly and without a hitch.

After the testimony of the fourteenth defendant, Antonia Drittenbass, the Swiss wife of Dobó, who confessed her crimes in broken Hungarian, the defense counsels came to deliver their plea. One after the other condemned our horrendous misdeeds, but implied that we were only the tools of the arch criminal Szőnyi, who already had to pay with his life for the crimes committed; their clients confessed freely to the charges, they deserved the harshest punishment, but the court should show mercy and mete out a just sentence—my counsel did not forget to mention my three-year-old daughter as an extenuating argument.

In his speech, the State Prosecutor Gyula Alapi summarized the horror story. In my stunned apathy, I only marveled the careful, elegant English pronunciation of the name of Noel H. Field, and I took sad note of his derisive remark that such depraved criminals as Hodos don't deserve to raise a family, they would only "poison the souls of innocent little children."

Then the members of the people's court left the room to deliberate on the verdict. It took them a very short time, and when they returned, they read the sentences ordered by the AVH—Ferenc Vági: death; András Kálmán, Iván Földi, György Demeter: life imprisonment; Gyula Kuti and János Dobó: fifteen years; Tamás Ács, Péter Balabán, György Somló: ten years; Endre Rosta, György Aczél, György Hódos: eight years; Antonia Drittenbass: six years; Rosa Demeter: five years of prison.

On my way out of the courtroom, I whispered to Vági: "I hope you don't take it seriously, it is only a theater." He looked at me and shrugged: "We are objects of history." Later, in the prison of Vác, I watched for four weeks the light burning day and night in his death cell. One night it went dark. The sentence had been carried out.

CHAPTER 10

THE REINTERPRETED
SHOW TRIALS IN ROMANIA

The Stalinist purges in Eastern Europe were dictated from Moscow down to the smallest detail: place, timing, victims, and charges were selected on the order of the Soviet MVD. However, there were deviations from the prescribed scenario; the apparent monolith of the Soviet empire had cracks that even Beria's terror machine could not bridge over. Perfect obedience was, in fact, achieved only in the model trial in Hungary and, apart from the flaw of Kostov's last-minute retraction of his confession, in Bulgaria. In Czechoslovakia, after a promising beginning, the process suddenly ground to a halt, but was restarted and ran its full bloody course without further mishaps. In Poland and East Germany, however, personal factors, world history, and political geography combined to delay the pace and change the depth of the schedule until, with the death of Stalin, the purges had to be interrupted and remained unfinished.

Romania was also a special case, though for quite different reasons. Factional disputes enabled the secretary-general of the Romanian communist party, Gheorghiu-Dej, to manipulate his Soviet masters and use the purge weapon handed to him in his own quest for power. The Stalinist principle of reinterpreting facts and events in the show trials was developed further by the Romanian party leader; he reinterpreted the show trials themselves.

In 1948, Stalin signaled the start for the preparation of satellite show trials against Titoists. Gheorghiu-Dej did not wait for stage directions from Moscow; he arrested Patrascanu and thus rid himself of one of his competitors for power in the land. In 1952 came the order to extend the purge to Zionists. Again, Gheorghiu-Dej did not hesitate. He chose his victims himself and, by purging Vasile Luca and Ana Pauker, rid himself of a "Moscow faction," the final obstacle on his way to unrestricted rule. He succeeded in changing the Stalinist concept of show trials from an instrument to secure Soviet hegemony over the satellites into one that secured his own hegemony in Romania. He was extremely careful never to put in doubt the authority of his master. Again and again, he demonstrated his servile allegiance to the Soviet Union and, since his plotting and scheming did not seem to endanger Soviet aims, Stalin and Beria allowed him to have his head. Romania became the only satellite in which the concept and the strategy of the show trials came from Moscow, but in which the tactics were left to the local Stalinist servant.

* * *

The history of all of the east European parties was permeated by factional infighting but the weakest of these, that of Romania, suffered the most from this tendency. It recruited its members primarily from the oppressed Hungarian, Jewish, Bulgarian, and Ukrainian minorities within the Romanian population. In its leadership, aliens far outweighed Romanians.[1]

To these ethnic differences were added the usual factional cliques. One set of leaders after another was accused, at various times, of being right or left deviationists, Trotzkyists, or revisionists. At the beginning, they were only dismissed; in the Thirties, they were physically liquidated, as were the theoretician Alexandru Dobrogeanu-Gherea, or the secretary of the Romanian Comintern section, Marcel Pauker, both of Jewish origin and both slain in the prewar Stalinist purges.

At the outbreak of the war, the Romanian communist party was divided into three principal factions. The prison group, headed by Gheorghiu-Dej, consisted mainly of workers arrested and jailed during the strikes of the short-lived revolutionary movement of the thirties. These were recent converts to the communist cause.

The second group comprised the old communist leadership installed by the Comintern. This group, in turn, was divided into two factions. The larger had escaped arrest in Romania by fleeing to the USSR. The Moscow Bureau, as they were generally called, consisted mostly of aliens such as the "Jewess" Ana Pauker, the "Hungarian" Vasile Luca, and the "Ukrainian" Emil Bodnaras, while the "Romanians" were represented by Teohari Georgescu. The Bureau enjoyed the full confidence of Stalin and Beria.[2]

The other, smaller faction of old communists remained in Romania and formed the leadership of the underground. The general secretary of the party, Stefan Foris, and Central Committee members Remus Koffler and Lucretiu Patrascanu, headed this group. It was this faction that prepared for the downfall of the pro-German Antonescu regime in the final phase of the war.[3] Foris and Koffler, both so-called aliens, organized the antifascist left within the Hungarian minority population. The Romanian Partascanu, a respected lawyer and son of a well-known writer, gathered around himself a core of university teachers, students, intellectuals, and artists. In accordance with the demands from Moscow to form an antifascist coalition, he succeeded in creating, together with the banned democratic bourgeois parties and the Social Democrats, a patriotic front demanding the overthrow of the Antonescu dictatorship and Romania's complete withdrawal from the war.

The Moscow bureau more or less ignored the prison group, but the Foris-

Koffler-Patrascanu faction was not trusted by them, either. Its two leading members, Ana Pauker and Vasile Luca, wanted Romania to capitulate only to the advancing Red Army. With the Soviets approaching the border, they argued that any alliance with reactionary circles would only delay the inevitable socialist takeover of the government. The prison group trusted neither the Patrascanu nor the Pauker factions. They found the intellectualism of the first suspicious and they were not prepared to accept without question the authority claimed by the Moscow faction, sitting in the faraway Soviet capital.

In March 1944, the NKVD, the Soviet Security Commissariat, directed the bureau to send Bodnaras and two other members to Romania with instructions to prepare the communist party for the coming Soviet occupation of the country. The three emissaries first contacted Patrascanu and assured him of Moscow's support for his efforts to form a broad anti-Nazi front in opposition to the Antonescu dictatorship. On April 4, they managed to hold a secret meeting inside the prison of Targu Jiu with the third faction, an event that marked the beginning of Gheorghiu-Dej's rise to the top of the political ladder.[4]

* * *

The young mechanic had been arrested in 1933 as one of the organizers of a railwaymen's strike in the Bucharest suburb of Grivita and he soon became the spokesman for the communist prison group. At the secret conference in April 1944 he took the opportunity to denounce to his comrades from Moscow, Stefan Foris, the general secretary of the underground party, as an agent provocateur. The Muscovites, who had lived in the Soviet Union since 1933 and watched there the purge of many foreign party functionaries named as spies and traitors, were easily manipulated, and at their suggestion the secret conference removed Foris from his position and replaced him with Gheorghiu-Dej. After the communists came to power at the end of 1944, Foris was arrested, kept in prison for two years, and hanged without trial. The murder was ordered not by Beria, but by Gheorghiu-Dej.

* * *

The transformation of Romania into a Soviet satellite did not put an end to the factional struggles carried on behind a false facade of unity. Gheorghiu-Dej was confirmed as general secretary of the communist party, and his "prison group" sat in the Politburo and in the Central Committee, but in the government they occupied relatively unimportant positions. Real power was concentrated in the hands of the members of the former Moscow bureau. Bodnaras, Georgescu, and Bodnarenko held the key posts in the army, the security police, and the Ministry of the Interior. The Soviet Union's two most trusted agents, Pauker and Luca, remained relatively in the background as ministers of foreign affairs and finance, but with their direct access to Stalin and Molotov, they dictated all of the important decisions in the Politburo, over the heads of the party and its general secretary.

The third faction was destroyed. Foris was murdered and his friend Remus Koffler was ousted from the Central Committee and disappeared from the political scene. Patrascanu remained isolated. When the Red Army entered the country, the new leaders emerging from Moscow and from the prisons were completely unknown to the general public. Patrascanu, however, enjoyed a certain degree of popularity among the broad democratic opposition, since he had been instrumental in the overthrow of Antonescu's fascist dictatorship shortly before the Red Army crossed the frontier. In the eyes of the masses, he had become the symbol of the party, the only communist to occupy a position, that of a minister of justice, in the first postwar coalition cabinet. He was also the only communist in the Romanian delegation sent to Moscow to arrange for an armistice. In the crucial years 1944 to 1945, "Patrascanu to power!" was one of the most popular slogans at demonstrations organized by the communists.

From the beginning, Gheorghiu-Dej looked askance at Patrascanu and in this mistrust he found willing allies in Pauker, Luca, and the Moscow faction. His liberal education, his culture, and his undogmatic intellect were seen by them as manifestations of bourgeois arrogance and his collaboration with the leaders of the democratic parties during the underground resistance and in the short-lived coalition cabinets of the postwar years roused in them suspicions of "contamination by the ideology of the class enemy."

Because of this mistrust and in spite of, or rather just because of his popularity, the first national party conference, held in October 1945, did not elect Patrascanu to the Politburo, although he remained a member of the Central Committee. In July 1946, Gheorghiu-Dej tested the atmosphere and, in his report to the Central Committee, launched his first open attack against Patrascanu. He criticized him for having taken a chauvinist position when, at a mass meeting of the Hungarian minority organization, Patrascanu objected to the flying of the red, white, and green Hungarian flag at the head of the parade, saying that the Romanian flag must precede all others. In this charge of anti-Hungarian chauvinism, the much more serious charge of anti-Soviet attitudes was tacitly but unmistakably implied.

With the curtailing of his party influence, the Patrascanu problem seemed to be settled. He retained the key government position of minister of justice and proved himself to be a faithful Stalinist. The spectacular trial of the opposition leader Maniu and eighteen other leaders of the National Peasant party was only the visible tip of the terror that swept through postwar Romania. In the first four years of the communist takeover, about 75,000 real or alleged enemies of the people were executed. The minister of justice was certainly one of the architects of the terror, even if he served in an auxiliary role behind the security forces led by Georgescu and controlled by the Soviet MVD.

*   *   *

Romania provided the initial impulse for the Stalin-Tito rift with Dimitrov's press conference in Bucharest, already discussed in the chapter on Bulgaria. The formation of a Bulgarian-Romanian customs union as a step toward the federation of the East European countries under Tito's leadership seemed to Stalin to be a challenge to Soviet hegemony over its satellites. On February 10, 1948, he summoned Dimitrov to Moscow and ordered him to stop discussing all plans for a federation. At the same time, he warned Ana Pauker to disassociate Romania from any Yugoslav orientation in its policies. Two days later, on February 12, the Romanian government ordered that all pictures of Marshal Tito be removed from shop windows. Soon, the warning from Moscow became more specific; the party was ordered to rid itself of nationalistic-chauvinistic elements.

Gheorghiu-Dej grasped the situation with uncanny instinct. He knew exactly with how much distrust his Romanian faction was regarded by the Muscovite troika of Pauker, Luca, and Georgescu. He also realized that unless he took some action immediately, he and his group might be tagged with the fateful label of Titoist.

Patrascanu was an ideal victim to be offered as a sacrifice on the altar of the witch hunt for anti-Soviet tendencies. He was politically isolated and robbed of his base within the party and of his contacts with the masses. His usefulness had ended with the party's departure from its policy of forming coalitions with the bourgeois democratic parties. He was an alien, irritating element for the Muscovites as well as for the Dejists. They were united in the conviction that, in view of the evolving anti-Tito campaign, the time had come for his liquidation. Gheorghiu-Dej had a free hand.[5]

The attack on Patrascanu came on February 22, 1948, at the first congress of the new Romanian Worker's Party, formed by the enforced merger of the Social Democrats with the communists. It was launched by Georgescu, while Gheorghiu-Dej kept himself discreetly in the background. He told the congress, with his victim sitting nearby, silent and seemingly indifferent, that Patrascanu had "fallen under the influence of the bourgeoisie," that "he had become an exponent of the bourgeois ideology," and that "by knowingly overestimating the forces of the class enemy, he capitulated before the reaction and its Western imperialist helpers." The congress unanimously accepted Georgescu's motion to remove Patrascanu from the Central Committee and from his post as minister of justice.

With the intensification of the Stalin-Tito conflict, Gheorghiu-Dej had to respond to increased pressure from Moscow for a purge. In May 1948, Beria ordered the MVD to unmask Titoists in the satellite countries and to prepare show trials. In contrast to the other peoples' democracies, Gheorghiu-Dej had an easy time of it because the Romanian victim had already been publicly identified. He succeeded in persuading Stalin and Beria that in Romania there was no need to launch a search for Titoists, their leader having already been found by him. Permission came from Moscow for the immediate arrest of Patrascanu.

Shortly afterward, on June 10, a plenary session of the Central Committee furnished the political justification for a show trial. Again it was a Muscovite, this time Vasile Luca, whom Gheorgiu-Dej pushed into the foreground. "The political position of Patrascanu is a typical example of the renunciation of the class struggle against the exploiters and of collaboration with the exploiting classes," he said. Patrascanu was charged with urging alliances, first with the bourgeoisie and then "with the entire peasantry, including the kulaks, the exploiting elements hostile to the working peasants." Patrascanu was accused of trying to falsify the history of the heroic struggle of the workers, he wrote slanderously about the alleged lack of influence of the working class, and he denied the leading role of the proletariat and attributed it instead to the bourgeoisie.

"With this policy of appeasement toward the exponents of the bourgeois-landlord reaction, with his line of nationalism and chauvinism, Patrascanu became the mouthpiece for bourgeois ideology in the ranks of our party," concluded Luca. "We resolutely reject his counterrevolutionary 'theories,' inspired by the interests of the class enemy."[6]

At the time of the plenary session, the investigations by the security organs under the direction of the MVD advisers were in full swing. In the cellar of Bucharest prison, the torture of Patrascanu began to make him sign confessions of his criminal activities. The progress was slow, however, because the interrogators were still largely in the dark about what crimes they had to invent. They could not yet anticipate the concrete outlines of the East European purge scenario. The premature arrest of Patrascanu took place two months before Tito's excommunication by the Cominform, so the initial charges against Patrascanu reflected only the actual state of the conflict as expressed in the letters of the Soviet communist party to the Yugoslavs. The accusations of taking a nationalist-chauvinist line, of the denial of the leading role of the proletariat, and of the alleged alliance with the entire peasantry, including kulak elements, established unmistakably the link with the Titoist heresy.

The mistake of the premature arrest was soon corrected. Beria ordered his team in Bucharest to coordinate the Romanian sector with the overall purges in Eastern Europe and to adjust the interrogation according to the blueprint supplied by Moscow. The script had to follow the exact scenario prepared for Hungary and Bulgaria. Patrascanu could not remain a mere political deviationist, he had to be transformed into a traitor, a criminal, and a police informer; he could not be an isolated case, but must be turned into the head of a gang of conspirators with connections to the Yugoslavs and the imperialists.

To prove the Patrascanu plot, Remus Koffler, friend and comrade-in-arms of the murdered General Secretary Foris, was arrested. Koffler had to confess that, together with Foris, he had been an informer for the monarcho-fascist police and that in 1941 they had recruited Patrascanu into their service. According to

Koffler's extorted statements, Patrascanu had denounced a number of leading underground communists and even provoked the arrest of Georgescu.

In addition to Koffler, the conspirators assembled by Soviet-Romanian security forces included some second-ranking officials of the Yugoslav minority organizations; some intellectuals only peripherally involved with politics; the economist and philosopher Belu Silber; the musician and folklorist Harry Brauner; the painter Lena Constante; and the architect Calmanovici. The former Romanian consul in Paris, H. Torosian, provided the necessary link to Western espionage organizations, the Deuxième Bureau in Paris and the British Intelligence Service. Yugoslav officials were reinterpreted into secret police agents and thus was established a link to Tito. Included in the group was Ion Mosony-Stircea, former commander of the Royal Palace Guard, who alongside Patrascanu played a prominent role in the arrest of Antonescu. Now he had to prove Patrascanu's collaboration with the monarcho-fascists.[7]

Patrascanu's show trial was scheduled to take place in the spring of 1950, when suddenly Beria ordered a postponement. It has never been made clear why he did this and some rumors that circulated through Bucharest at the time laid the responsibility to excessive torture applied to Patrascanu that drove him to the edge of insanity. It is more probable that immediately after the Rajk and Kostov trials, which resulted in the purging of hundreds of top party and government officials, the Soviet stage directors judged the Romanian version to be but a pale and inadequate copy of the originals. They demanded a wider and deeper purge and urged the inclusion of the proven suspect categories of home communists, Spaniards, and Westerners.

Pauker and Luca immediately began a campaign against the Romanian volunteers who had served with the International Brigade in Spain. Many of these occupied important positions in the party and the government. Some were even members of the Central Committee and the Politburo, as were Petre Borila, chief of the army political directorate; Leonte Rautu, head of the Agitprop department and leading theoretician of the party; and Valter Roman, minister of posts and telegraph. Especially critical was the position of Central Committee member Gheorghe Vasilichi, a railway worker who had been arrested together with Gheorghiu-Dej in the Grivita strike of 1933. After his release from prison, he had joined the International Brigade and later spent the war years in France, from which he returned home to become a close personal friend of Patrascanu. To Beria and Pauker, they were all potential spies, to be dragged into show trials. Much later, in 1961, Borila and Roman stated that only the resistance of Gheorghiu-Dej averted their arrests and spared their lives. Their statement seems to be credible. Gheorghiu-Dej protected them in order to protect himself and his faction.[8]

He must have been frightened of the Soviet-Muscovite pressure to extend the purge. He knew full well from the Rajk and Kostov trials that among the proven suspect categories, the underground communists imprisoned by the old regime were especially vulnerable. They were constantly reinterpreted into being police spies, and he and his prison group clearly fitted the pattern.

Gheorghiu-Dej could only prevent widening of the Patrascanu affair by dividing the Moscow faction. Not only the Spaniards and Westerners under attack, such as Borila and Rautu, were prepared to join with Dej, but even the Minister of Defense Bodnaras, and security chief Bodnarenko changed allegiances and thus left the Muscovite troika of Pauker, Luca, and Georgescu increasingly isolated. At a time during which Stalin looked with growing suspicion on communists of Jewish descent, the former close relations between the Soviet dictator and Pauker, daughter of a rabbi, became increasingly strained. The timing of the pressure to broaden the scope of the list of victims proved to be wrong. The bureau broke up, the influence of its powerful central core weakened, and by May 1951, when the party celebrated its thirtieth anniversary, Gheorghiu-Dej was, with Stalin's support, its uncontested master, no more a mere figurehead for Pauker and Luca. One year later, in May 1952, he was strong enough to begin the purge of the Muscovite faction, as we shall see.

The Patrascanu trial was postponed a number of times. During 1950, it was due to the cunning sabotage of Gheorghiu-Dej who kept the victims limited to their original number. During the following year, with the slow, steady weakening of the troika, a new and unexpected supply of victims appeared to become available; the planned merger of the Patrascanu and Luca groups was promising, at last, to provide a set of representative defendants for a proper show trial. The interrogation of Patrascanu took a new turn; now Soviet and Romanian security officers began fabricating protocols that sought to link him with his former accuser, Luca.

The purge of the Muscovite faction had scarcely concluded when, in September 1952, the first rumors began to circulate about Stalin's rapid physical decline and the beginnings of struggles for power among those who might succeed him. These caused Gheorghiu-Dej to halt his preparations and wait for the outcome of developments in Moscow. Stalin's death and the execution of Beria, the first hesitant steps toward a reconciliation with Tito, and above all Khrushchev's pressure on the satellites to revise their show trials, created a completely new situation for the Romanian leadership. The prematurely begun and long-delayed Patrascanu affair had to be concluded as rapidly as possible.

In May 1949, Gheorghiu-Dej forestalled Stalin by arresting Patrascanu in order to avoid being accused of Titoism. Now, nearly six years later, he forestalled Khrushchev by executing Patrascanu to protect himself from having to rehabilitate an enemy who, during the time of de-Stalinization, might endanger his control of the country.

In March 1954, the indictment was finally completed and those charges in which the defendants confessed their links to Tito were dropped. According to the new version, Patrascanu headed a group of spies and conspirators after having been recruited by Foris and Koffler to serve as a police informer for the fascist Siguranta. This subjected him to blackmail by the imperialist espionage agencies that brought him into their service, specifically to undermine the unity of the Central Committee by following an anti-Soviet, nationalistic line.

In the secret show trial, held in Bucharest April 6–14, 1954, Gheorghe Tatarescu, the former leader of the Liberal Party, was dragged from his prison cell to present his memorized deposition, according to which, during the Paris peace conference in 1946, Patrascanu had been instructed by his masters in Western intelligence to detach Romania from the Soviet Union and bring it into the Western orbit. Patrascanu, broken physically and mentally by six years of prison and torture, slipped suddenly from his role of confessed criminal and was said to have exclaimed: "Such a scum of history they have brought to this trial as a witness against me, a lifelong communist. If such an individual is needed to prove that I am not a communist, it is only evidence of the low level of the Romanian party which has to use such elements, evidence of the total lack of proof against me."9

The unexpected outbreak on the part of the principal defendant did nothing to change the predetermined verdicts, dictated to the military court by Gheorghiu-Dej. Patrascanu and Koffler were condemned to death; Silber, Stafanescu, and Calmanovci given life in prison; Mosony-Stircea and Torosian sentenced to fifteen years; and Brauner and Constante to twelve years.

* * *

We now turn to the most important of the show trials, that of the Muscovites.10 The premature arrest of Patrascanu served to sharpen the latent tensions between Gheorghiu-Dej and the Pauker faction. Contrary to later official explanations, these strains did not arise around questions regarding the correct Leninist line, much less about a first attempt to shake off Soviet influence on Romania, themes that were often stated later in Romanian and Western literature. There were no ideological differences between the two Stalinist factions. Dej was, if possible, even more slavishly devoted to his Moscow masters than were Pauker and Luca. At the Cominform conference in Bucharest in July 1949, it was Gheorghiu-Dej whom Stalin selected for the task of honor of denouncing Tito. In the following year, Dej ordered the deportation of the Serb and Croat minorities as Titoist agents, and he spearheaded the forced collectivization of agriculture in the course of which 80,000 peasants were hanged or imprisoned and an even greater number were sent without trial to concentration camps.

The schemings and intrigues of Gheorghiu-Dej had as their purpose the removal from power of his three fellow members of the party Secretariat, Ana Pauker, Vasile Luca, and Teohari Georgescu. Luca's Hungarian descent and the Jewishness of Pauker proved fortunate for their enemies. But the fact that all three had returned from living in the Soviet Union and had excellent personal relations with Stalin, Molotov, and Beria remained an obstacle that was overcome only with the opening of the Slánský trial in Prague. It was there that the previously untouchable Muscovites first proved to be vulnerable. The Hungarian bourgeois nationalism of Luca was defined to Stalin as the equivalent of the Slovak bourgeois nationalism of Clementis and his comrades, and Ana Pauker was described as a potential zionist agent in Romania.

There was, however, one significant difference. In Prague, it was Stalin and Beria who forced upon Gottwald the arrest of the bourgeois nationalists and the Zionists. In Bucharest, it was Gheorghiu-Dej, operating with manipulative genius and uncanny political instincts, who used the Soviet rulers as his tools in ridding himself of his rivals for unrestricted power in Romania.

It is difficult to separate fact from fiction in what were later offered as explanations for the purging of the Moscow group.[11] In the initial version of these, Gheorghiu-Dej asserted that he achieved the de-Stalinization of the Romanian party even before Stalin's death. The later version of his successors claimed that the elimination of the Muscovites restored the independence of the party and of the country from Soviet, Jewish, and other foreign influences.

In reality, the second phase of the purge had nothing to do with either de-Stalinization or de-Sovietization. Gheorghiu-Dej began his struggle for power very cautiously. After splitting the Moscow group and isolating the troika, he risked an initial attack on them in the summer of 1950. On June 23, an article by him was printed in the Cominform journal, *For a Lasting Peace,* criticizing the mistakes made in the recruiting of new party members. Without naming specific leaders, even though everyone knew he was referring to Pauker, he claimed that the expansion of the membership by nearly 200,000 individuals meant that the party had been opened to exploiting and hostile elements, morally corrupted people, careerist, fascists, bourgeois nationalists, and the like and had great damage inflicted upon it.[12]

This first foray was followed by arrests in the Hungarian and Jewish minority organizations. Just prior to that time, the Hungarian-born Luca had been the main accuser of Patrascanu on grounds of anti-Hungarian chauvinism, now he was accused of demonstrating Hungarian chauvinist tendencies and Gheorghiu-Dej appointed a trusted follower, Alexandru Moghioros, to stand as a watchdog by his side. In the Jewish Democratic Committee, the hunt for enemies began as early as 1949, and during the following year dozens of Jewish leaders were arrested, including some relatives of Ana Pauker previously thought to be untouchable.[13]

Aside from these visible signs, much more dangerous attacks were launched behind the scenes. Pauker and Luca mobilized their old friends from the Comintern and the NKVD and denounced to them Gheorghiu-Dej as a disguised Titoist who, masquerading as a Stalinist, followed an anti-Soviet line. Two or three years earlier, this would have put Gheorghiu-Dej into the dock, but in 1950 and 1951, it was Pauker and Luca who belonged to new suspect categories. Their way to Stalin was blocked. Gheorghiu-Dej countered their attempts to reach their old friends by going himself to Moscow and accusing Pauker, Luca, and Georgescu of fomenting factional intrigue.

There can be no doubt that in this competition for Stalin's favor, Gheorghiu-Dej was the winner; without making sure that he had the highest Soviet support, he could not have gone over from employing the cautious tactics of attrition to the bolder policy of open attack. He offered Stalin three candidates for a show trial, all top party leaders instead of the relatively insignificant Patrascanu. However, he did not fully achieve his aims. Someone, probably Molotov, intervened on the side of Ana Pauker, and Beria rushed to the defense of Georgescu. Their political purging could not be prevented, but their lives were spared. Vasile Luca was sacrificed.

The frontal attack on the troika opened on February 29, 1952, three months after Slánský's arrest in Prague. At a session of the Central Committee, Gheorghiu-Dej accused the Ministry of Finance and the national bank, both under Luca's control, of grave mistakes and frauds in the application of the currency reform. Luca disregarded previous warnings given by the Central Committee, charged Dej, and followed a policy of relaxing the proletarian dictatorship. Pauker and Georgescu were also sharply criticized for shielding Luca; they had to share responsibility for allowing the class enemy to occupy high positions in the economy and thus preventing the prompt correction of the mistakes.

Luca was forced to offer the ritual self-criticism; he thanked the party for exposing his rightist deviationism and promised to correct his mistakes and to faithfully follow the Stalinist policies of the Central Committee.

But for Gheorghiu-Dej, this was only a beginning. He carried his attack from the inner circle of the Central Committee to the broad public and prepared the political atmosphere for a show trial. A letter was sent to every party organization in the country informing them of the controversy and ordering them to mobilize the masses for the coming fight against rightist deviationism. As a further step, he appointed a special party commission to investigate the case of the three victims. On March 13, the commission summoned the troika for a hearing. Luca, supported by Pauker and Georgescu, retracted his self-criticism and denied having made any rightist errors. The Muscovites had realized that compromise was no longer possible and elected to put up a fight.

But it was too late for that. At its plenary session, held on May 26, the Central Committee condemned Luca for breaking his promise to follow the party line, for rebelling against Central Committee decisions, and for trying to drag other members of the Central Committee down the same right-opportunist road. He was also accused of sabotaging the currency reform, undermining the collective farms, and protecting capitalist trade. The Central Committee voted unanimously to expel Luca from the party, and its Control Commission was ordered to examine the deeper roots of his mistakes.

At the same time, the Central Committee severely criticized both Pauker and Georgescu. The committee accused them of deviating from the correct Leninist-Stalinist line and said that their opportunistic policies were reflected in their lifestyles "on the slope of aristocracy," further isolating them from the masses. Ana Pauker, continued the resolution, helped and encouraged the rightist deviations of Luca and Georgescu, she opposed the collectivization of agriculture, and thus caused grave damage to the economy. She was, therefore, to be removed from the Politburo and the party secretariat. However, in view of her having acknowledged some of her errors, Pauker was permitted to remain a member of the Central Organization Bureau and to retain her government post as minister of foreign affairs.

In the case of Georgescu, the Central Committee was less lenient. The resolution said that his conciliatory attitude toward Luca masked an opportunist, rightist spirit, he had taken no measures to counter capitalist speculators, his lack of proletarian vigilance allowed enemies of socialism to perform, undisturbed, their subversive activities. It was decided to oust him from the Politburo and from the Central Committee and to dismiss him from his government functions as minister of the Interior and president of the Economic Council.[14]

It is not known when Vasile Luca was arrested, probably very shortly after the Central Committee meeting of May 26, 1952. At the June 29 meeting, Gheorghiu-Dej reinterpreted Luca's political errors into criminal acts and determined with that the ideological direction of the show trial. Luca knowingly retarded the development of heavy industry, he placed saboteurs and hostile elements in the banking and financial administrations, he encouraged capitalist trade and profiteering, in the field of agriculture he supported wealthy peasants by enrolling tens of thousands of kulaks as "middle peasants" and thus exempting them from taxation. His criminal activities, so Dej concluded, were responsible for the underfulfillment of the economic plan and for the strengthening of the class enemy.

With the arrest of Luca, at long last a leading communist could be sacrificed, a catch worthy of the other prominent victims of the Stalinist purges in the satellites. The young Hungarian carpenter—his original name was László Lukács—participated in the Hungarian revolution of 1919, escaped to Romania, and became a founding member of the party. He spent the underground years in and out of prison. The last time he was arrested was in 1938 in Czernovitz, where two years later, with the Soviet annexation of Bessarabia and Northern Bukovina, he was released and joined the Moscow bureau of the Romanian communist leadership.

In the prison of the security police, Luca's political career took on quite a different color. He was tortured and forced to sign statements confessing to having been since 1929 a paid informer for the Siguranta, with the additional assignment of supporting the treacherous Trotzkyist clique of Marcel Pauker. Ever since, he had participated in a factional struggle against the Leninist line of the party, as a diversionist, his subversive activity was carried out in the company of the traitor and Siguranta agent, Stefan Foris. After the liberation of the country, he entered the service of the imperialists and, at the command of his new bosses, he sabotaged the economic progress of the state with the aim of restoring capitalism in Romania.

With Luca, the security police arrested Deputy Finance Minister Alexandru Jacob, President of the National Bank Dumitru Cernicia, and Deputy Minister of Foreign Trade Ivan Solymos.[15] It was intended that this group would be placed in the dock together with the Patrascanu group, in prison already for four years, in order to stage the Romanian Slánský trial.

Parallel with the torturing of Luca and his coprisoners in the cellars of the State Security prisons, the political liquidation of Ana Pauker proceeded rapidly. A rumor campaign was launched; she had contacts with foreign intelligence through Israel where her father lived, she smuggled part of her fortune out of the country and deposited it in a Swiss bank, and so on. On June 5, 1952, she was dismissed from her post as minister of foreign affairs, and on September 12 she lost her last positions in the party and in the government. She was, however, spared the final and ultimate humiliation; the protective hands of Stalin and Molotov saved her from prison and execution. Ana Pauker disappeared from public view, and her death in 1960 was passed over in complete silence.

Publicly the Pauker affair was never connected with the anti-Semitic witch hunt raging at that time all over Eastern Europe. She was never publicly accused of Zionism and, in contrast with Czechoslovakia where the "de-Jewification" purge reached its bloody climax, Gheorghiu-Dej appointed Simion Buglici, a Jew, as head of the Foreign Ministry, succeeding Pauker. A Bessarabian Jew, Iosif Chisinevschi, rose after Pauker's downfall to the most powerful position in the Secretariat of the Central Committee, and Leonte Rautu, another Bessarabian, remained head of the Agitprop and chief ideologue of the party.[16]

* * *

The tortures of Luca and his gang of conspirators and spies were not yet ended when Stalin died in March 1953. With his death, Gheorghiu-Dej buried his plans for a great public show trial. The Patrascanu group was again separated from the Luca group and tried in March 1954 before a military court with the results already described. Six months later, on October 4, 1954, there came the turn of Luca at a time when, in neighboring Hungary, the survivors of the Stalinist show trials were already free and exonerated, and the rehabilitation of the murdered victims, the repudiation of the Rajk trial, had already been announced.

Contrary to Hungary's Rákosi, however, the Romanian murderer retained his absolute power. To release Luca from prison, to revoke the trumped-up charges, would have meant the equivalent of committing political suicide. There was no retreat for Gheorghiu-Dej if he intended to survive. As with the case of Patrascanu, the trial had to take place without attracting any attention, not to make political capital from it, but to enable the Luca problem to finally disappear.

On October 10, 1954, Luca was found guilty of sabotage, conspiracy, and espionage and sentenced to death; on appeal, the verdict was commuted to life imprisonment. His codefendants received prison terms ranging up to twenty-five years. Luca died in prison in 1960 at the age of sixty-two.

*   *   *

"Once Pauker, Luca and Georgescu were expelled from the party, the dead hand of Stalinism was lifted," said Gheorghiu-Dej in December 1961. "We de-Stalinized during Stalin's time, in our country there are no grave injustices to be forgiven, no one has to be rehabilitated posthumously."[17]

Gheorghiu-Dej died in March 1965. Six months later, the party appointed a special commission to investigate the show trials. As a result of its work, the Central Committee and the Supreme Court declared the verdicts to be null and void. Foris, Patrascanu, Koffler, and Luca, together with all of the survivors, were fully rehabilitated.

"All of the charges against those comrades were without foundation and proved to be complete falsifications, concocted by illegal investigation methods."[18]

Personal Notes V: March 1950–April 1952

The promised villa turned out to be the old prison of Vác, near the border of Czechoslovakia, and the six weeks lengthened to four and a half years. My new apartment was located in the solitary confinement section. A tiny cell, No. 12, its contents included two sacks filled with straw dust, a bucket, a water jug, a wash bowl, and innumerable bedbugs who sucked my blood, but luckily seemed to prefer that of my cellmate and old friend, G.

We had no books, no cigarettes, no contact with other prisoners, and no names; I was Number 60—buried, forgotten, locked away in a hell hermetically sealed off from the outside world. We had no work, we had no walk. Every morning, the cell door was opened to allow the bucket to be emptied and a tiny slice of bread and ersatz coffee to be passed to us. What a feast it was when occasionally we were given a thin flour soup kept hot by a layer of tallow for breakfast. The normal slop we received was the least of my problems at Vác. I am a small eater, so I shared my portion of the disgusting mess of beans, lentils, cabbage, or dehydrated potatoes fit only for animals, with my always-hungry cellmate. I did so again at dinner, which was a variation of lunch.

Once a week we were shaved by the prison barber, a sturdy war criminal, the former leader of a fascist firing squad. Also once a week, toilet paper was distributed and a tray pushed from cell to cell by a paramedical prisoner, a priest sentenced in the trial of Cardinal Mindszenty. He smeared some red fluid on my skin, infected by dirt, malnourishment, and a lack of fresh air. Every time the cell door opened, for whatever reason, we had to jump to attention and report respectfully that the number of its inmates was two. That was the only contact we had with our jailers.

After a couple of months, our isolation was lessened and some of us were brought together to the "mill," where fifty prisoners were gainfully employed tying together short pieces of yarn and winding them up on a wheel. There I again saw some old friends, such as my former cellmate Reisman and other familiar faces from a faraway, unreal previous life. Their faces were haggard, pale, with shifty, frightened eyes. I also saw them in the mornings when, for fifteen minutes, we were led single-file for a walk in the courtyard, hands folded behind our backs, heads bent down.

For this one step out of our total isolation, we had to pay a costly price. We exchanged the deathly silence of our solitary cells for the incessant shouts of our jailers: "Don't talk! Don't look up! Don't turn around! Don't lag behind, you fascist murderer!"

At night they would burst into our cell. "Get up! Face the wall!" They searched the tiny space for hidden treasures such as pieces of yarn, scraps of paper, pencil stubs, or a rusted nail that might be used to commit suicide. Any forbidden object, any sign of communication between human beings was punished with "short iron" for up to six hours, sitting in the prison corridor with hands fettered to feet while every passing prison guard kicked you.

Half a year later, we were transferred from the solitary confinement block to the main building of the prison. My new home was cell number 69, where I shared quarters with nineteen other prisoners, all of us jammed into a small space, all of us Rajkists. The extent of the terror we experienced increased with this move. From the moment that our cell door opened in the morning until it closed behind us after the distribution of the stinking brew called dinner, we were in constant danger. No one knew when or why he might be singled out for two or three days in the dark cell, for beatings, short ironing, or forced exercise in the corridor until collapse.

During our interrogation, such tortures served a purpose, but in the prison they made no sense. There was nothing more our tormentors wanted from us, we were reduced to mere numbers, removed from the rest of society. It was terror for its own sake and its presence was assured by the person of Major István Lehota,

promoted from chief jailer in the AVH cellars in Andrássy Street to prison
director at Vác.

The days were hell, but the evenings and Sundays offered an escape. In large
measure, I survived those years sanely because I was no longer alone. In the
loneliness of the cellar in Andrássy Street, my mind was completely numbed. In
the detention cell in Markó Street, the first contact with my fellow victims
Vietoris and Reisman strained my belief in the party, but did not destroy it. As
soon as I was again confronted by my interrogators, my doubts dissipated and I
clung to my faith in the party like a drowning man does to a life preserver. In the
prison at Vác, I had no lifebelt. I knew now that I was being cheated, used, and
thrown away on the dustbin of communism. In my whispered conversations with
G—we spoke in Swiss-German so that our jailers could not understand even if
they listened at the door—I tried, for the first time, to analyze with a clear head
what had happened to us, to unmask the hideous conspiracy, not of invented
imperialist spies, but of the communist party that knowingly, cynically sacrificed
its sons on the altar of a lie. We called our prison Atilla's tomb, after the ancient
king of the Huns who was buried in a secret place and whose gravediggers were
then killed so that they might not reveal where he lay. Our hitherto incomprehensible fate started to make some sense, and the true villains and victims were
revealed.

In cell 69, the last missing pieces of the mystery fell into place. In solitary
confinement I still had my lingering doubts; perhaps some of the details of the
concocted conspiracy might just contain some kernels of truth. Now all doubts
disappeared. Our twenty former communists were a mixture of victims from the
Swiss, French, and English groups; Forgács, a chemical engineer, had returned
to Hungary from Chile, the Spaniards Mátyás, Ráth and Cséby returned from the
Soviet Union, Hegedüs and Rex were Yugoslavs. Ernő Villányi was neither of
those, his arrest was solely due to being the brother of András Villányi, deputy
minister of trade, who was hanged in a secret follow-up trial. None of us had
committed any crime. Földi and Kálmán, the two witnesses against Szőnyi in the
public trial, now served us as witnesses to the fact that even the main defendants
were innocent victims.

From there it was a small step to the realization that the criminals were not
those who had swung on the gallows or were rotting in prison, but the rulers in
the Kremlin and their Hungarian puppets in the party and the AVH. The purge
was not a mistake, not an administrative abuse of power by the security officials,
or even by Rákosi or Stalin. It was communist policy. This revelation laid bare
the system itself, revealing like a surgical operation the innermost mechanism
hidden behind the facade of a deceptively beautiful promise. Our quasireligious
faith withstood the tortures of the interrogations; it collapsed under the collective
proof of our innocence. In the hell of the prison, we regained the freedom of our
thoughts.

Cell 69 was my real political university. Buried alive in Attila's tomb I saw the true face of Stalinism, undistorted by the mendacious ideological clichés of Orwellian newspeak. We knew more about Stalinism than anyone else because we were, at the same time, its victims and champions. Even in prison we used Marxist terminology to analyze it because that was the only idiom we understood. We sang the proletarian rallying marches (in subdued voices so as not to be heard by our proletarian jailers) because they were the only songs we knew. None of us, however, kept our illusions about the system.

After the Stalinist show trials were declared null and void and we were fully rehabilitated, a few among us turned around again and came to occupy leading positions in the party, the economy, and the government. They forgot the insights opened to them in prison. Post-Stalinism doesn't use the knife anymore, as a general rule; it is resorted to only in emergency situations. The pain killers and mind-altering drugs, the symptomatic treatments administered to a sick society fraudulently called socialist, restored in them, if not the faith irrevocably lost, the hunger for power and privilege offered them once again by this society.

I do not want to harm them by revealing the cynicism of their double turn-arounds. I did not remain in Hungary, so I cannot pass judgment on them. Nor can I fully explain the sad, ugly, social and psychological mechanisms behind this pitiful mixture of self-delusion, spinelessness, and compromise. One extreme example, however, should not pass unmentioned. L. M. left political exile in Belgium to join the International Brigade in Spain. The Soviet Union rescued him from a French internment camp, and he spent the war years in the Soviet Union, returning to Hungary with the Red Army to serve as a colonel in the political department of the Ministry of the Interior. His accounts of life in the Soviet Union were, for me, one of the most shocking eye-openers I encountered in cell 69. It was from M. that I learned firsthand about the Stalinist terror, of the poverty and backwardness of the socialist paradise, of the huge gap between slogan and reality. After our release from prison, the victim became victimizer. M. joined the AVH and took an active part in the arrest and interrogation of the communist writers who played a role in the anti-Stalinist uprising in 1956.

Other more prominent and much deadlier examples are, of course, Kádár in Hungary and Husák in Czechoslovakia. Their transformations from Stalinist victims to post-Stalinist butchers are a worthwhile subject for a psycho-social study.

M. was not my only mentor on the subject of Soviet reality. Lajos Cséby was born in the southern part of Hungary that, after World War I, was annexed by Yugoslavia. His father was one of the founders of the trade union movement and in 1919 the younger Cséby, barely out of school, joined the short-lived communist revolution in Hungary. He managed to escape from the White terror to Yugoslavia, although his father was not so fortunate and was murdered by counterrevolutionaries.

In Yugoslavia, Cséby worked as a leader of the Hungarian minority organization until 1932 when the party sent him to the Military Academy in Moscow. In 1936 he was sent to Madrid as an adviser to the International Brigade and two years later returned to the Soviet Union where he fought in the Red Army. He organized the Hungarian propaganda broadcasts of Radio Moscow and the political indoctrination of the prisoners of war, linking them with the partisan fighters in Hungary.

After the war, Cséby became president of the Partisan Union in Hungary, with the rank of colonel-general. His Yugoslav connection earned him arrest as a Titoist at the same time that his sister was arrested in Yugoslavia as an anti-Tito Stalinist. In cell 69, Cséby told me about the purges in Moscow, about the execution of Béla Kun and the other Hungarian communist leaders, and of the murder of the entire Polish section of the Comintern. "Only the benches remained," he said.

After our release, he was given back his rank and his position. In 1956, when I decided to leave Hungary, I asked M. to give me and my family a passport because I could no longer live in an atmosphere of lies. He refused. I turned to Cséby and he arranged it for us.

"You are right," he told me. "I would also leave if I could, but I am old, a lifelong professional revolutionary. I am not good for anything else. I have to stay and keep my mouth shut."

It was in cell 69 that I learned about tortures compared to which my own on Andrássy Street seemed like child's play. The AVH apparently did not regard me as important enough, so I was spared the extreme treatment of the barbarous initial phase of tortures. It is even possible that my first interrogator, the nameless lieutenant, had his secret doubts about my part in the crimes he was supposed to extort, and saved me from the third-degree methods employed by his colleagues. Even in the closeness of the cell we tried not to talk about those horrors, but the picture emerged slowly from countless involuntary remarks. Even now I am unable to write about the specifics of my own lesser hell, but for those who are interested in the grisly details, I recommend the excellent memoirs of my fellow victim, Béla Szász, *Volunteers for the Gallows*. He describes with admirable detachment the particulars, from the savage beatings and the salt feedings of the first days, the weeks without food, water, and sleep, the excruciating pain of broken ribs and injured kidneys, to the rhythmic convulsions induced by electric currents and the swish of rubber truncheons in the "bathtub," not to mention the crouching, crawling, vomiting, delirious agony under the kicks and blows of sadistic torturers. And his ordeal was less than those endured by Rajk, Szőnyi, Szalai, and the other prominent actors in the show trials before they confessed.

The friendship of our evenings eased the terror of those prison days, but it could not mitigate the pain of my hopeless, complete isolation from the outside world. We were not permitted to send or receive letters, to say nothing of visitors. During my interrogation, I was told many times that my wife had been arrested and that I would recognize her cries under torture in a nearby room. Shortly before my trial, I was assured that those had been only threats—"an unfortunate trick of my predecessor" was the phrase used by my friendly psychiatrist, Faludi. Marta, he said, was awaiting with impatience my quick return to our home. But I knew that Faludi was a liar. Was she really free? What was she thinking? She had no word from me and didn't know if I was alive or dead. Would I ever see her again?

In one respect, Faludi spoke the truth. The length of our sentence was a mere formality. With such knowledge as we possessed of the workings of the show trials, we could not hope to leave our nether world alive. As weeks, months, and years passed, the life we had once led receded into a foggy, blurred dream. Cell 69 offered a hiding place in Attila's tomb, an illusion of refuge, but every morning, inexorably, inescapably, inhumanity took over and that was the only reality, fated to go on and on until, at last, my nameless corpse should one day disappear in the prison cemetery.

CHAPTER 11

THE INTERRUPTED SHOW TRIALS IN EAST GERMANY

The Soviet scenario for the Rajk trial left no doubt that there would be a follow-up in East Germany. On September 19, 1949, in Budapest, Szőnyi confessed that in Switzerland, during the war, the U.S. master spy Noel Field and the Yugoslavs recruited not only Hungarians, but other exile groups into their service, including "a German Trotzkyist group whose leader was Miss Politzer."[1]

This was the first indication that there would be a trial in East Germany. At the same time, it indicated the first confusion in connection with Berlin as Stalin's intended staging area for the satellite purges: There was no Miss Politzer among the leading German emigres in Switzerland. Yet it is inconceivable that Szőnyi misspoke; every word of his testimony was precisely arranged, every name mentioned was purposefully planned. Szőnyi had been in close contact with the German exile group and a long list of names of people now prominent in the party and the government, extorted from Szőnyi and Field, was in the hands of the Soviet security organs in Moscow, Berlin, and Budapest. The fact that Szőnyi was told not to divulge them demonstrated the uncertainty that Stalin and Beria must have felt in the fall of 1949 about what methods to be used in divided Germany.

Among the communist exiles in Switzerland, the German group was by far the most important.[2] Already in the first years of Nazi rule in Germany, it included several hundred people, and its strength grew rapidly after Hitler's armies destroyed one exile center after another. As Vienna, Prague, Paris, and Marseille came under Gestapo control, neutral Switzerland became its main headquarters in Western Europe. Contacts were established with the resistance movements and with the underground communist cells in Germany itself. Pamphlets, newspapers, and propaganda material were smuggled across the frontier. Among the Politburo members in Western exile, Franz Dalhem was arrested in Paris, Paul Merker escaped to Mexico, and the third one, Paul Bertz, found refuge in Switzerland and took over command.

One of the Swiss group's most important tasks during the years 1940–1942 was to open and maintain communication lines with the exile center in Vichy, France, which was not yet occupied by the Germans. For this highly dangerous mission, their main instrument was Noel Field, whose Unitarian Service Committee (USC) offices were in Geneva and Marseilles. In 1940, Field met Bruno Goldhammer, one of the leaders of the German communists in Zurich. The next year the Swiss party put him in touch with Maria Weiterer in Marseilles, and she led him to Merker, Bertz, Lex Ende, and Willy Kreikemeyer, the leaders of the German emigres in the West. The Swiss group gave Field the names of German communists held captive in French internment camps; the USC, with open access to the camps, provided them with medicine, food, and clothing. Hundreds of internees owed their lives to Field.

Field's help was also used for political purposes. His position as the American director of an international humanitarian organization allowed him, until the German occupation of Vichy, France, to cross the frontier and commute unmolested between his Geneva and Marseilles offices. He functioned as a courier between the Swiss and French exile centers. Besides this invaluable service, Field also helped his German comrades in Switzerland by giving them financial assistance from the funds of the USC.

The contact man between Field and the exile centers was Leo Bauer in Geneva. A brief incident involving the two men, which seemed at the time to be unimportant, later acquired a more ominous significance. In the fall of 1942, Field put Bauer in touch with Robert Dexter, director of the USC office in Lisbon, Portugal. Dexter worked also for the United States intelligence organization OSS and made the suggestion that Bauer pass on political and economic information about Nazi Germany. In exchange, he offered financial help for the German anti-Nazis in Switzerland. This collaboration, so he said, would be of mutual benefit and serve the common goal of the fight against Hitler. Bauer did not have time to inform the party leadership of this suggestion, and a few days after his conversation with Dexter, he was arrested by the Swiss police for illegal political activities. His direct contact with the OSS was interrupted and never reestablished.

After the occupation of Vichy, France, the Marseilles branch of the USC was closed, but Field continued to support his German friends through his Geneva office. Shortly before the end of the war, he rendered them a final service. He used his long-standing acquaintance with Allen Dulles, director of the OSS in Berne, to include a number of communists in a group of German emigres whom the OSS parachuted into Germany with the aim of taking over the crumbling Nazi administration and paving the way for the advancing Allied armies.

After the war, Field often visited Germany to see his old friends from Switzerland and France, and also to explore the possibility of getting a job at a university or research institute in the Soviet occupation zone. His German comrades, whom Field had helped financially and politically at great personal risk during the war, did not return his help. They were sympathetic but noncommittal while the Soviet administration, which they contacted, refused even to consider having an American living and working in the midst of their zone. Field finally disappeared from Germany. His ghost returned years later, changed beyond recognition, to pick up in East Germany the thread of the tissue of lies prepared by Stalin at the Rajk trial.

* * *

At the time that Szőnyi was giving testimony in Budapest about a German spy organization, one peripheral member of it was already undergoing months of torture in the cellars of the Hungarian AVH. It was not the mysterious Miss Politzer, but Ibolya Steinberger, the Hungarian wife of a former German emigrant, Berndt Steinberger.[3] He had been a young student of economics and a member of the communist exile group in Zurich where he met Ibolya, a wholly nonpolitical woman, through his contacts with the Hungarian exiles. They married after the war and returned to Leipzig where Steinberger finished his studies and worked as a lecturer at the university. In the spring of 1949, Ibolya returned to Hungary to visit her parents. On the last night before her scheduled return to Leipzig, she stayed at the apartment of András Kálmán. That same night, Kálmán was arrested by the AVH. The policemen returned a few hours later to ask Ibolya if, in Switzerland, she had known someone named Field. When she told them that she had heard his name mentioned, they ordered her to dress and come with them.

Mrs. Steinberger was of no use to the Hungarian and Soviet interrogators. Her political role was so insignificant that eventually the Soviet advisers instructed their Hungarian colleagues not to put her on trial, but to isolate her in the infamous concentration camp of Kistarcsa.

The files containing her statements were transferred to the Soviet security offices in East Berlin. In the fall of 1949, Berndt Steinberger was arrested in Leipzig and was taken to the Soviet prison of Karlshorst in Berlin. He became the first German victim of the Stalinist purge, to be followed by many more.

At the time of his arrest, there existed no East German state, and as a result no East German State Security Service. The function of the political police was entrusted to the Internal Section of the Soviet military administration in Germany, a branch of the MVD under the command of General I. A. Serov, who had had an important role in the Stalinist purges of the Soviet party in the thirties. The East German Political Commissariat of the People's Police (K5) performed only auxiliary services for its Soviet masters. The judicial and penal systems for political offenses were also in the hands of the Soviets, but their military tribunals were controlled by the MVD.[4]

This situation changed on October 7, 1949, with the transformation of the Soviet Occupation Zone of Germany into the German Democratic Republic (East Germany). This resulted in the creation of the Ministry of State Security and the

Security Police (SSD), but "special cases" remained firmly in the hands of the MVD and the Soviet military tribunals in East Germany; police and justice organs of the new nation were reduced to the role of Soviet handymen.[5]

The Titoist conspiracy was definitely such a special case. In the Karlshorst prison, Steinberger completed the task begun in Budapest by Field and Szőnyi, that of naming all of the members of the German spy group in Switzerland, and after only a short period of torture he confessed his anti-Soviet activities in the service of Field and U.S. intelligence. The preparations for a German Rajk trial could get under way.

* * *

Contrary to the Stalinist purges held in Sofia, Prague, Budapest, and Warsaw, planning in Moscow for an East German version did not begin in May 1948. At the time the Soviet Union had to deal with the Allied Control Council for all Germany on matters relating to the political future of the country. The question of its neutralization or partition was still undecided. The future of the Soviet occupation zone, and with it the communist leaders of the Socialist Unity Party (SED), depended not upon the crude methods of the secret police, but upon cautious political maneuvering. Unlike the people's democracies, the zone was not a satellite state, ruled by remote control from Moscow. Here controllers sat in the heart of Berlin. The leaders of the SED were unmediated recipients of Soviet military orders and their absolute submissiveness was secured, so to say, administratively. Slavish obedience did not yet have to be enforced by judicial constructions.

One and a half years later, the situation had changed radically. The partition of Germany became a fact, and the antagonism between the United States and the Soviet Union developed into the Cold War. With the creation of the German Democratic Republic, the way was opened for Stalin and Beria to extend the purge to their newest satellite. At the same time, however, their hands were tied to some extent by the division of the German communist movement into two parties, the SED in the East and the KPD in the West, the latter being physically removed from their control. This situation forced upon them an unavoidable compromise that determined the character, range, and depth of the first phase of the East German Stalinist purges.

* * *

Immediately after Steinberger's arrest in September 1949, MVD General Serov issued two directives to Walter Ulbricht, secretary-general of the SED. The first ordered him to establish a special committee at the Central Party Control Commission to investigate the wartime ties linking German communists to Field. The second instructed the Central Cadre Department to remove from sensitive party and government posts certain categories of people, among them communists who were caught in Yugoslav or Western prison camps or who had lived in the West and who therefore could have been recruited as agents by the imperialists or the Titoists.[6] Serov also gave Ulbricht the list of communists named by Field, Szőnyi, and Steinberger as linked with Western intelligence.

The special party committee under Hertha Geffke, a trusted agent of the Soviet security organs, interrogated dozens of high- and middle-ranking communists. They all were compelled to write detailed accounts of their connections with Field. After the revelations of the Rajk trial, most of them had no choice but to offer more or less sincere self-criticism stating that they had been careless, failing to detect the true nature of Field's activities, but at the same time, they asserted that they had believed their wartime collaboration to be in the best interests of the party.

There were three exceptions to this pattern. Maria Weiterer, Field's first communist contact in Marseille, remained skeptical even after the Budapest trial.

"I knew Noel and Herta Field as honest, sincere persons and I don't believe that their loyalty to the Soviet Union had been feigned," she bravely wrote. "I personally think of them always with deep gratitude and respect."

Hans Bergmann, an old union organizer, who in Switzerland had been the chairman of the Soviet-inspired Free Germany Movement, seemed to have a sharper political instinct; after the first abusive roasting by the Geffke committee, he fled to West Berlin. The third suspect, Paul Bertz, chose another form of escape. He had been a member of the Politburo of the communist party and a top leader of the exile organizations in France and Switzerland. Bertz did not await the outcome of the inquiry, but committed suicide.[7]

Parallel to the party probe and in close cooperation with it, the MVD and its East German handymen of the SSD launched their secret investigation. The protocols of the Geffke committee were handed over to the Soviet security organs, the depositions were politically reinterpreted by experts schooled in the Rajk trial, and they selected from among the three dozen Fieldists the most promising candidates to be the victims of a show trial.

A lucky break played into their hands in rounding off the prefabricated fiction of an imperialist espionage net. Erica Wallach, whom the Fields saved from the turmoil of the Spanish Civil War—her fate has been outlined in the fourth chapter on the Field connection—decided in June 1950 to search for her vanished foster parents. From Paris, she called her old friend from the Swiss exile group, Leo Bauer, at that time the chief editor at the East German radio.[8] The call was monitored by the MVD and Bauer's Soviet superior instructed him to invite Erica to visit East Berlin. Bauer knew what the consequences of the letter would be, but he did not find the price too high in order to demonstrate his loyalty to the party. For the MVD, the imminent arrival of Erica Wallach was a welcome gift; she could be turned, as were her foster parents in Budapest, Prague, and Warsaw, into a linchpin of the German version of the spy scenario.[9]

At the same time, Moscow instructed its East German governors to begin the political preparations for a show trial. At the Third Party Congress of the SED on July 20–24, 1950, Wilhelm Pieck, president of the GDR, reported: "The Rajk trial proved beyond a doubt that the agents recruited by Field had to fulfill certain political tasks set by Allen Dulles and that Field's helpers infiltrated also into the German emigrant groups. . . . Our duty now is to sharpen the vigilance in our party and to eliminate from its ranks the Trotzkyist agents." A resolution stressed the same point. "The trials against Rajk in Hungary and against Kostov in Bulgaria furnished the unequivocal evidence that the Tito clique, on the orders and in the employ of the Anglo-American imperialists, maintain in all democratic and freedom loving nations a widespread net of agents to execute the dirty business of warmongers."[10]

On August 24, 1950, the Central Committee issued a lengthy report "about the connections of former German political emigres to Noel H. Field, director of the Unitarian Service Committee." It summarized the results of the inquiry of the Geffke committee in the version reinterpreted by the MVD. Every contact with Field was transformed into a collaboration with U.S. intelligence and into a service for the class enemy. The communists in Swiss and French exile were charged with a lack of vigilance that allowed the penetration of spies into the party organizations and the divulgence of confidential information to the imperialists. Eleven party functionaries were mentioned by name. Four of them, Bruno Fuhrmann, Hans Teubner, Walter Beling, and Wolfgang Langhoff, were stripped of their positions; seven others, Bruno Goldhammer, Willy Kreikemeyer, Paul Merker, Lex Ende, Maria Weiterer, and Paul Bertz, "in the meantime deceased"; and Leo Bauer, "now unmasked as a longtime American agent," were expelled from the party.[11]

Bauer, Goldhammer, and Kreikemeyer could not read the resolution; they had been arrested the previous night, August 23, and locked up in the newly constructed prison for political detainees on Schumann Street. Here they were joined by Steinberger, transferred from the Soviet prison after months of torture and interrogation. The next day, Fritz Sperling was locked up with them. He had spent the Hitler years first in a concentration camp and then in exile in France and Switzerland. In 1945 he returned to the U.S. zone of Germany. As secretary of the party's executive committee, he became one of its most influential leaders. To supplement the East German Fieldists, the MVD needed a representative communist from the Western zones, so Ulbricht was told to summon Sperling to East Berlin for a conference. He was arrested on his arrival August 24.[12]

Two days later, Erica Wallach landed at the West Berlin airport at Tempelhof. She immediately tried to call Leo Bauer and, when she could not get in touch with him, went to party headquarters in East Berlin, hoping to find out what happened to her foster parents. No one wanted to speak to her and when she left the building she was arrested in the street. On the same day, security police arrested Gitta, the wife of Leo Bauer. Her sister, Hilde Dubro, happened to be present, so they took her also.

Here one previous arrest should be mentioned, seemingly independent of the Field case, that of the second most powerful man in the West German party, Kurt Müller, deputy to its chairman, Max Reimann. Müller had been leader of the communist youth organization in the Weimar Republic. In 1931 the party sent him to Moscow where he worked in the German section of the Comintern. Müller later became one of the first victims of the early Trotzkyist purges in the USSR. He was fortunate; at a time when dozens of German Comintern function-aries were arrested, they only banished him to Gorki. In the spring of 1934, he was allowed to leave the Soviet Union to join the underground communist movement in Germany. That September, the Gestapo arrested him and he spent eleven years in concentration camps. Five years later, the MVD unearthed his name among the suspects in the Trotzkyist center in the Comintern and selected him as a victim in the German Rajk trial. On March 22, 1950, Ulbricht lured him under false pretenses to East Berlin, but instead of a party meeting, he was driven straight to State Security headquarters and became the first inmate of the new prison on Schumann Street.[13]

Müller and the Fieldists were selected as the core of the spy group and their interrogation and torture were used to prepare the net for capturing more and more imaginary agents and conspirators. Bauer, Goldhammer, Kreikemeyer, Sperling, and Steinberger were relatively unimportant communist functionaries, but their close connections to Field made them promising starting points for the spectacular catch of a German Rajk. Erica Wallach was assigned the role of a beautiful American superspy, a Mata Hari whose sexual attraction lured men into the imperialist trap. And the outsider, Kurt Müller, furnished a link to the Trotzkyist aspect of the conspiracy.

Paul Merker, the most prominent communist among those expelled from the party in August 1950, was spared for the time being, the arrest of a member of the Politburo requiring more incriminating evidence to be extorted from Bauer and his comrades. Merker was banished to a small East German town and there earned his living as a waiter. The MVD kept him in reserve for later use. His fate is described later in this chapter.

Why Maria Weiterer and Lex Ende escaped arrest could be explained only by examining the secret MVD archives that are, of course, not available to histo-rians. Weiterer was stripped of her positions in the party and in the women's movement and given a low-grade job as a bookkeeper. Lex Ende, one of the leaders of the exile center in Marseilles, became editor of the party newspaper,

Neues Deutschland. After the August resolution, he was banished to a uranium mine, and there he died, six months later, suffering from maltreatment, hunger, and exhaustion.

*   *   *

The program for the intended victims was prescribed in the MVD scenarios in the detention prisons in Budapest and Sofia. They were interrogated night after night; the beatings and tortures brought them step by step closer to the breaking point. No more mention was made of ''lacking vigilance,'' or ''blindness for the class enemy,'' or of some arcane political-ideological deviations. They now had to confess to crimes never committed. Müller had to admit that back in 1933 he had conspired with a certain Trotzkyist criminal Fedotov to commit terrorist acts and to plan the murder of Molotov and other Soviet leaders. The MVD invented for him a secret meeting in Paris with Trotzky's son, Lev Sedov, and reinterpreted his eleven years in a concentration camp as being spent in the service of the Gestapo as an informer. For the period after his liberation, the MVD changed Müller into an agent of the British intelligence service with the task of undermining the position of party chairman Reimann and, later, to sabotage the unmasking of the Tito clique in the West German communist press.

This last charge was intended to link Müller with the six Fieldist-Titoist victims. Their confessions were pale copies of the protocols in Budapest. During their emigre years in France and Switzerland, they were recruited by Field as agents of U.S. espionage. After the war, they were ordered to return to Germany to build a spy net in the service of a far-reaching Titoist-imperialist plot against the Soviet Union and the socialist countries.

From time to time, their tortures were interrupted by friendly exhortations about their duty to the party, and by promises of leniency, even forgiveness, if they agreed to accept the charges. The role of Kádár in Hungary, Chervenkov in Bulgaria, and Bacilek in Czechoslovakia was played in East Germany by Erich Mielke, deputy minister of State Security. He visited all the victims and he cynically appealed to their communist convictions to make the sacrifice of a full confession. Erica Wallach, who had left the party years ago, was even dragged to a prison dinner with a Soviet MVD general. During a sumptuous repast that included wine and vodka, she was offered an immediate release if she disclosed to him the members of her spy net.[14]

The basic concept of interrogation and stage management was identical with the Budapest model, adapted to the new performing site, with Beria's script translated not into Hungarian but German. There were, however, basic differences; factors outside Beria's control distorted the original concept.

At the time of the arrests, the German Democratic Republic was only ten months old, in transition from a Soviet military administrative district to a satellite country. It was not even a member of the Cominform. This exceptional position was also reflected in the treatment of the victims. In the people's democracies, the interrogations were conducted by the native security services, while the Soviet advisers kept in the background and intervened directly only in exceptional cases. In East Germany, the roles were reversed. The SSD was kept as an auxiliary police, the MVD regularly transferred the victims to the Soviet prison in Karlshorst for interrogation and torture, and even in the SSD detention prison on Schumann Street interrogations were usually conducted in the presence of an MVD officer.

The decisive element distorting the normal pattern of a Stalinist purge was, however, the partition of the country and the existence of the West German Federal Republic. The double purpose of the terror, the intimidation of a potential opposition against Soviet hegemony and the elimination of communist cadres infected by Western values was accomplished by the party purge and the arrest of groups of the Fieldists, but there remained an uncertainty in Moscow as to whether the culmination of the purge, a public show trial, could possibly be staged in partitioned Germany without causing damage to the overall interests of the Soviet state. Furthermore, the fact that its sphere of influence was restricted to the eastern part of the country put the MVD in a position completely different from that it enjoyed in Hungary, Czechoslovakia, Bulgaria, and Poland.

Stalin's hesitation and the fetters imposed on the MVD explain the fact that, contrary to the prescribed course in the satellite countries, the first detentions in East Germany were not followed by a steadily expanding circle of arrests and that only second-ranking communists were caught in the purge. It explains also why the name of Franz Dahlem remained unmentioned in the August declaration of the Central Committee.

Dahlem was an ideal victim candidate for a Stalinist show trial. Before joining the communists in 1922, he was a member of the Independent Socialist Party, an organization characterized as Trotzkyist by the Comintern. He fought in the International Brigade of the Spanish Civil War and, together with Merker and Bertz, he was a leading member of the wartime Politburo in Paris. He was liberated by the Americans from the concentration camp of Mauthausen. He was a close friend of the arrested Kreikemeyer and of the banished Ende. He knew Erica Wallach, and after the war he interceded with the Czechoslovak party on behalf of Noel Field to grant him a residence permit. Dahlem thus fit in most of Stalin's suspect categories and he would have been, for Beria, a perfect German Rajk, the main defendant of a show trial in East Berlin. The MVD was busy extorting incriminating evidence against him from Müller and Bauer, but outwardly Dahlem remained untouchable. His name was erased from the SED resolution because of the doubts and hesitation in Moscow about the depth and the range of an East German trial.

* * *

There were few early arrests centered on the organization of the German Rajk trial and the public denunciation of Tito; but the East German purge was not confined to candidates for a show trial. Hundreds of communists were arrested, expelled from the party, and dismissed from their jobs for the mere suspicion of Western contacts or Yugoslav ties. The Soviet occupation authorities did not consider most of them as special cases so the MVD left the small fry in the care of the East German security organs. Their interrogation was not tied to the Fieldist-Titoist-imperialist plot. Their arrests, tortures, and convictions were carried out in secret, their names remained unmentioned. They were, nonetheless, as much the victims of the Stalinist purges as their comrades who were prepared for the show trials.

The only trace of those nameless victims came years later, in 1956, when oblique statements in the party press mentioned past "abuses committed by the security organs," the "harsh sentences against unjustly accused comrades" that have been annulled, and the "mistakes" rectified. For many of the approximately three hundred communists mistakenly labeled as Western spies and Zionist agents, the corrections came too late; their lives were ruined or they perished in the prisons.[15]

*   *   *

Amid the mass arrests of 1950–51, the interrogation of the candidates for the show trial took its prearranged course. One of the contemplated defendants, however, had to be crossed off Beria's list. Willy Kreikemeyer died in the detention prison of the tortures to which he was submitted. The murder of Kreikemeyer and the death of Bertz, driven to suicide, marked the beginning of the casualty list of the Stalinist purges in East Germany.

The remaining prisoners were prepared for their roles. Deputy Minister Mielke told them at the beginning of 1951 that a show trial would be held soon, and as late as the summer of 1951, the interrogators spoke of an imminent "great German trial." At that time, all the detainees had already confessed and signed the first incriminating protocols admitting anti-Soviet and espionage activities.

In the summer of 1951, Stalin suddenly decided to drop his plans for a German Rajk trial. The main reason stemmed from purely practical considerations. The mechanics for transplanting a Titoist conspiracy from Hungary to East Germany did not work under the conditions of the partitioned country. A considerable number of German communists who escaped from the Hitler terror to France and to Switzerland, settled after the war in West Germany and occupied important political and cultural positions in the Federal Republic. Beria could lure Fritz Sperling to East Germany, but it was impossible for him to trap all the dozens of former emigrants who had been in contact with Noel Field or who were financially helped by the Unitarian Service Committee.

In this connection, I refer to the Rákosi letter mentioned in the Slánský trial in Chapter 8, in which the Hungarian communist leader urged his Czechoslovak colleague Gottwald to turn the hesitant beginnings of the arrests into a wholesale purge, before the show trial of Rajk was publicly staged. "We came up against the difficulty," Rákosi wrote, "that Czechoslovak names will appear by the dozens at the hearing. . . . All those people are still at liberty. They will protest vehemently about the things said in court and will try to undermine the credibility of the charges."[16]

The difficulty in East Berlin was similar to that in Budapest two years earlier. A partial show trial in East Germany, a publicly staged horror story full of obvious lies and distortions, would have certainly aroused vehement protests in the ranks of the West German communist party and undermined the credibility of the charges. It would have happened with much more devastating propaganda effects than in a country in the orbit of the Soviet empire. The partial show trial would have unmasked the whole; therefore, it could not, it should not take place.[17]

* * *

After the decision in Moscow, the now embarrassing affair was liquidated in a typically Stalinist manner. The atmosphere in the prison changed dramatically, the nightly interrogations to extort further and further confessions stopped, and the pressure eased. Suddenly, in the summer of 1952, all the former candidates for a show trial were officially handed over to the Soviet authorities. In September, after more than two years of incarceration, they were notified that a Soviet warrant for their arrest had been issued, as if they had just been detained, and the interrogations started from the beginning. This time, they were no longer accused of a German Titoist-imperialist conspiracy, but were prepared in a Soviet prison for a secret trial by a Soviet military tribunal. The cases of Leo Bauer and Erica Wallach were connected and the others were tried individually, all of them being charged by the Soviet state prosecutor, according to paragraph 58 of the penal code of the Soviet Union, for espionage, anti-Soviet agitation and propaganda, organization of counterrevolutionary activities, and support of the international bourgeoisie.

The military trials took place in December 1952. Leo Bauer and Erica Wallach were sentenced to death by a firing squad; Goldhammer, Müller, Sperling, and Steinberger received terms of twenty-five years of forced labor. A half year later, the two death sentences were commuted to twenty-five and fifteen years of forced labor, respectively. Neither the trial nor the sentences were made public; the six victims vanished without a trace into the archipelago of the Soviet Gulag.[18] The aborted first phase of the show trials ended in deep silence.

* * *

In the summer of 1951, it was merely the plan of a German Rajk trial, but not of a German show trial, that was discarded in Moscow. The center of Stalin's suspect categories shifted gradually from Titoists to Jewish communists; the most abominable villains were no longer Dulles and Ranković, but Morgenthau and Ben Gurion; the main enemy became the "Zionist agency of American imperialism" that penetrated the leadership ranks of the young socialist countries with Trotzkyists, spies, and wreckers. The shift, its motives, and its influence on the Stalinist liquidations were dealt with in Chapter 8.

Parallel to the bloody purges in Czechoslovakia, the Soviet MVD set out in East Germany to resume and finish its interrupted task in accordance with the new conditions. As in Prague, Tito and Field became mere supporting actors in an all-embracing show, and the MVD got freedom of action to arrest any communist under the labels of Zionism, Trotzkyism, or bourgeois nationalism. With the elimination of the restrictive category of Fieldists, there was no need to worry any longer about the reactions of West German communists, and the road to the top leadership of the SED became wide open.

After Stalin's decision to drop a German Titoist trial, the interrogation of the initial victims in the prisons in East Berlin took a new turn. The Field connection retreated into the background, and the detainees had to sign protocols containing evidence about communist leaders in the East and in the West, especially about the next two victim candidates intended for arrest, Paul Merker and Franz Dahlem. But no politician was above suspicion; even the life of Ulbricht, the Muscovite general-secretary, was reinterpreted for the files of the MVD, handy in case of any future need.[19] This new series of interrogations might explain the fact that the secret trials of Bauer, Müller, and their comrades were repeatedly postponed, Beria needing to extort as much incriminating material as possible about all the leading communists before his detainees disappeared into the Soviet Gulag.

There was a more immediate need. The protocols had to serve as a basis for a new show trial. The outlines of the changed scenario were drawn in Moscow in the middle of 1952. In it, Merker would play the role of the leader of a Zionist spy group recruited by U.S. intelligence while in exile in Mexico. He was instructed to return with his group to Germany and, in collaboration with Bauer's Fieldists and Müller's Trotzkyists, to form a widespread conspiracy within the party leadership to detach East Germany from the Soviet Union.

In September 1952, on Beria's orders, the German sector of an imaginary East European plot was inserted in the protocols of the purge victims in Prague. On November 21 came the starting signal from Czechoslovakia. In the Slánský trial, André Simone confessed his criminal ties to Merker during his Mexican exile, Geminder mentioned the conspiratorial contacts he and Slánský maintained with the German Trotzkyist Merker, and the next day Arthur London unmasked his German accomplice Merker as a "Trotzkyist and a collaborator of Noel Field."

Paul Merker was immediately arrested. At the same time, Ulbricht instructed a special commission of the SED to translate Merker's crimes into party jargon. In December 1952, the Central Committee published a resolution about the "lessons from the trial against Slánský's conspiratorial center."

"The unmasking of the Zionists as agents of the American imperialism unmasks at the same time the treacherous role of the spy Merker," said the resolution.

"During his emigration in Mexico, Merker converted the exile journal *Free Germany* into a Zionist publication in which he advocated the interests of Jewish monopoly capital and demanded restitution for the Jews. He abandoned the correct Marxist-Leninist theory on the national question and lowered himself to the petit bourgeois, opportunistic platform of considering the Jews in Germany as a national minority and Zionism as a national movement. After his return from Mexico, he tried to bribe comrades of Jewish descent with donations from the American Joint Distribution Committee, in order to enlist them in the service of imperialist espionage. The agent Merker revealed himself as a subject of the American finance oligarchy, an enemy of the Soviet Union; he adheres to the same ideological platform as Tito, the fascist hangman of the Yugoslav people."

The same resolution denounced Merker's accomplices, his comrades in the Mexican exile: Alexander Abusch, general secretary of the East German cultural union; Erich Jungmann, editor of a party newspaper; and Leo Zuckermann, an aid to State President Pieck and director of the Institute for Legal Research. The Merker network was also linked to Fritz Sperling, "this paid spy of the Americans," and to "the long time Trotzkyist party wrecker and British agent" Kurt Müller. An ominous meaning sounded from the formulations in which no names were mentioned, like "Merker and his aides and abettors." In particular, the threat that "the policy of surrender pursued by some leaders of the emigrant communist organisation in Paris during World War II has yet to be examined in its connections," left the door wide open for the naming of additional criminals and spies.[20]

The name of Fritz Dahlem was again withheld from the resolution—Stalin still opposed his public inclusion in the conspiracy net—but everybody who could read between the lines had no difficulty in decoding the hint underlying the nameless accomplices as pointing unequivocally at Merker's friend and comrade-in-arms in the Paris exile leadership.

The preparations for the new show trial were slow to begin. Abusch and Jungmann were removed from their positions and expelled from the party, and every day they feared arrest. Dr. Zuckermann did not wait for the outcome and saved himself by escaping to West Berlin. Merker's interrogation by the East German and Soviet security team did not open any new avenues for a purge and his alleged contacts to Jewish organizations proved to be a mere figment of imagination in faraway Moscow; he did not know any of his Zionist collaborators. In their efforts to speed up the police interrogation, the Soviet authorities instructed Ulbricht to order the reexamination of the pasts of all "comrades of Jewish descent." Especially scrutinized were the board members of the Union of the Victims of the Nazi Regime (VVN). This time, however, the partition of Germany and particularly the open demarcation line between East and West

Berlin obstructed the Stalinist terror in the same way as in the case of Dr. Zuckermann. The VVN directors of East Berlin, Leipzig, Dresden, and Erfurt all managed to avoid arrest by escaping to the West.[21]

After the arrest of Merker, Ulbricht began to press Moscow for the speedy inclusion of Franz Dahlem in a German show trial. As mentioned, Beria had selected Dahlem for the role of the German Rajk as far back as 1950, but the uncertainties in Germany's future forced him to restrict the project of a show trial to the liquidation of the Field group. At that time, even Merker was only expelled from the party and banished from the capital, but Dahlem, second in command after Ulbricht, remained untouched.

The new pressure for a show trial seemed to offer Ulbricht a welcome opportunity to rid himself of his rival.[22] The latent tensions between the two East German leaders did not arise from ideological differences—both were staunch Stalinists and obedient followers of every hint from Moscow—but from their different political backgrounds. Ulbricht was a grey, cold party apparatchik who survived Hitler and the war in comfortable Moscow exile. He saved his skin in the Stalinist purges of the thirties by collaborating closely with the NKVD and denouncing to them his comrades. Dahlem had a quite different career: emigration to the West, participation in the Spanish Civil War, jail in France, concentration camp in Hitler's Germany. Until 1953, he had been saved from the purge by the support of Stalin, whose ulterior motive was to foster a division in the satellite party and to sustain a counterweight against Ulbricht in order to use the tensions for his own ends. By the beginning of 1953, however, the sick, old Stalin was no longer a secure support. He could not stop the inherent dynamics of the purge, and Beria lifted the barriers for Ulbricht to settle accounts.

In February 1953, Ulbricht attacked Dahlem at a meeting of the Central Committee and succeeded in forcing him into abject self-criticism. Dahlem had to admit to grave errors in the political line of the prewar Paris underground organization, especially to a false evaluation of the Stalin-Hitler pact. This, however, did not satisfy Ulbricht. He rejected the admissions as completely insufficient and instructed the Central Control Commission to reexamine Dahlem's political activities after the war.

The results, edited by Ulbricht, were made public at a session of the Central Committee on May 14, 1953. According to the report, Dahlem had been utterly blind to the attempts of imperialist agents to penetrate the party, he supported the effort of the spy Field to settle in Czechoslovakia, he tried to protect Lex Ende from party expulsion, and he helped Yugoslav agents occupy responsible positions in the East German economy.

"Those actions, seen in connection with mistakes committed during the war, cannot be assessed as accidental," said the report. The Central Committee decided to relieve Dahlem of all his functions and to remove him from the Politburo and the Central Committee.

"The Control Commission is instructed to carry on the inquiry," announced the foreboding last sentence of the resolution. This formulation indicated in Stalinist jargon the prelude for an imminent arrest.[23]

But it was too late. The Dahlem resolution came two months after Stalin's death, at the beginning of the power struggle within the Soviet leadership for the succession, only forty-three days before the arrest of Beria, Ulbricht's main protector and ally. In Czechoslovakia, the automatic impulse of the bloody purge carried the show trials further, but in East Germany the second phase of the Stalinist purge was, at the time of Stalin's death, still in an initial, even embryonic stage. The terror machinery stopped suddenly, the second show trial aborted the same way, even if for quite different reasons, as the first. Paul Merker remained in prison, but his Soviet and German interrogators knew that the police investigation had arrived at a dead cnd. There could be no continuation, much less an expansion. The construction of a German Slánský had to be abandoned, like that of a German Rajk three and a half years before. The second and last German show trial did not take place.

*   *   *

"In our country, there was no Rajk trial, Beria's agents could not cause damage here because they were not allowed in," later lied Ulbricht, Beria's most influential agent in East Germany.[24] He did his utmost to follow the Hungarian and the Czechoslovak example, and it was by no fault of his that his turn came too late, that only Willy Kreikemeyer had been tortured to death, only Paul Bertz and Lex Ende had to die, that only a dozen German communists had to endure for fivc or six years the hell of Soviet labor camps, that the life of a mere couple of hundred nameless communists had been ruined in his prisons.

It was not Ulbricht, but Khrushchev, who ordered in October 1955 the release of Erica Wallach, Bauer, Goldhammer, Sperling, Steinberger, and Müller from the Siberian Gulag. Erica Wallach returned to her family in the United States, Bauer and Müller wanted no part any more of the communist regime; they chose to settle in West Germany. Goldhammer, Sperling, and Steinberger stayed in the German Democratic Republic. Ulbricht tried for years to obstruct their rehabilitation and he ceded only to the pressure of the de-Stalinization campaign from Moscow. Merker spent two years in prison and it took another year until Ulbricht was forced to exonerate him, and even then only from the criminal but not from the political charges. The full rehabilitation of Dahlem was announced in a one-sentence party communique, but his exclusion from the Politburo remained in force.[25]

In a formal respect, Ulbricht was right. There was no Rajk or Slánský trial in East Germany. The two-phase plan of Stalinist show trials miscarried as a result of Germany's partition and a lack of time.

*   *   *

Steinberger was arrested again in 1956, barely one year after his return from the Siberian camp, in connection with the so-called Harich affair, together with a group of oppositional communists who wanted to remove Ulbricht from the party leadership. He was sentenced to four years in prison. However, this new purge lies outside of the scope of this book. The Harich affair was not an imaginary, trumped-up conspiracy, but a genuine oppositional movement within the communist party, and thus does not fit the character of the Stalinist show trials. The post-Stalinist purges, as those of Harich, Schirdewan, and Wollweber in East Germany, of Imre Nagy and his comrades in Hungary, or of the group around Dubček in Czechoslovakia belong to a different category of communist repression and terror.

Personal Notes VI: April 1952–June 1954

One April evening, we were forbidden to go to bed. At midnight, all of the cell doors were opened and we were ordered out into the corridors, down the steps, out into the courtyard lit by searchlights. Then, amid a row of armed guards, we were hustled into trucks. Three hours later, we arrived at another courtyard and the sequence was reversed, at the end of which we were pushed into individual cells and the doors locked behind us.

I had no idea where I was. Did they lock me up in solitary confinement? A few days later, I received a cellmate, László Rákosi, no relative of our bald, "arse-headed" leader. From him, a former Social Democrat, I learned for the first time of the mass arrests of his comrades. Within a few days, I also discovered that we were now residing in a prison in Kőbánya, a suburb of Budapest, which was now run by the AVH as a high-security political penitentiary. It was nicknamed "Star Prison" because of its five wings joined at the center.

Our little Rajkist collective at Vác was now dispersed, but I had no more need of a political university. I was now a graduate, one among thousands of locked-up enemies of the state; gone were the conceited elitism, the arrogance of belonging to bearers of the absolute truth. My postgraduate studies in the Star Prison provided me only with the knowledge that except for the war criminals of the fascist era, I did not meet, among the motley collection of conservatives, liberals, socialists, or just plain random victims of the terror, a single genuine spy, saboteur, or conspirator. All of us were imprisoned on trumped-up charges. One of my cellmates, Jenö Varga, a clerk in the Ministry of Interior, told me that a friend of his once asked him to deliver a sealed envelope to the British Embassy. That was the closest I came to contact with a real criminal, and even in this instance, I am certain that he recited only his extorted false confession because he was afraid to tell me the truth. Who knew? A former communist might be an informer for the police.

Looking back from my new home, Vác appeared to be a mere antechamber to hell. We exchanged the mill for the button factory. Work began at six in the morning and continued until ten at night. Even my sleep was stolen from me, since I awoke time and again during the night because of cramps in my legs from standing sixteen hours in ill-fitting convict's boots. We worked for piece rates and were theoretically entitled to cigarettes and additional food, promised us if we achieved 80 percent of our "norms." We never received anything, of course, since as soon as we approached those norms they were increased. It was not only cramps that kept me from sleeping, but also the howls and cries of prisoners enduring the short iron treatment. The guards had an absolute right to beat and torture us as they liked. We were punished if we produced too little, if we stood up or sat down without authorization, if they thought we were laughing, if we looked into their eyes or if we looked away; the pretexts had no limit, the terror no end.

There were also collective punishments. At noon, we usually received a watery, sour, stinking cabbage for lunch. After a while, I got nauseous from the smell and, despite my hunger, I preferred to go without eating. I must have shared this repugnance with many others because one day, after the distributions of cabbage, all of the button workers were assembled in the courtyard. One hundred portions were uneaten, said the prison director, Antal Bánkuti. Those who had taken part in the revolt should step forward. Four or five prisoners stepped out of the line.

"I will tell you who are the Trotzkyist spies, fascist criminals, and mass murderers," Bánkuti shouted, and he called out one hundred numbers at random. We had no names, of course. Those men, one after the other, had to run the gauntlet between two lines of jailers armed with rubber truncheons. The beatings continued inside the building, and we who were still outside heard the sounds of blows and cries for hours. Meanwhile, Bánkuti raged on like a maniac. "I am God here! I am Lucifer! I will show you what is meant by the dictatorship of the proletariat!"

The next outbreak of mass terror occurred when a prisoner succeeded at escaping. The run through the gauntlet was repeated and this time no one was spared. We were lined up in the corridor and beaten with steel-buckled leather belts until many of us collapsed. That same night, the jailers went from cell to cell beating the prisoners who were still able to stand. The following night, the collective beating was repeated and then we were deprived of food and water for two days.

A few weeks later, another prisoner attempted to escape and this time he was caught at the prison entrance. To witness his punishment, one representative from each work brigade was called to the director's office and there watched the prisoner being beaten to death.

Whatever else he might do, it seems that murdering prisoners was forbidden to Bánkuti because he then disappeared from our sight and later, we learned, was arrested himself and sent to prison. His successor was an old acquaintance, István Lehota, the chief jailer in the AVH cellars and then prison director at Vác.

The terror, however, did not ease. There was no refuge in the Star Prison as had existed for me in cell 69. And here, unlike Vác, we were constantly rotated. After my first cellmate the socialist Rákosi, came Varga, the "British spy;" then Barna Konkoly-Thege, a high officer in the prewar army who had sought to serve the new regime faithfully until he was caught up in the purge; he was followed by Sándor Majoros, a lieutenant in the military counterespionage who was a victim of the infighting between rival organizations in the State Security system. I don't remember the others, as we were in no condition, either physically or mentally, to form close friendships when we dragged ourselves back to our cells late at night.

Back in Vác, the prison director had made us fill out forms listing our professional skills. The authorities were particularly interested in engineers, and near the end of our time in Vác, such people were withdrawn from the mill and sent to work elsewhere. These included my friends, the Swiss Földi and Demeter, the French Pikler and Perczel, and others. In the evenings, they returned to cell 69, bringing with them cigarette butts and pieces of lead pencils, which I used to learn Russian from my former Red Army comrades, sacrificing my rare toilet paper in the cause of education.

In the Star Prison, the professionals among us did not show up for work in the button factory and soon my old cellmate G., a chemical engineer, also disappeared. Then I began to notice the absence of other friends from the French, English, and Yugoslav groups and learned, through the prison grapevine, that they had been placed in special cells. The AVH put them to work designing new prisons and subcontracted them to industry although they remained with us. Those who had language skills were employed translating confidential foreign material into Hungarian, texts from Western or Yugoslav newspapers or books deemed too subversive to be handled by anyone other than a prisoner silenced and buried forever.

In January 1953, I said farewell to the button factory. I was transferred to a tiny cell in another part of the prison. There I was given a table, paper, pencils, a dictionary, and a book, a novel by the French author Roger Peyrefitte. I have forgotten the title of the novel, but it was about lovers, homosexuals, and spies in and around the Greek embassy. Some completely illiterate AVH bureaucrat must have selected it for translation on the basis of its title because by no means could it have been of any value to a security agency. For me, it meant deliverance from sixteen-hour workdays, from sadistic guards, and from many of the other horrors of the Star Prison. I even received a daily ration of five cigarettes and some food rations. I didn't even care that, after three years, I was once again in solitary confinement.

It was a rather thick book, and I tried to stretch out the translation time as best I could, fearing that there might not be any to follow. But I had not even finished with it when, one month after my transfer, a prison officer ordered me to pack my things, leave the book behind, and follow him.

This time I was led to an engineering office. Compared to anything I had undergone in Hungarian prisons, it was a paradise. The AVH had constructed a new prison annex, nicknamed the "little hotel," and for us prisoners the name was apt. The corridors were floored with thick carpeting, our cells were large, bright offices with drawing boards, there were desk lamps we could turn on and off at will, we had beds without dirty straw mattresses, and real flush toilets instead of buckets. We even received books to read, not only technical literature but novels, real novels, in addition to the ubiquitous Soviet works of the "socialist realism" school, all about overachieving workers and tractor drivers. During the day our cell doors remained open so that we could visit neighbors, albeit ostensibly for technical consultations. We even earned money. Most of it was deducted for our upkeep, but some remained to buy cigarettes and to supplement the prison diet. The jailers left us in peace; our accommodations and privileges and, above all, the awesome paraphernalia of engineering—desks, compasses, bow pens, rules, T- and setsquares and copy machines—apparently inspired such respect among the young peasant boys recruited for the job that they even spoke some human words to us. It was like a miracle.

There was one problem. I had not an iota of knowledge about engineering. I had been transferred only because my Rajkist friends insisted to the prison authorities that my "technical knowledge" would be of valuable assistance to them. I worked with my eternal cellmate, G., and marveled at the patience he displayed while introducing me to the secrets of industrial design and architectural drawing. We worked for piece rates, and he lowered his own production in helping me to achieve my norms. Here I again met some of my old friends from cell 69, but I also made new acquaintances: architects, electrical engineers, mechanical engineers, and even a former Nazi minister of public construction and a well-known communist professor of oil engineering.

The sudden leap from terror, hunger, and pain to the semicivilized environment of the "little hotel" was an immense relief, but also a serious shock. I began to think and to feel again, and realized with horror that in three years, the AVH had succeeded in transforming me from a human being to a subhuman vegetable. It was now "normal" to me to be alive in prison under endurable conditions; freedom had become so unreal that I never even spoke about it. I forgot how to hope. The prison was now my home, and my former life appeared only in my dreams where, night after night, I walked the streets with Marta, breathing fresh air. Freedom became a fantasy so painful that I even tried to repress the dream. Forget it, I told myself, you will be free on the day that you learn how to fly through steel-meshed, opaque windows.

From time to time, prisoners would be taken to the AVH headquarters for questioning about suspects selected for arrest or already being tortured in the cellars. Late in March 1953, one of us returned from the Andrássy prison with the electrifying news that Stalin had died. With it, we allowed ourselves a brief outburst of hope; the nightmare might be coming to an end. After all, it seemed logical that an amnesty would be granted to political prisoners. Nothing happened. Perhaps, we reasoned, they are waiting for May Day, a logical time for such an announcement. Weeks, months passed, and our daily routine remained the same. Stalin, dead or alive, was unreal. The only reality was our prison without an exit. Don't think, don't speculate, and above all, don't hope. It does nothing to you except hurt. We didn't know anything about what was happening outside the prison walls, about the slow emergence of Imre Nagy, Khrushchev's protégé, in the struggle against Rákosi and in the de-Stalinization program. Inside, nothing changed.

Then, in November 1953, our isolation suddenly ended. We were permitted to write a postcard of no more than sixteen lines, our first message to the outside world since our sentencing. I was feverish. What should I tell Marta? How should I address the card? Is she free and well, is she still living in our apartment? I wrote her that I was healthy and that I hoped to be released in six years, and perhaps even sooner for good behavior. I didn't know where she lived now, if she had been evicted or fired from her job, but I was sure that the AVH would find her and deliver the card. For weeks I lived in a trance, waiting day after day for a reply. No letters came—to me or anyone else. Had it all been another of AVH's methods of torture?

At the beginning of December, we were told we would be granted a visitor. Shorn bald, in grey convict's clothing, we were escorted to a huge cage surrounded by a dense wire screen. Four feet in front of the screen stood our relatives. Marta was beautiful. I was so shaken and moved that I could hardly speak a word. At best, I could hear her in the cacophony of shouts and cries; she was well and so was our little daughter. She lived in the same apartment and held her same job. After ten minutes it was over, and we were marched back to our cells. My life left with her. There was so much I wanted to tell her, so much I wanted to hear, so much to know, so much unsaid.

That Christmas, I received a package of food and then a letter and, in the spring, a second food package. I waited to see my wife again, but then we were told that visits had been temporarily suspended. What happened? Was it, perhaps, an administrative error, now corrected, to have allowed us to reestablish contact with our families? Would they once again seal up Attila's tomb?

Then, in June 1954, permission was granted for another visit. For prisoners who surpassed their work norms, the reward would be 30 minutes in a private room. I worked feverishly and achieved a level 25 percent over my norm, for which I was immensely grateful to G. I was warned beforehand to sit at opposite ends of the table from my wife, but as soon as I entered the room, I rushed to hug and kiss her. The warden looked the other way, pretending not to notice this breach of regulations. Marta was tanned, she had just returned from a vacation in Lake Balaton. She looked happy. Was it joy on seeing me or was she only pretending or was there hopeful news of which I was still unaware? We were not permitted to discuss my case, so I spoke little except to ask dozens of questions about her life, our daughter, and my mother and sister. I was starved for every word, and when she left and I was brought back to my cell, the prison seemed a different place than it had only that morning.

*   *   *

Marta told me nothing of what she had endured those past five years. The AVH men who came for me in July 1949 warned her not to mention my arrest to anyone and she did keep silent until September, hoping every day for my return. When she finally heard my name mentioned in the radio report on the Rajk trial, she fainted. There was no further need for secrecy.

Marta was fortunate. Her director at the Institute for National Health, András Havas, was an old communist, a Muscovite who had been arrested in the USSR during the Stalinist purges of the 1930s and spent eight years in the Gulag. He told her: "If you have faith in your husband, wait for him. Keep quiet, do your job, and I will keep an eye on you." He did not speak to her for some years, but it was he who saved her from dismissal and supported her quietly as best he could. He saw to it that she was promoted and her salary raised, and made certain that her research papers were published in the scientific journals. The party secretary at the institute was also sympathetic. When, in September 1949, a mass demonstration was organized around the slogan "The rope for the traitors!", Marta asked to be excused from the event. How, after all, could she shout for the death of her husband?

"You just show up," he said. "You don't need to shout, but go and show your face." To her coworkers, mostly professionals from the prewar era, Marta became a heroine overnight, a victim of the hated communists.

In December 1949, she was summoned to AVH headquarters on Andrássy Street. She was certain that she was about to be arrested, but they only inquired after her friends.

"I have none," she told them. "They have all been arrested."

They asked her what she thought about me.

"I don't think anything until you tell me why he is here, of what crimes is he accused."

They told her to leave a package of underwear for me, since it was cold in the cellars. She did so, but of course I never received it. The interrogation probably had as its purpose to frighten her and it succeeded in accomplishing that. For the entire night she sat on her bed, awake and shivering.

The fear remained with her through all of those difficult years. All of our former friends shunned her, they crossed to the other side of the street to avoid meeting her, they got off a bus if she got on it. We had a three-room apartment in Budapest. Soon after my arrest, a policeman with his wife and child moved into one room. Then an AVH man with his family moved into a second room.

"Don't dare to complain, lady," they told her. "Otherwise, you will be sent where your husband is."

Marta was a strong and brave woman. In her one remaining room, alongside her six new co-tenants, she kept quiet, did her job, found some new friends, raised our daughter, struggled to make ends meet, and never lost faith in me, hoping against hope for my return.

Other women were less fortunate. Among our friends, Paula, the Swiss wife of András Kálmán, the parents and the bride of Balabán, and the girlfriend of Kuti were all dismissed from their jobs, thrown out of their apartments, and banished from Budapest to the countryside. G.'s wife was left without work and without a roof over her head before she managed to return to Switzerland. The wives of Szőnyi, Demeter, and Dobó were arrested together with their husbands, the Swiss wife of Dobó, Toni Drittenbass, died in prison of insufficient medical treatment. The French wife of Péter Mód committed suicide shortly after the arrest of her husband.

These were bitter, hard years for Marta, five years of poverty, humiliation, and sadness. Hope came only at the end of 1953 with my initial postcard, the first indication she had that I was still alive. After our first visit, she was both happy and frightened. I hardly spoke; perhaps my teeth had been knocked out. She looked at my sunken cheeks, my empty eyes, my body wasted away.

"He won't survive it," she told a friend.

But the thaw began to spread from Khrushchev's Moscow to Budapest. Imre Nagy came to power in Hungary and a liberating scent of change was in the air. The AVH tenant in her apartment smelled it and moved out hurriedly. Soon afterward, Marta found a friendly couple willing to exchange rooms with the policeman and his family. The labor camps were closed and more than 100,000 internees set free, deportations were stopped, and the banished families began returning to Budapest. In March 1954, AVH Chief Gábor Péter was sentenced to life in prison and in July, János Kádár, the minister of the Interior during the Rajk trial, was released and rehabilitated. Publicly, the Rajk trial could not be criticized, but as the deadly weight of Stalinism began to lift from Hungary, the end of Marta's private nightmare no longer seemed an unthinkable possibility.

CHAPTER 12

THE POLISH WAY OF SHOW TRIALS

"No show trials of Polish communists were staged," wrote Zbigniew Brzezinski in his scholarly study *The Soviet Bloc,*[1] a statement that has been repeated in many academic and other works about this period. The statement is incorrect. There were many bloody show trials in Poland, the difference in the Polish experience being that the trial that was intended to be the culmination of the process, that of Władisław Gomułka, could be averted. Poland was not an exception to the rule, but a variation of it, a unique and special case.

Poland was the only satellite state in which the Stalinist purge began at the very top, with the fall of the secretary-general of the communist party. This represented a deviation from the usual plan prescribed by Beria, to begin at the second or third ranks of party leaders and then expand the terror into both higher and lower echelons, thus engulfing wider and wider circles of officials. Those at the very top of the satellite regimes, Rákosi, Ulbricht, Gottwald, Gheorghiu-Dej, and even Dimitrov, remained untouched.

Gomułka's case was an exception to this formula. In the early summer of 1948, at the height of the conflict with the Yugoslav party, he was seen by Stalin as a menace. Gomułka was no Tito; he never questioned Soviet hegemony in Eastern Europe, but he had his own ideas about Poland's place in the structure. To begin the purge with him was, from Stalin's point of view, an absolute necessity, but given certain facts about the histories of both Poland and its communist party, it became a source of failure as well.

When the ax was directed at the head of the party, the move triggered within the other party leaders, like an experiment in Pavlovian conditioned reflex, a defense mechanism aimed at self-preservation. They felt that if they were to remain alive, the blow must be blunted, diverted. They struck out right and left, but tried to preserve the center; they attempted to postpone the inevitable in a subtle, cunning way, inherited from their forefathers. After five years of procrastination, the evasive maneuvers were no longer necessary. Stalin's death absolved them from trying and executing Gomułka. They saved him, however, at the price of sacrificing hundreds of lower ranked communists, tortured to death, executed in secret trials, or jailed on trumped-up charges. They managed to avoid the main show trial by staging surrogate ones.

* * *

The specific features of the Polish purges were determined by two tragic historical legacies. Since its birth as a nation, Poland had been forced to struggle for its independence against two mighty powers, Germany and Russia. At the end of the eighteenth century, Poland ceased to exist, partitioned among Germany, Russia, and Austria. After World War I, Poland was reborn, but only after a short war with the Soviet state. In 1939, the Hitler-Stalin pact secretly agreed to a new partition of Poland, and it disappeared once more until 1945.

World War II gave the Poles no reason to change their anti-Russian feelings. In the eastern provinces, annexed to the Soviet Union after the war, one and a half million Poles fell victim to their new rulers, imprisoned or executed as spies or sent to the prisons of the Gulag as bourgeois exploiters. Well-remembered was the Soviet slaughter of 4,100 Polish army officers in the woods of Katyn, and the Poles have not forgotten how Stalin ordered his armies to stand for two months on the outskirts of Warsaw while the Germans killed 150,000 who were fighting to liberate the city from within, in an uprising lead by the Home Army, the resistance group based in London.[2]

After Hitler's defeat, the eastern parts of the nation were annexed by the Soviet Union, which compensated Poland for its loss by adding to its territory the German provinces of Silesia and Pomerania to the west. This did nothing to alleviate the hatred of the Soviet Union, instilled by centuries of experience with the neighbor to the east. If the ruling communist party installed by the arch enemy wanted to gain at least the passive cooperation of the masses, it had to take into account the fiercely nationalist and anti-Russian feelings of the population. It had to follow a Polish way.

The twin slogans of communist patriotism and independence were adopted by the Comintern after the German invasion of the Soviet Union and were mandatory for all of the communist parties of the occupied nations.[3] It was a difficult policy shift for them, and especially for the Polish party, which was born in 1918 from a merger of left wing socialists and social democrats, both of which advocated the incorporation of Polish territories in a revolutionary Russia. To them, the restoration of Poland was a bourgeois illusion or, as Rosa Luxemburg, the Social Democratic leader, formulated it, "impossible under capitalism, unnecessary under socialism."[4] In 1920, the Polish communist party supported the Soviet offensive into Poland and, though under pressure from Lenin it later changed its "Luxemburgist" stand, the party's policy toward the nation remained ambiguous. It supported Soviet claims on the eastern provinces of Poland and, at a time when Moscow was courting the Weimar Republic as the next potential link in the chain of nations joining the world revolution, advocated the cession of western Poland to Germany in order to score points for the German communists.[5] Only when Hitler came to power did the party, again under instructions from Moscow, try to shed its anti-Polish image as a Soviet instrument.

Immediately after World War II, Gomułka adopted a policy calling for a Polish way to socialism, one that did not, on the surface, seem to differ from similar policies that spoke of German or Romanian or Hungarian ways to socialism. There was, however, a basic difference. For Gomułka, operating under the conditions set by the deep-seated and long-standing hatred of Poles for anything Soviet, this was not a temporary, tactical move but a policy with long-range implications. Unlike Tito, he did not oppose Poland's integration into the Soviet empire, but contrary to his satellite colleagues and to the policies of Stalin, he was firmly convinced that he had to use methods that took into consideration the realities of Poland, that the Soviet objectives could best be reached by not copying Soviet methods. It was a heresy that had to be purged.

The target of the purge having been determined, the timing suggested itself with the unfolding of the much more dangerous Titoist heresy. Under Stalin's rules, the process promised to be a clear-cut, smooth operation.

Once again a heritage, not this time of the Polish nation but of the Polish communist party, upset Moscow's plans. For the Soviet Bolsheviks, their Polish brother party had always been a despised, unreliable, suspect burden. Within the Comintern, the name "Polish" was synonymous with insubordinations and deviations of every kind. This started at the birth of the party with Lenin's ideological struggle against Luxemburgism and turned, under Stalin, into a much more dangerous witch hunt. In 1924, the Comintern dismissed the Polish party leadership for "right wing opportunism," and two years later accused their successors of supporting Pilsudski's fascist coup. Then came the menacing charge of Trotzkyism, resulting first in the claim that the Polish party leaders were influenced by Trotzkyist criminals and then the accusation that the leaders themselves were followers of Trotzky, a charge that resulted in the liquidation of virtually the entire Polish party leadership in the Great Terror. Rightists and leftists alike were slaughtered, followed by the entire Polish section of the Comintern. From 1933 to 1938, all of the leaders of the Polish party, among them twelve members of the Central Committee, most of the party intellectuals, and several hundred of its prominent functionaries, were murdered. The only ones to escape were those fortunate enough to spend those years in the prisons of fascist Poland, or those with exceptionally close ties to the NKVD, the Soviet secret police. The Polish communist party ceased to exist. Its formal death sentence came at the end of 1938 when the Comintern declared it dissolved.[6]

The trauma caused by this mass killing never left its few survivors. The chilling memory decisively influenced the course of the postwar Stalinist purges and show trials.

* * *

The national trauma placed Gomułka in the role of purge victim; the communist trauma saved his life. He was one of the fortunates who spent the years of the Stalinist bloodbath in Polish prisons.[7] He escaped his captors in the chaos that followed the German invasion of 1939 and found his way to Soviet-occupied territory. The Russians gave him an office job in a stationery plant in Lvov. The NKVD, the Soviet security service, was not interested in this minor functionary, a union organizer and secretary of a regional party committee. When Hitler overran the rest of Poland in 1941, Gomułka remained in Lvov and waited for instructions. There was no Polish communist party to join; the only resistance movement, the Home Army, organized by the government-in-exile in London, was as anti-Soviet as it was anti-German. In 1942, Stalin decided to parachute a handful of trusted NKVD proteges, led by Marceli Nowotko, Pawel Finder, and Boleslaw Molojec, into Warsaw to resuscitate the organization under the name of the Polish Worker's Party (PPR).[8] Finder remembered Gomułka from prewar times and appointed him secretary of the Warsaw party committee. With most of the leaders dead, it was a simple matter for Gomułka to climb to the top of the party hierarchy. He became a member of the Central Committee and, in November 1943, after the death of Nowotko and the murder, by the Gestapo, of Finder, Gomułka was elected secretary-general of the PPR. He was not Stalin's choice, but only Nowotko and Finder knew the secret code for radio communication with Moscow and the appointment was made in the short period during which there was no radio link between the underground party and its Soviet bosses.

The murder of Nowotko illustrates a dark aspect of the communist wartime experience that, much later, influenced the course of the purge. Under instructions from the NKVD, he established contact with the Gestapo and denounced to them partisans of the rival Home Army. Molojec, the third leading member of the Moscow emissaries parachuted to Poland, discovered that his superior was collaborating with the Gestapo, refused to believe that it was on instructions from the NKVD, and murdered him as a traitor. After the murder, Molojec was condemned by a party tribunal and executed. The Gestapo connection was a sordid game, played by both sides, to get rid of their rivals in the underground resistance. After the war, thousands of Home Army leaders went to the gallows for allegedly or actually collaborating with the Germans. But their secret Gestapo connections tainted also the pasts of a number of communists, making them easy targets for the Stalinist purgers who conveniently forgot the role played in this matter by the NKVD.[9]

As a counterforce to the underground Home Army, Gomułka organized the "People's Guard" under the command of his friend, Marian Spychalski. Spychalski had joined the communists in 1931, and after the outbreak of the war escaped with Gomułka to Lvov, returning with him to Warsaw. His People's Guard became the military arm of the communist party.

Shortly afterward, Bolesław Bierut, a Soviet protégé, turned up in Warsaw.

He was also one of those who survived the slaughter of the 1930s in a Polish prison. After the German invasion, he escaped to the Soviet Union where his close contacts with the NKVD obtained a leading position for him in the Comintern. Bierut would have been the logical Soviet choice of succeeding Nowotko, and he was placed on the Central Committee after his arrival in Warsaw at the end of 1943, but he came on the scene too late to displace Gomułka.

* * *

Without this brief history of the Polish communist party, the specific course of the postwar purges would be impossible to follow. The rest of the necessary prelude can be briefly described. At the beginning of 1944, as the Soviet armies neared the Polish frontier, a National Council for the Homeland (KRN) was formed in Warsaw with Bierut as its president. Parallel to the Bierut-Gomułka-Spychalski troika in Warsaw, there was created in Moscow the Union of Polish Patriots with two trusted NKVD agents, Jakub Berman and Stanisław Radkiewicz, as its most prominent members. In March 1944, a KRN delegation led by Spychalski went to Moscow to coordinate the policies of the Moscow and Warsaw centers. On July 21, with the Red Army capturing its first Polish city, the two factions gathered in Lublin and formed the Polish Committee of National Liberation, which on December 31 became the provisional government. Bierut was appointed president, Radkiewicz became minister of public security, and Berman the deputy prime minister, entrusted by the Politburo with all security matters and the overseeing of the Bezpieka, the secret police. Spychalski was made chief of staff of the army and later the deputy minister of defense with the rank of general. Gomułka occupied the real center of power as secretary-general of the PPR and, in the government, he held the post of vice premier as well as minister of the territories recovered from Germany. These were to be the main actors in the forthcoming show trials.

* * *

On June 3, 1949, Gomułka addressed a closed session of the PPR's Central Committee. His subjects were the mistakes of the prewar communist party, its sectarianism and its irresolute attitude toward national independence, mistakes that, he said, could only be overcome by demonstrating the patriotism of the new party and by following a Polish way to socialism.[10]

The themes were well known to the Central Committee: patriotism and the Polish way having formed the cornerstone of party policy since it assumed power. It paralleled the policies of Moscow, and when Gomułka time and time again assured his countrymen that the Sovietization of Poland, collectivization of agriculture, proletarian dictatorship, and one-party rule were nothing but "fantastic, provocative insinuations by the enemy," he was only repeating the Soviet-sanctioned slogans of the time.

It was not the content but the timing of Gomułka's speech that made the difference. On June 3, the Stalin-Tito conflict was nearing its climax and the hostile tone in the correspondence between the Soviet and the Yugoslav central committees warned all of the fraternal parties that the era of separate national roads to socialism was now ended. No variations were to be tolerated by Moscow. Bierut received an order from Stalin and Beria to arrange for the liquidation of Gomułka, whose speech, applauded enthusiastically on its delivery, was attacked only a few days later as a "conscious revision of the Leninist evaluation of the history of our movement."

Stalin's displeasure with Gomułka dated back to the founding of the Cominform on September 22, 1947, in the Polish town of Szklarska Poreba. Among all of the delegates, the host, Gomułka, was the only one who was cool toward the plan to create a new international movement under the old Soviet command, and he also openly opposed a resolution calling on all of the nations present to collectivize their agriculture. He was overruled, but Stalin remembered the first satellite leader who dared to defy him. Gomułka stuck to his position on the Polish way. His deviation had nothing anti-Stalinist, nationalist, or liberal about it. Without questioning Stalin's general line, he did not believe that Poland could withstand even the temporary economic strains that would result from collectivization, and he was convinced that—given the intensity of Polish nationalism and the traditional hatred of all things Soviet—the party and, for that matter, Moscow as well should for the time being placate such prejudices rather than try to meet them head on.[11]

He stuck to his position too long. When, in the spring of 1948, Tito's much more basic defiance triggered the concept of the East European purges, Beria did not have to invent a Polish victim for the show trials. Gomułka was the natural target.

Shortly after the June 3 speech, Beirut convened the Politburo and delivered a sharp attack on Gomułka. The Polish leader's downfall developed step by step from that time on, although from Beria's point of view it did so in an exasperatingly unprofessional way.[12] After the first attack and Gomułka's refusal to offer any self-criticism, he should have been arrested, according to the Stalinist blueprint. Then, while in prison, his mistakes could have been reevaluated into criminal activities. But the reality of Poland's situation blocked this course. The two genuine Muscovites in top positions, Radkiewicz and Berman, responsible in the government and in the party for security matters, were not strong enough, Gomułka had a majority in the Central Committee and Bierut tried to maneuver between the two factions. However, they all remembered the mass slaughter of the thirties, the physical liquidation of the prewar communist leadership. When, in the summer of 1948, Beria urged Gomułka's immediate arrest, Bierut evaded the pressure by promising Stalin that he would end the secretary-general's political power.

He kept his promise, using impeccably Stalinist methods. In July, he gained a majority in the Politburo by evoking the Soviet charges against Gomułka, and in August Gomułka began to apologize in some vague, general terms. This concession was unacceptable to Stalin, and the Politburo prepared a resolution on Gomułka's "rightist-nationalist deviation," accusing him of having advocated an alliance with the reformist wing of the socialists, of opposing collectivization, of favoring the kulaks, or wealthy peasants, and of not condemning strongly enough Tito's treason. On September 2, Gomułka capitulated and accepted the resolution. Bierut could not and did not want to go further. On the same day, he announced triumphantly, "After hearing Comrade Gomułka's speech, the Politburo decided that his self-criticism is sufficient and satisfactory." It seemed as though the indictment was ended. On the next day, September 3, Gomułka was dismissed from his post of secretary-general and from the Politburo, a number of his friends, Kliszko, Bieńkowski, Loga-Sowiński, and others were purged from their positions of power among the party leaders, the native majority was removed from the Central Committee, being replaced by men loyal to Bierut, Beirut himself was elected secretary-general. In January 1949, Gomułka's Ministry of the Recovered Territories was dissolved, he was made to resign as vice premier, and he was tucked away in an office of a state insurance company. He remained a member of the Central Committee, but he was treated as an outcast, stripped of all political power and influence.

After the Rajk trial in Hungary, Bierut had to retreat one step further and, on orders from Moscow, he summoned a plenary session of the Central Committee on November 11, 1949. Gomułka was now accused of a lack of vigilance in allowing spies to infiltrate his ministry, of having followed a political line similar to that of Tito, and there were even insinuations that he might have been involved in the wartime murder of Nowotko. Gomułka was expelled from the Central Committee and a few months later was compelled to resign from his last government position. He lived in obscurity in the resort town of Krynica, shadowed by the secret police.

*   *   *

In spite of all the pressures, Gomułka remained free and alive, but Beria did not give up, he merely changed his tactics. Simultaneously with the show trials staged in Hungary and Bulgaria, he began to apply his purge pattern to Poland. If he could not liquidate the top man immediately, he intended to achieve his goal in a roundabout way.

Beria attacked from all sides. In July 1949, while in Budapest, the torture of the victims chosen for the Rajk trial was in full swing; the Hungarian communist leader Rákosi dispatched his deputy chief of security, Ernö Szücs, to Warsaw with a list of Polish members of the Field group, communists who had spent the war years in exile in the West.[13] He handed over to Bierut twelve names of persons who, according to the confessions extorted from Noel Field, Tibor Szőnyi, and other members of the Hungarian Swiss group, were American intelligence agents recruited by Field in Switzerland and in France. The Hungarians urged their immediate arrest, a request that was passed on to the Tenth Department of the Bezpieka, the top-secret branch of the secret police.

The Tenth Department was headed by Anatol Fejgin and his three deputies, Josef Swiatło, Henryk Piasecki, and Kazimierz Michalak. It dealt with imperialist spies and Trotzkyist agents who had infiltrated the ranks of the party. It was formally the responsibility of Deputy Security Minister Roman Romkowski, a confidential agent of the NKVD, and through him it had its private channel of communication with Moscow, sometimes even behind the backs of Bierut and Berman. To assure MVD control, special Soviet advisers were directly attached to the department and it became the central instrument of the Stalinist purge in Poland.[14]

The control of the Bezpieka by the Soviet MVD was as tight as in all the other satellite countries. The initial organization of the Polish secret police was set up by the MVD General I. Serov; the Minister of State Security Radkiewicz was assisted by the MVD adviser General Lalin; Colonel Fejgin, the head of the Tenth Department, was advised by the MVD Colonel Nikolashkin; while Swiatło and his investigating team followed the directions of another MVD officer, Colonel Soldatov. Of the twenty departments of State Security, eight were headed by Soviet officers directly, all the others by Poles trained and controlled by Soviet agents.

In September 1949, the Tenth Department arrested the imperialist agents named by the Hungarians. The most prominent among the initial eleven victims was Colonel Leon Gecow, delegate of the Ministry of Defense to the International Red Cross. The remaining ten were Mrs. Gecow, Szymon Jakubowicz, Tonia Lechtman, Jan Lis and his wife, Jerzy Kawa, Jerzy Nowicki, Janusz Sokolowski, Paulina Born, and H. Held.

The eleven were soon joined by a twelfth, Anna Duracz, who had fought together with Tonia Lechtman in the Polish communist underground in France. There, she met Noel Field and his wife, Herta, who supported the Polish comrades in their fight against the Nazis, and they established a line of communication linking the Poles in exile in Switzerland and in France. After the war, Duracz became the secretary of the head of security, Jakub Berman. In February 1949, Noel Field came to visit her in Warsaw to ask Berman to put him in touch with an old acquaintance, P. F. Yudin, then the Soviet representative in the Cominform. Field was trying to clear up doubts regarding his wartime activities and to disperse, once and for all, the distrust he encountered everywhere in the satellite countries. Berman made sure not to see him, but let him know that he could leave a letter for Yudin with Duracz and that he could expect a reply on his next visit to Warsaw.

After Noel Field's arrest, the Tenth Department moved to arrest Duracz as well. Berman tried to save her, since he was afraid that this might mark him as the next purge victim. However, Stalin personally insisted on her arrest and he was forced to yield. The menace of a Field connection hung over Berman's head for some years. Time and again, Stalin demanded his arrest, but Bierut kept him at his side.[15]

Another fortunate coincidence worked for the Bezpieka in its attempt to round up all those who might have been connected with Noel Field. In the summer of 1949, Noel's brother Hermann wrote letters to his Polish friends Mela Granowska and Helena Cyrkus, asking for their help in getting him a visa to visit Warsaw. He wanted to find out what had happened to Noel, who had vanished in Prague. The two women forwarded the letter to the Bezpieka and, with the approval of Bierut, were ordered to lure Hermann Field to Warsaw. He arrived in mid-August, could not find out anything, and on his way to the airport to leave the country, was arrested by Swiatło.[16]

In the first weeks after their arrest, members of the Field group were interrogated day and night, but even under torture they admitted to no connection with an alleged Titoist-imperialist conspiracy. At the beginning of September, Swiatło went to Budapest and interrogated Noel Field, Brankov, Szőnyi, and two other members of the Hungarian Swiss group, Vági and Kálmán. By that time, shortly before the beginning of the Rajk trial, they had broken under AVH torture and repeated to Swiatło the confessions they had made, admitting to being spies and telling how they and their Polish comrades had been recruited by American intelligence. When asked for proof, they could not supply any details.

The interrogations in Warsaw went on for some years by an investigating team of the Tenth Department headed by Swiatło, Fejgin, and their brutal aides like Kaskiewicz and the worst of the sadists, Jósef Rozański. Hermann Field was kept in the cellar of a suburban villa in Miedzeszyn, owned by the Tenth Department. The others were held in a special section of the Mokotow prison. Colonel Gecow died under torture, Anna Duracz attempted suicide by cutting her wrists, and Tonia Lechtman was hung by her hair and driven close to insanity. The Bezpieka, however, was not satisfied with extorted confessions about connections with Field; it wanted to establish a link between Gomułka and the Titoist-Fieldist conspiracy, a method that had successfully been applied in Hungary and Czechoslovakia. In Poland it proved to be a dead end, since even with all of the beatings and torture suffered by the accused, no such link could be created. None of the victims knew Gomułka or had any dealings with him.[17]

After more than three years of unproductive interrogation, Beria tried another technique. In November 1952, he ordered Bierut to send Swiatło and his boss, Romkowski, to Prague to interrogate Slánský and Arthur London in order to establish a link between Field, Gomułka, and the Czech defendants, soon to be tried. The Bezpieka emissaries returned from Prague no more successful than they had been in Budapest. Now the pressure on the Polish Field group took a new turn aimed at extorting evidence against Jewish communists in keeping with the ongoing anti-Semitic witch hunt ordered by Stalin. From Anna Duracz, the interrogators tried to obtain evidence even against Jakub Berman. For the prisoners, the Field contact and the Gomułka connection faded into the background.

*   *   *

In the purge's initial phase, from June 1948 to August 1949, Bierut and the group around him succeeded in diverting Soviet pressure for Gomułka's liquidation and restricting arrests to members of the Field group. In the fall of 1949, however, the situation changed. In Romania and Bulgaria, the trials against Patrascanu and Kostov were under way, in Czechoslovakia and East Germany plans were made to expand the trials of the Field group into a full-scale witch hunt, and in Hungary's Rajk trial Gomułka was publicly named as Tito's man in Poland. Bierut was pushed into a corner. He had to try to protect Gomułka from arrest in order to avoid a second Stalinist destruction of the party, but on the other hand he could not stop at the arrest of the relatively unimportant communists of the Field group; he had to sacrifice a leader of the second rank.

Gomułka's friend and comrade in arms, Marian Spychalski, had been a likely candidate for the role of victim for a long time. He was one of the earliest leaders of the communist anti-Nazi resistance and, after the war, as vice minister for defense, he played a decisive role in the "Polonization" of the senior officer's corps in the army and also in the military counterintelligence, which until that time was largely under direct Soviet control. The changeovers had been accomplished with the approval of Moscow, but what had been Soviet policy in 1945–46 became an anti-Soviet attitude in 1948. The MVD pressed for his arrest. Bierut had to give way. He demoted Spychalski to a post with the Ministry of Construction and gave the Tenth Department permission to begin an investigation. Beria and the MVD saw in Spychalski a road by which to reach Gomułka.[18]

But first the road to Spychalski's liquidation had to be arranged. In August 1949, the secret police arrested Alfred Jaroszewicz and Wlodzimierz Lechowicz, Spychalski's friends from underground days whom he had placed in leading government positions after the war. They were accused of having been agents of Poland's prewar intelligence service, the Deuxième Bureau, and of having penetrated the party in order to conduct subversion and espionage.

In reality, Jaroszewicz and Lechowicz had been Soviet agents since the 1920s and joined the Deuxième Bureau on orders from their Soviet controller. During the war, the NKVD put them in contact with Spychalski, who used them to obtain information from the enemy.[19]

The arrests were a convenient lever in the hands of the Bezpieka. Spychalski was first blackmailed into joining the political attack against Gomułka and, later, at the anti-Gomułka plenum in November 1949, he became a target himself.

There had been a tolerant attitude toward the enemies of the people, to the agents of the Deuxième Bureau, said Bierut. "Who was most responsible for this state of affairs? Comrade Spychalski, as Chief of the Intelligence Department of the People's Guard and the People's Army. Comrade Gomułka, as Secretary General of the party, with whom Comrade Spychalski coordinated these harmful acts."[20]

Spychalski was under tremendous pressure. He was confronted, not only with false accusations extorted from Jaroszewicz and Lechowicz, but he was also vulnerable because of his brother, Jósef, a high-ranking prewar officer the London government sent back to Poland, where until his murder by the Gestapo he directed the Cracow district of the Home Army. Spychalski maintained contact with his brother in order to coordinate the struggle of both the reactionary and the communist undergrounds against the common enemy. Now he tried to save himself by attacking Gomułka and by offering an abject self-criticism. "I have made mistakes, comrades, grave mistakes. I am guilty, extremely guilty. I have done enormous harm to the party."[21]

Beria, however, was not interested in humiliating, but in liquidating Spychalski. The net was tightened by arresting two senior officers of the People's Army, Mieczyslaw Waczak and Piotr Mankiewicz, on the charge of having been agents of the Gestapo. The truth was again distorted; the two officers had been in contact with the Germans on the direct order of the communist underground to collect information, but in the cellars of the Mokotow prison they were tortured into confessing that Spychalski instructed them to deliver their comrades to the Gestapo.

Then the Bezpieka threw Hedda Bartoszek into prison, a heroine of the wartime communist underground, an adjutant of Spychalski. She was accused of having been a Nazi collaborator and a Gestapo informer in the concentration camps. The tortures she endured in the communist prison destroyed her reason. She began to draw pictures of herself dressed in a Nazi uniform, beating concentration camp inmates. The drawings served as evidence for her interrogators, and Bartoszek eagerly agreed to furnish more. She not only confessed, but even after her eventual release she refused to accept her innocence. She spent many months in a mental institution before she returned to a semblance of sanity.[22]

The net closed in the spring of 1950 with the arrest of General Stanislaw Tatar. During the war, he had been chief of staff of the Polish armed forces in the West. In 1946, he decided to return to Poland from England and convinced several senior officers to do the same. Some of them even joined the communist party. The Soviet MVD ordered the Polish security forces to arrest Tatar, and with him some three dozen other generals, and to extort from them confessions of a conspiracy against People's Poland in the service of British intelligence. The main objective was, however, to incriminate Spychalski and, through him, Gomułka.

At last, in lay 1950, Spychalski was arrested by the Tenth Department.[23] He was first confined in the villa at Miedzeszyn and then transferred to the Mokotow prison. Spychalski was savagely tortured and soon reduced to an obedient puppet. Driven close to insanity, he was forced to salute every person he saw in order to knock out of his head the notion that he was still a general. However, it took his interrogators long months to convince him that amid all of the traitors around him who had already confessed to their crimes, he must have been, even if only unwittingly, a part of the imperialist plot, an objective accomplice of Tatar and of British intelligence. From this admission it was only a short step to understand that his association with traitors and spies, in a correct political interpretation, made him a traitor and spy himself. In the interest of the party, he eventually signed the requisite protocols. He confessed that he had been recruited by British intelligence to infiltrate agents and saboteurs into the communist resistance movement and that later he had done the same in the People's Army of socialist Poland. The road was now open to the holding of a show trial.

On June 1, 1951, the trial against "Stanislaw Tatar and his gang of conspirators and spies" was begun in the full glare of publicity, including the radio broadcasting of a part of the proceedings. In their well-rehearsed confessions, the nine main defendants admitted to having been in the service of the Anglo-American imperialists in order to create dissention in the army and to sell information about the armed forces to foreign intelligence agencies.

The defendants were mostly noncommunists, but the trial was actually aimed at "traitors in communist masks." To turn their indictment into a dress rehearsal of a future Gomułka show trial, the script writers lined up a great number of arrested communists as witnesses who were carefully coached to deliver memorized testimony, implicating not so much Tatar and his co-defendants, but "spies and traitors penetrating the party leadership."

The MVD and its Polish colleagues chose Spychalski as their trump card. He was dragged from his prison cell to serve as the main witness and, from the first day of the courtroom proceedings, there was no doubt that he and through him, Gomułka, were intended to be the chief culprits. Tatar confessed that Spychalski suggested to his brother that he join the communist People's Guard with the intention of placing a leader of the Home Army into the communist underground. At his return to Poland from London, he said, he had arranged a conspiratorial meeting with Spychalski and two agents of British intelligence, Colonels Pickens and Perkins.

Gomułka was still a free man when Spychalski testified that, in the underground, he had been in contact with the defendant General Frantiszek Herman and that after the war he had recommended to Gomułka his admission to the new Polish army. Then the prosecutor asked if he had told Gomułka that Herman had been chief of intelligence in the Home Army. Spychalski responded: "I told that to Gomułka and he expressed his agreement.'' Later, Spychalski admitted that he had arranged, with Herman's representative, a meeting between Gomułka and Jan Rzepecki, the leader of the WIN, a right wing guerilla group that continued to fight against the Polish government after the war. Herman corroborated this statement by saying that ''Spychalski and Gomułka did seek my help in contacting the ringleader of the WIN bandits. Gomułka even promised Rzepecki immunity from arrest.''

The prosecutor's closing speech, on July 29, did not attempt to hide the real target of the show trial. ''The vile activities of these spies and saboteurs were brought about by the right wing nationalist policies. Their instrument in the military was Marian Spychalski. . . . It is no coincidence that the imperialists and the emigré London clique put their trust in Gomułkaism and Spychalskism in the hope that Poland, like Titoist Yugoslavia, would fall into their hands.''[24]

The verdicts were handed down on August 13, 1951. Generals Tatar, Herman, and Kirchmayer were sentenced to life in prison and the others received terms of ten to fifteen years. This ''leniency'' was quickly corrected in a trial that followed that of Tatar. In the ''case of the nineteen,'' as it was called, of twenty-two defendants in a secret trial, nineteen were sentenced to death. In this trial, the witnesses at previous trials, communists and Home Army officers, stood before a military tribunal. They were kept in death cells for long months and only much later, after Stalin's death, were they executed to make sure that the trumped-up proof given at the Tatar trial disappeared with them.[25]

Spychalski was one witness who was not placed in the dock. He was kept in reserve for Gomułka's impending liquidation.

On August 14, one day after the Tatar sentencing, the party newspaper *Trybuna Ludu* published an editorial that was quite explicit about what might be expected to follow. ''In their treacherous work, the group of spies received support and encouragement from the right wing nationalist clique of Gomułka who is, through Spychalski, directly linked with this diversionary activity.''[26]

But Gomułka did not read either the verdict or the editorial, having been arrested by Swiatło on August 1, 1951.

*   *   *

Spychalski was not the only one to be arrested in preparation for the Gomułka trial. In September 1949, Czesław Dubiel, Gomułka's deputy in the Ministry of Recovered Territories was arrested as a Gestapo spy. Later, another suspect was rounded up, Boguslaw Hrynkiewicz, a Soviet NKVD agent who, during the war, formed an underground group within the party to supply information on the Home Army to the Gestapo. His group raided the Home Army's archive center in Warsaw; the files concerning communists they gave over to Spychalski and Gomułka, and the material on Home Army men they saw that the Gestapo received. In 1949, six years later, Hrynkiewicz was tortured in the Mokotow prison to force him to "confess" that he had collaborated with the Gestapo on the orders of Gomułka.

Soon came the turn of Colonel Wilkonski and Lieutenant Colonel Wojnar, two commanders in the western provinces who had received Gomułka's order to shoot all looters when the Polish army entered the western territories detached from Germany. Now they were accused of anti-Soviet activity, instigated by Gomułka.

Shortly after the arrest of Gomułka, the Soviet MVD advisers directed their Polish colleagues of the Bezpieka to arrest Alexander Kowalski. He had been trained in Moscow, parachuted into Poland during the German occupation, and later elected to the Central Committee. In the prison of Mokotow, the interrogators tried to extort from him a statement accusing Gomułka of having arranged the murder of Nowotko in 1943 (at that time secretary-general of the PPR) and of delivering his successor, Finder, into the hands of the Gestapo in order to take over the top post in the part for himself. When Kowalski refused to incriminate Gomułka, he was forced to submit to intensive treatment, with the result that he lost his mind. He was taken to an insane asylum and died there shortly thereafter.

The same charge was demanded of Waclaw Dobrzynski, a lieutenant colonel of the Bezpieka. It was his misfortune that Nowotko had lived in his home for some time. Now he was arrested and tortured to extort an admission that Gomułka had tolerated Gestapo agents within the party and thus contributed to Nowotko's murder. Dobrzynski was a security officer of the old school. He refused to sign, and was beaten to death by the notoriously brutal interrogator, Captain Kadzior.[27]

* * *

With Gomułka's arrest, the Polish target of the Stalinist purge had been reached at last. His selected codefendant, Spychalski, had been broken; a thick file full of incriminating evidence, extorted from dozens of arrested victims, was ready for use. Beria could look forward with some confidence to the next chapter of the script, the breaking and conviction of Gomułka.

His assistant stage managers in Poland did not, could not follow his scenario. The trauma of the recent bloodbath in Moscow was stronger even than the pressure of the MVD. Another decisive factor leading to cautious resistance was the anti-Semitic campaign launched from Moscow that was reaching its peak at the time of Gomułka's arrest.

The pressure by the Soviets to purge Jews from the ruling communist apparatus began in 1949.[28] It was started in an area where Soviet control was strongest, the military. In 1949–51, most of the Jewish political officers and commanders were ruthlessly dismissed. The anti-Jewish campaign soon became an integral part of the Stalinist purge. In 1949, the Bezpieka arrested Leon Ferszt who, in the wartime underground, had contact with the "Gestapo agent" Jaroszewicz.[29] Ferszt was a Central Committee member of the prewar communist party. After the liberation, he held a high post in military intelligence. In the cellars of the prison, he became the key to the arrest of the majority of the general staff's intelligence section. Fourteen officers of high rank, all of them Jews, were charged with forming a spy ring within the army in the service of the imperialist powers.

The Bezpieka selected General Wacław Komar, chief of the military intelligence department, to be the head of the conspiracy. Komar, a veteran communist, had joined the party in his teens, and fought with the International Brigade in Spain. Accused of organizing a spy ring, he told his interrogators that he had no need of a spy ring since all military secrets passed through his hands anyway. As this argument proved futile, he named among his agents all of the top party leaders, including Berman and even Bierut and promised to unmask them at a public trial. The group was tried by a secret military tribunal. One of the defendants, Colonel Stanislaw Bielski, could not appear since he had committed suicide. Major Henryk Godlewski was sentenced to death, General Komar received a life sentence, and the others were given prison terms of from ten to twenty-five years.[30]

After that of the military, a similar anti-Semitic purge was carried out in government departments. A considerable number of highly qualified civil servants and industrial managers of Jewish origin were dismissed. When, on Stalin's order in the spring of 1951, the purge of Czechoslovakia began to engulf the Jews, the top Jewish party leaders in Poland understood the message; it was now their turn to be swallowed by the Stalinist terror.

From among the 3.5 million Jews of prewar Poland, only 50,000 survived the Holocaust and about 170,000 returned to Poland from the Soviet Union in which they had found refuge during the war. After the war, a disproportionately high number of the leading party and government positions were occupied by Jews. Hilary Minc was responsible for the economy, Berman and Radkiewicz for security, Roman Zambrowski for state administration; together with the non-Jewish Bierut, they held the important levels of power in their hands. The head of the secret police, Romkowski, was Jewish, as were the chiefs of the Tenth Department, Colonel Fejgin, and two of his deputies, Swiatło and Piasecki.

It was not a unique situation. In Hungary, Jews were also predominant among the top office holders. In both Hungary and Poland, the virulently racist, anti-Semitic prejudices of the population, fanned and incited by the prewar, semi-fascist regimes, drove Jewish workers and intellectuals to the communists, the only party that had put up an uncompromising fight against the preparers of the Holocaust. It was the victory of the Red Army that saved, at the last minute, a small fraction of Jews from the Nazi exterminators. In Hungary, the staging of the Rajk trial preceded the postwar anti-Semitic turn that the purges took and therefore it did not affect the top Jewish communists. In Poland, however, Gomułka's arrest coincided with the witch hunt against the "Zionist agents which penetrated into the party leadership." The trauma of the previous blood-bath now intensified in the face of this new threat. When, six months after the Slánský trial, Swiatło was sent to Prague in another futile effort to gather some real evidence against Gomułka, a high Czech security officer asked him: "When will you also finish with all those Jews?"[31]

*   *   *

Gomułka's arrest was delayed for three years, from June 1948 until August 1951. Only at the height of the Stalinist witch hunt was the Polish party leadership forced to give in to Stalin's demands. After August 1, 1951, they tried to avoid putting him on trial; they hedged, they temporized, they found pretext after pretext to gain time in the hope that something miraculous would occur to save them from sitting at his side in the dock as codefendants in a Trotzkyite-bourgeois-nationalist-Zionist plot. The period of procrastination lasted years, and then the miracle occurred: Stalin died. Bierut, Berman, Minc, Radkiewicz, Zambrowski, the "men from Moscow," the hard-core Stalinists, and the clique around them survived. They remained intact because they had succeeded in keeping Gomułka alive.

Gomułka was not thrown into a damp prison cell; he was placed in Miedzeszyn, near Warsaw, in a special villa under the control of the Tenth Department. He lived in a large, comfortable room with barred windows, ate good food, and had the party newspaper *Problemy* to read. As Colonel Swiatło, the defected deputy chief of the Tenth Department, later revealed in his broadcasts on Radio Free Europe, during Gomułka's first three months in detention, no one from the party or even the Bezpieka wanted to talk with him and no one interrogated him. At last, at the end of October, Deputy Security Minister Romkowski and the chief of the Tenth Department, Colonel Fejgin, were assigned to begin the interrogation. We know about the period only until Swiatło's defection in December 1953, but it was then, and remained so afterward, a highly unorthodox instance of Stalinist procedure. During those two and a half years, Gomułka's examinations did not fill more than fifteen working days. He was not given any physical abuse or torture. He did not admit to anything more than he had stated publicly to the Central Committee, he did not go a step beyond the self-criticism he had been forced to make three years earlier. When confronted with the false incriminating evidence extorted from Spychalski, Lechowicz, Jaroszewicz, Komar, and the other arrested communists, he refuted the fabricated charges and went over to the attack, accusing Bierut and his clique of collaborating with the Nazis during the occupation.[32]

There are many legends circulating in Poland and printed in Western literature about why Gomułka was not forced to confess, why he did not become the star defendant at a show trial. It was suggested that he stubbornly refused to admit false charges, even when asked to do so for the sake of the party; that he was one of the few modest, politically and personally honest communists against whom no genuine incriminating evidence could be found; that he knew of too many shameful events in the past and that his accusers were afraid that a Gomułka trial might turn into a public indictment of Bierut and his supporters.

All of these explanations completely miss the point. Had Gomułka been tortured in the same way as were Rajk, Slánský, and the other victims, he would have reacted just as they did and signed all of the documents presented to him. The alleged fear of a possible courtroom retraction or of counteraccusations is an equally unbelievable argument in the light of Kostov's fate in Bulgaria. The Stalinist stage managers knew very well how to deal with such a situation.

In *The Soviet Bloc,* Brzezinski asserts that the weakness of the Polish communist party enabled Bierut to evade a Gomułka trial by his pleading to Stalin that a virulent purge would further undermine the communists' position and harm the unfinished process of consolidation.[33] This argument is no more valid than the others; the Hungarian and Romanian parties were as weak as that in Poland and they did not spare Rajk or Kádár or Patrascanu or Luca.

The Polish Stalinists did not force Gomułka to the breaking point because they did not want to do it. They saved his life in order to save their own.[34] Bierut forbade the use of torture by the Bezpieka, knowing very well that it was the only way to get him to confess to crimes never committed. Berman and his security apparatus cooperated fully. Up to that time, they felt secure enough to sacrifice Gecow and the Field group and all of the random victims selected to provide incriminating evidence. They did not hesitate to torture some of them to death, to extort false confessions from others, and to keep many of them in prison indefinitely for future use, without trial. They wrote trial scripts in advance and arranged for pre-agreed verdicts and sentences and even for secret trials and military tribunals in the Mokotow prison before frightened, servile judges.

Bierut, Berman, Radkiewicz, Fejgin, Romkowski, Swiatlo and the others knew perfectly well which methods to use to obtain confessions. The great white Bezpieka building on Koszykowa Street in Warsaw had among its torture chambers a room called "the bear's walk." Its floor was electrically heated, and prisoners were forced to walk across it, barefoot. There was a room filled with contraptions that gave a high but not lethal electric shock, and there was a refrigerator room where naked prisoners were doused with cold water. The torturers also used the primitive method of hanging women by their hair and kicking them in the groin, and they used sadistic variations of old-fashioned beatings. They played humiliating games with their prisoners to extinguish any lingering flame of human dignity, a favorite being to force the victim to jump about on hands and knees and bark like a dog.[35]

The methods were all available to practice on Gomułka but he remained in the villa, unharmed and unbroken. After the Stalinist purges in Czechoslovakia burst all barriers and threatened everyone, Muscovite, Jew, nationalist, internationalist, the Polish leaders took fright. The past trauma of the party leadership awoke the possibility, even the probability, of a second extermination.

The answer to the question of why the Polish leaders, foremost among them Bierut and Berman, spared Gomułka, is evident. No answer can, however, be given to the question of how they succeeded in stalling so long in the face of heavy Soviet pressure. Even an opening of the secret party archives would be unlikely to provide an answer since the tacit conspiracy to save Gomułka's life must have been hatched without leaving a written trace. It is known that Stalin was impatient with Bierut for his constant stalling and that Bierut went through the motions of reproaching the security services for working inefficiently to obtain incriminating proofs. It is also known that Beria and the MVD advisers constantly pressed their Polish counterparts to extort from Gomułka the required confessions. Every time, Stalin and Beria received the obedient but evasive answer that evidence was still being collected and that the trial would begin soon.

The arrest of Gomułka was made public knowledge only three months after the event, in a small paragraph in a newspaper article announcing that a parliamentary commission had examined the evidence "in connection with certain activities directed against the state as revealed in the course of the trial of Tatar and others, and gave permission to begin criminal proceedings."[36] In the secrecy of the villa in Miedzeszyn, no real effort was made to unmask those certain activities. Outwardly, however, the Polish leaders did their utmost to convince the Soviet Union and the Polish people that the case was essentially wrapped up and closed. During 1952 and the first half of the next year, in party seminars, in books, speeches, newspaper articles, and elsewhere, Gomułka and Spychalski were treated as if they had already been convicted of the most hideous crimes. "It is today absolutely clear that it was hypocrisy, dishonesty towards the party, opportunism, hostility to the USSR and the building of socialism in Poland which joined Gomułka and Spychalski with the agents of imperialism in Belgrade and Budapest," wrote Bierut. Over and over again, they were made responsible for the murder of the wartime communist leaders Nowotko and Finder, they were unmasked as agents in the service of foreign powers. Behind the scenes, Bierut quietly sabotaged the transformation of Gomułka into a criminal, but publicly he declared his "nationalist mistrust of the USSR led Gomułka straight into the imperialist camp in the footsteps of Tito and his band of spies."[37]

*   *   *

With the death of Stalin on March 5, 1953, Soviet pressure for a Gomułka trial eased and then stopped completely. Gomułka's name disappeared from the press; he became an unperson. Bierut, Berman, and the Bezpieka suddenly found themselves in a reverse situation. Now they could not exonerate Gomułka, Spychalski, and all of the other communist victims without endangering themselves. They quietly cleared up some loose ends, showing that they remained faithful to the Stalinist model. In May 1953, they ordered the execution of the nineteen army, navy, and air force officers sentenced to death in the follow-up to the Tatar trial. A few months later, the final public show trials were staged. They began with such minor party functionaries as Pajor, Ojrzynski, and Nienaltowski, imprisoned for four or five years, during which time they served as professional witnesses incriminating other defendants. Now they were in the dock themselves, repeating their own confessions of having been Gestapo agents, but with one significant change. Now there was no mention of the names of Gomułka and Spychalski. This chain of show trials ended with that of Jaroszewicz and Lechowicz. Here, too, the stage managers were careful to delete any mention of the names Gomułka and Spychalski that had, of course, been used freely by the same defendants when they served as witnesses at the Tatar trial.[38]

The show trials of these communist witnesses held in prison for years amid complete silence as to their fates, were now given considerable publicity in order to intimidate those liberal elements within the party who might think that because Stalin was dead, so was Stalinism. The noncommunists needed no such demonstration; the trial of Bishop Kaczmarek as a U.S. spy in September 1953 and, soon after, the arrest of Cardinal Wyszynski along with nine bishops and several hundred priests were message enough.

The process of de-Stalinization urged by Khrushchev could not be delayed. Bierut was in a quandary. He did not know what to do with the surviving communist victims, with Gomułka and Spychalski, with the high-ranking officers and the party functionaries, with the Fieldists and their American master spy Hermann Field. He waited for a new miracle from Moscow.

It was a hesitant, piecemeal retreat. In the spring of 1954, the Politburo, pressured by Khrushchev, appointed a commission of inquiry to review the political trials of communists. In the case of the Field group, the decision was soon made simple by the Hungarian comrades whose own review in August 1954 exonerated Noel Field and his agents. On October 25, Hermann Field was set free. Mrs. Markowska, a member of the inquiry commission, apologized profusely in the name of the Polish government for the inconvenience of five years of imprisonment and torture. After a medical checkup and with a $50,000 compensation in his pocket, he drove to the Warsaw airport on November 19 and boarded an airplane to Zurich. At the same time, Anna Duracz and the eleven surviving Fieldists were released and fully rehabilitated. Their party membership was restored.[39]

Beginning at the end of 1954, the surviving victims of the Tatar and Komar show trials, the convicted agents and the jailed witnesses, began to reemerge from prison, first in a trickle and then in a broad stream. The fates of Gomułka and Spychalski remained undecided for a long time. At the third Plenum of the PPR in January 1955, it was admitted that "many innocent people were arrested and imprisoned," and that "there were cases of shameful and infamous methods of investigation." But when the Central Committee demanded to know the truth about Gomułka, Bierut did not answer questions. The inquiry commission set up to investigate the abuses of the security police had not yet come to any conclusions on the Gomułka case, he explained.

By that time, Gomułka and Spychalski were already free. In December 1954, they were transferred first from Miedzeszyn and Mokotow to a hospital and then quietly released. They disappeared from public view.

Gomułka's rehabilitation was dragged out for another year and a half. He was no more an imperialist agent, but remained a "rightist-nationalist deviator who abandoned the correct Marxist-Lenist line." It was only the Poznań uprising at the end of June 1956, the first armed revolt of the people against oppression, that opened the door for his return to political life. On August 5, 1956, he was readmitted to the party, and the storm of the "Polish October" swept him back into power. Poland was in uproar, and Gomułka emerged as everybody's hope; the nation remembered him as the champion of the Polish way; for the party, he was the only alternative to an utterly discredited leadership. History proved the party right; the abused imperialist spies saved it from the wrath of the people and from Soviet retaliation. Gomułka became secretary-general, Spychalski was his minister of defense, and Komar took office as commander of the Internal Security Corps. It was this resurrected first Stalinist guard that averted the disintegration of the Polish communist party and maneuvered the rebellious country back into the Soviet orbit. The circle was completed, the former victims rose once again to control the nation in the service of the Soviet Union.

Personal Notes VII: July–September 1954

In mid-July of 1954, I was summoned to the prison office. This was to be a very unusual interrogation, different in almost every way from any I had previously undergone. In those, I had been questioned about persons in whom the security police were interested. This time, the AVH officer did not name anyone, but instead asked me if I still had any friends who had not been arrested. A strange question, I thought. Have they run out of suspects? To answer it, I had to rack my brains because virtually all of my friends were in prison. Finally, I thought of one who was not. His name was Imre Patkó, a childhood friend who worked as a journalist at the central party newspaper.

"Tell me about him," said the officer. I became even more confused. Something must be very wrong. If they want to interrogate me about Patkó, why don't they go about it as directly as usual? I told him what I knew, but I saw that the officer took hardly any notes; he was scarcely listening to me.

When I was finished, he suddenly turned to me. "And you, why are you here?"

I was stunned. If I told him the truth, I thought, I might be put in a punishment cell and have to leave the comforts of the "little hotel" as a stubborn, unrepentant criminal.

"You must know," I answered, "you have my statements."

But he persisted. "What were you sentenced for?"

I tried to evade a direct answer. "You have certainly read the charges. Espionage and conspiracy."

"Did you really commit those crimes?"

Now I knew. At long last, the correct question.

"No."

"Then why did you confess?"

"I was tortured. I never committed any crimes."

He began to pack his things.

"What will happen to me now?"

"I made a note of your statement. You go back to your cell." He stood up and called for the warden.

I was perplexed. What could all of this mean? Why did he interrupt the interrogation so suddenly? Would this bring me punishment or freedom?

I didn't have long to wait. Three weeks later, they came and drove me off in a Black Maria with small cages the size of telephone booths. This time, the van did not stop at the headquarters on Andrássy Street, but at a building unknown to me. I learned later that it was a new investigating prison of the AVH on Fő Street.

They locked me into a tiny cell, a bed with a mattress on one side and a toilet in the corner. The food was inedible; there were no books and no cigarettes. A punishment after all, something more horrendous than I could imagine?

But the very next day I was taken to an office. A young man in civilian clothes sat behind a desk. He stood up and introduced himself.

"I am Lieutenant X"—I have forgotten his name—"we will now begin to reexamine your case."

It was the first time that an AVH officer had ever told me his name. I was astonished at the degree of indifference with which I reacted to the whole amazing turn of events. Perhaps I had simply forgotten how to rejoice, and fear was the only emotion I was capable of feeling after five years of terror.

For five days we met in his office. I told him about all of the phases of the interrogation, the truth, the entire truth. At first it was difficult, even embarrassing, for me to explain to an AVH officer how his colleagues falsified my statements, to make him understand why I confessed to abominable crimes, but he listened carefully and, as he wrote his notes without interrupting me, it became very easy.

Then we began from the beginning, transforming his notes into a typewritten statement. Nothing was embellished, nothing changed, nothing omitted. Even the notorious political reinterpretation was repeated, though now with a contrary meaning. When we came to a certain passage of my original statement and he dictated, ". . . after being tortured, I admitted to the false charge. . .," I objected that I wasn't tortured at that specific time, only slapped a couple of times.

"That is immaterial," the lieutenant said. "Your confession was extorted under threats and as the result of physical maltreatment. What difference does it make what sort of maltreatment it was?"

I remembered the enormous difference, but he was right.

I signed the statement. It was still not joy that I felt, but a kind of calm satisfaction, or perhaps a kind of peace. The nightmare was ending. I could wake up, the pieces of my broken life would be reassembled into a sane and complete whole.

*   *   *

I was not released yet. We were transported back to a special wing of the Star Prison. We received double portions of food: tomatoes, garlic, paprika, fresh fruits. It was the healing, fattening cycle all over again to make us regain our human shape. But even with the special treatment, we were still prisoners. We waited day by day for our imprisonment to end. We knew nothing about the political events outside our prison, of the ups and downs of the power struggle between Imre Nagy and Rákosi during the spring and summer of 1954. We didn't know how lucky we were; had Rákosi succeeded in forcing Nagy out two months before, our release could have been postponed for years.

On September 1, 1954, we were driven back to the prison on Fő Street. There we met in a huge entrance hall, all of the surviving Rajkists. In one corner, there was a giant heap of clothing. In the center of the hall stood István Lehota, the prison director.

"You are going to be released," he said. "Choose from among the pants, shoes, shirts, underwear, and you will receive your release paper."

I changed from prison garb to clothes that more or less fit me. They handed me my savings earned in the "little hotel" and, to my utter surprise, the wedding ring and watch I had deposited with them five years ago at the time of my arrest. I also received an official document of the Ministry of the Interior consisting of a single sentence: "György Hodos, detained on September 1, 1954, is to be released, effective immediately." The date on the piece of paper read September 1, 1954. One thousand, eight hundred and eighty three days had been politically reinterpreted into a single day.

Lahota stood by the entrance door. I ignored his outstretched hand, the blood carefully washed away.

I was standing on the street, a free person. I didn't feel any joy yet, just a deep sense of peace. I was going home. Should I take the streetcar? But I had some money in my pocket, so I shared a taxi with my coconspirator, Balabán, and my spy boss, Rosta.

The car stopped in front of my house. A cleaning woman opened the door and looked at me with suspicion. I explained that I used to live in the house and she let me in. I looked around. It was a curious eerie feeling, as if I had left only yesterday, as if the dates on the release paper were the true ones and the five years only a bad dream.

I took a hot bath and sat on the balcony. Then I saw them coming up the road, my wife and a group of children. They were coming home from the opening ceremony for the new school year. Marta looked up, saw me, and cried, "Oh my God, your father has come home." When they burst into the apartment, I kissed and hugged my wife, and then, looking at the half dozen little girls, asked, "Which one is mine?" Zsuzsika was two years old when I last saw her; now she was seven and a half. How could I have recognized her? At that moment, as she stood in the corner of the room, shy, bewildered, and with a deeply mistrusting look on her face, only she reminded me of the five years stolen forever from my life.

CHAPTER 13

CONSEQUENCES AND CONCLUSIONS

Present history is the consequence of the past, but only one of its possible consequences. Stalinism did not develop inevitably from Leninism; the course of the Bolshevik revolution left open other alternatives, and should the course indicated by Bukharin have prevailed, Soviet socialism would have taken a very different turn.[1]

The cautious, uneasy process of de-Stalinization and the revision of the show trials dictated by Khrushchev left the satellite countries with several alternative courses of action. Their situations following the death of Stalin differed in many ways from that of the Soviet Union. Stalin may have died, but his lieutenants in the satellite states were still alive and in power. In the months after his death, they all tried to follow the course set by Moscow as far as it seemed safe to do so, but soon their paths parted. Poland, Hungary, and Czechoslovakia tried to transform the half-hearted disengagement from Stalinism into a radical break with the past in an attempt to create a humanistic, liberal socialism. Romania, Bulgaria, and East Germany, on the other hand, beat a hasty retreat and erased their own vicious legacy by denying and repressing it.

In all of the satellite countries, pressured by Khrushchev, the fabricated trials, the terror verdicts had to be revised by the very same Stalinists who produced them. This basic contradiction characterized the process of revision and had to lead, sooner or later, to either a violent or a subtle new oppression. All of the satellite leaders were forced to declare the verdicts of the show trials null and void, to exonerate their murdered victims, and to rehabilitate the survivors. The first move was made by Hungary in the summer and fall of 1954, but the shock waves produced by the revelations were so great that the frightened colleagues of Rákosi soon felt the need to pull back. The genie, however, once released, could not be placed back in the bottle. In April 1956, a hushed-up process of rehabilitation took place in Bulgaria, East Germany followed in July, and in August it was the turn of Poland. The popular revolutions in October 1956 in Poland and in Hungary disrupted the process temporarily and only many years later did the murderers, pressured by internal and external forces, continue their balancing act of, at one and the same time, admitting their crimes and attempting to conceal them. In September 1965 Romania surreptitiously rehabilitated its victims, while in Czechoslovakia a partial, reluctant revision of the show trials was dragged out until August 1963 and the complete truth was revealed only in April 1968, after the old leadership responsible for the purge had been removed and the Prague Spring brought promise of a socialism with a human face.

*   *   *

Show trials were not only integral parts of Stalinism, they were also its most cruel, deadly form of expression, and as such they became the focal point of the struggle over de-Stalinization. Rajk, Kostov, Slánský, Gomułka, Merker, Patrascanu, and their comrades had all been Stalinists when they were selected by their master to be symbols of resistance to Soviet hegemony and thus cast into the role of traitors deviating from the one and only true doctrine. De-Stalinization invested them with a new role and changed them into symbols of a socialism devoid of terror, oppression, and lies. The horror aroused by the revelation of the purge atrocities gave new meaning to the false accusations of the past; the fabricated charges suddenly turned against their creators.

The assistant script writers of the purge trials who survived the principal authors were well aware of the dangers to them inherent in a revision of the verdicts. In Romania, in East Germany, and in Bulgaria, they succeeded in reducing the process of rehabilitation to an internal struggle behind closed doors, a dispute between the recalcitrant local party leaders and their new masters in Moscow, and they were very careful to keep the protracted wrangling hidden from both party members and the public. They placed the blame initially upon Beria, then on an impersonal personality cult, finally they published short notices in the party press about the exoneration of the victims from criminal charges and declared the matter ended, the mistakes corrected, and socialist legality restored. The victims were sacrificed for a second time on the altar of a new lie. In Romania, Gheorghiu-Dej charged his former victims, Pauker and Luca, with responsibility for the Stalinist purges, thus turning their liquidation into a matter of political suicide. In Bulgaria, Kostov was first rehabilitated and then his liquidation was deleted from the party history; in the introduction to a 1978 edition of his speeches and writings, no reference is made to his downfall or execution. In East Germany, the purges and show trials were relegated to figments of Western propaganda, following Ulbricht's infamous statement: "In our country, Beria's agents could not cause any harm."

*   *   *

The Polish way was quite different. As already described, the surviving victims of the purges came back into power in the wake of a popular revolt. For Gomułka, the victory was a completely passive event. He watched idly in the shadows as the surging tide of anti-Stalinism elevated him to the top of the nation as a symbol of a human, Polish socialism. But throughout it, he remained a conscientious, hard-working party apparatchik, unimaginative and darkly suspicious of intellectuals and dreamers. He used the immense confidence that people placed in him to lead the nation back into an oppressive, post-Stalinist system in collusion with the new Soviet rulers. The victim of Stalinist terror did not fulfill the hopes invested in him; he turned out to be a false symbol. The student revolt of 1968, which aimed at a socialism true to its promises, was directed against Gomułka's government and the uprising of the hungry, exploited dock workers in 1970 put an end to his career. Ten years later, at the beginning of the Solidarity movement, Gomułka was a forgotten man; there was no longer any connection between the former symbol of a Polish way and the latest outburst of its indestructible ideal.

The real Gomułka was forgotten. His legend however, born in the anti-Stalinist struggle for his release and his rehabilitation, remains at the source of the Solidarity movement. "In a sense, we are all children of October 1956, when Władysław Gomułka returned to power", says Adam Michnik, the most influential theoretician of the Solidarity underground. "The present is part of the process that began in 1956, a process of antitotalitarian self-organization of society, which is the only road open to democratic changes in the future."

* * *

In Hungary, the shock that accompanied the revelations about the show trials became the single most important cause of the revolution of 1956. As everywhere in the satellite empire, de-Stalinization began in Hungary when, in June 1953, Khrushchev summoned Rákosi to Moscow and forced him to appoint Imre Nagy as prime minister and to readmit him to the Politburo. Nagy had been purged as a right wing opportunist at the time of the Rajk trial. In July 1954, Rákosi was forced, again under Soviet pressure, to release from prison and fully rehabilitate János Kádár and his codefendants, and two months later the Rajk trial was denounced as a "provocation of Beria" and its surviving victims began to emerge from the prisons.

The struggle for de-Stalinization began on very unequal terms. Rákosi and his allies had a tight hold on the party apparatus and the secret police, and Nagy remained isolated within the leadership despite the immense popularity of the reform measures he supported. After the release of Stalin's victims, the tide of power was suddenly reversed, and exposure of the tortures leading to the false confessions spread quickly among the rank and file party members. Their reactions furnished the spark that set alight the torch of liberty held high by writers, poets, university students, and other intellectuals, the "conscience of the nation," as they had been called during the many centuries of Hungarian history. The initial call for the "correction of past mistakes," so easily manipulated by

Rákosi, developed its own momentum and resulted in an overwhelming demand for punishment of the murderers and for a socialism without subservience to a foreign power, without lies, and without distortions.

The revolution broke out on October 23, 1956, but it had already made itself evident on October 6 at the funeral of Rajk and the other murdered victims. For the crowd of 200,000 that gathered around the coffins it was not only a day of mourning, but also a day of reckoning. It was the first open, mass demonstration against the regime, for the overthrow of a murderous system. Only a few among those who attended his delayed funeral recalled Rajk as a Stalinist, but one exceptional witness to the proceedings whispered to a nearby friend, "If he had lived to see this, he would have ordered the police to fire at the crowd." For the mourners as well as for the entire nation, Rajk had become the hero of anti-Stalinism, a symbol of freedom, independence, and social justice.

The surviving victims, gathered around Nagy, were the inspiration for and provided the political organization of the revolution, the Trotzkyists Kádár, Kállai, Donáth, Losonczy, Haraszti, and Ujhelyi, and the Rajkists Ádám, Heltai, Mód, Szász, and the widow Julia Rajk. Only at the final phase of the revolution, when its elemental forces ripped the command from the hands of Nagy and the uprising began to take an anarchic turn beyond any control, did the paths of its initial leaders part. One group, headed by Kádár, deserted to the Soviets. A second group, around Nagy, was arrested and many of them hanged or shot after a subsequent trial.[2] A third group continued to fight on in an underground movement even after Kádár was placed in power by the Soviets.

Even Kádár's desertion, partly voluntary and partly under coercion from the invading Soviet forces, could not erase the role of the show trials in inspiring the revolutionary forces of 1956 or their symbolic meaning for Hungary today. The Kádár government is well aware of this smouldering fire under the ashes, which is why it suppresses any open discussion of the Stalinist purges and substitutes, instead, empty phrases like "violation of socialist legality" and "personality cult." The symbol retains its validity, not only in the abstract, but also in a very tangible sense. László Rajk Jr., son of the murdered leader, is one of the central figures in the opposition who does not believe that socialism can be reduced to a full dish of goulash.

*   *   *

In Czechoslovakia, the imprint of the show trials on post-Stalinist history was even more decisive, from the earliest stages of de-Stalinization up to the present. There, the resistance to attempts to rehabilitate the victims was especially stubborn. Gottwald died two weeks after the death of his master in Moscow, but the organizers of the bloody purges, Novotný, Zápotocký, Čepička, Bacilek, and Kopecký remained in power and sabotaged the attempts forced upon them by the Soviets to reverse the trial verdicts. The victims were released at a dilatory, hesitant rate and many of them remained in prison for long years after Stalin's death. Inquiry commissions set up to right the previous wrongs were under constant pressure from the murderers to delay the process. In September 1957, the execution of Slánský was still labeled "justified"; a few years later, he was labeled responsible for his own purge. In 1963, he and his murdered comrades were exonerated from criminal charges, but not from political and ideological mistakes. Their full rehabilitation became possible on April 29, 1968, only after the downfall of Novotný and his supporters.

The history of the Prague Spring is too well known to need repeating here. The ghosts of the murdered communists and the struggle of the survivors to repeal the fabricated charges against them became the starting signals for a process of liberalization and for the reemergence of the victims into the political life of the nation. Slowly the bridges to the democratic traditions of the prewar party that had been destroyed during the reign of terror were rebuilt. The exonerated victims formed the rallying point of a mass movement linking the fight for the de-Stalinization of the party to the realization of a socialist system with a human face.

The Prague Spring was mainly the achievement of the former victims. Smrkovský, Svoboda, Husák, Goldstücker, and their comrades were among the leaders of those who prepared the downfall of Novotný and his allies who were supported by Khruschev and Brezhnev. They helped to elevate Dubček and a new group of communists with no blood on their hands to positions at the top of the party hierarchy, and shared power with them. They became, together with Dubček, the principal victims of the Soviet intervention of August 20, 1968.

In contrast to Hungary, there were only isolated defections to the Soviets. With the exception of Husák and the insignificant Fieldist Vilem Nový, all of the former victims had leading roles in the resistance against the Soviet invasion. They remained faithful to the ideals of the Prague Spring. In today's gray, oppressive atmosphere, the rulers of the country have relegated them to the status of non-persons, they have been silenced to an inner exile or compelled to leave the country as they were during the German occupation. Despite all attempts at suppression, they remain a powerful political force. Slánský, the Stalinist, could not rise from the dead to become a symbol of freedom, but the survivors of the show trials did not require any political reinterpretation. The double victims of the terrorist oppression of Stalin's time and the normalized oppression of the Husák era embody the connection, the continuity of two lies, and keep alive the hope for a new spring.

* * *

Stalinist show trials do not belong to the past alone. In Albania, in China, in Cambodia they extend deep into the present. In Eastern Europe, however, they form a seemingly closed chapter of history. Fabricated trials against opposition elements within the party were dropped because they became, in the hands of Stalin, an instrument with which to subjugate the party itself. The collective leadership in the Kremlin never again wants to fear for its life at the hands of a despot. The former monolithic structure of the Soviet empire has slackened somewhat; each of the six satellite countries has put on a slightly different face and their elbow room has become considerably increased, but they are still kept on a leash, even if a much longer one than in the days of Stalin. They, too, do not want to have recourse once again to terror against their comrades; neo-Stalinism is possible without show trials, as the example of Romania demonstrates.

The significance of the show trials for the present time, does not lie in the conceivable danger of their repetition. The Polish revolt, the Hungarian revolution, and the Prague Spring form an unbroken chain between the fabricated terror trials of yesterday and the realities of today, and not only in Poland, Hungary, and Czechoslovakia. The victims, living or dead, are a constant reminder of a past the rulers want desperately to bury under a headstone labeled "personality cult." The personalities behind this cult, Rákosi, Novotný, Gheorghiu-Dej, Chervenkov, Ulbricht, and Bierut, become diffused in this empty phrase, and the new generation scarcely remembers their names. But their victims are remembered, for they are the symbols of revolutionaries who dedicated and sacrificed their lives for an ideal yet to be fulfilled, at a time when bureaucrats administer a caricature of those ideals.

But there are deeper reasons that the ghosts of the show trials cannot be erased from the consciousness of the peoples of these countries, despite all the attempts of their rulers to remove them from history. The victims of the past remain an explosive political factor because the radical breach with Stalinism was halted and oppressed by external and internal forces.

In the Soviet Union, Khrushchev's erratic attempts at de-Stalinisation were strangled. As long as he signaled, with the liquidation of Beria, the end of the random terror and the omnipresent danger of arrests and executions, the majority at the top of the party stood behind him; as soon as he tried to introduce major changes in the Stalinist system, he was toppled.

Gorbachev seems to be resuming Khrushchev's aborted attempt. The transformation of Soviet society assumes a new direction. He tries to reach beyond the beginnings of the Stalinist era to rid himself of the suffocating heritage of sixty years of aberration, to pick up the brutally broken thread leading back to the late Lenin and the murdered Bukharin.

The fate of Eastern Europe depends on his success. If the economic, political and ideological straight-jacket of Stalinism and its epigones is not cast off, the imposed subservient bonds of a client state are not severed, origins and history of the post-war show trials have to be suppressed and falsified, the ghosts of the victims will remain a threat to the rulers, a ferment for freedom and democracy.

NOTES

PREFACE

1. Koestler, Arthur, *Darkness at Noon,* New York, 1961, pp. 78–79.
2. *Darkness,* pp. 161–162.
3. *Darkness,* p. 175.
4. *Darkness,* p. 75.

1. INTRODUCTION

1. Yugoslavia, the initial target of the Stalinist purges, is excluded from this book. Tito's purges of the "Cominformists" (communists who sided with Stalin or merely disagreed with the break) belong to a different category, as genuine and not imaginery, fabricated opponents were hounded and imprisoned. That does not mean, however, that the Yugoslav purges were either more humane or more just than those of Stalin. The two prominent victims, Politburo members Hebrang and Žujović, were jailed shortly before the conflict broke into the open. Hebrang committed suicide in the prison, Žujović stayed for two and a half years in solitary confinement and was released in September 1950 after recanting his pro-Soviet views (in 1966, he was even readmitted to the party). From 1948 until its dissolution in 1962, about 12,000 "Cominformists" were sent to the infamous internment camp of Goli Otok, an uninhabited, inaccessible island in the northern Adriatic, many of them for merely dropping critical remarks in private conversations, for reading illegal leaflets, or for listening to the shortwave radio. They were beaten, put to hard labor, and had no visitation rights, and many died of the extremely cruel treatment. Thousands escaped internment but were fired from their jobs, families were disrupted as pressure was put on wives to divorce their "traitor" husbands. See Djilas, M., *Rise and Fall,* New York, 1983, pp. 235–245.
2. As an arbitrary choice, see Ambrose, S., *Rise to Globalism,* New York, 1980; it offers a concise outline of the escalating East-West antagonism.
3. National Security Council directive NSC 10/2 of May 1948.
4. For covert operations in Western Europe, see Barnet, R., *The Alliance,* New York, 1983, pp. 140–143. For covert operations in Eastern Europe, see Powers, T., *The Man Who Kept the Secrets: Richard Helms and the CIA,* New York, 1979, pp. 46–50. For a detailed account of the Albanian operation, see Bethell, N., *The Great Betrayal,* London, 1984.
5. Medvedev, R., *On Stalin and Stalinism,* New York, 1949, pp. 153, 157. Mikoyan

was accused of being a "Turkish agent," the writers Ilya Ehrenburg and Alexey Tolstoy were called "international spies." Medvedev, R., *Let History Judge,* New York, 1971, p. 157.

6. *Let History Judge,* pp. 309–310.

7. *Let History Judge,* pp. 493–497. Also Medvedev, R., *On Stalin and Stalinism,* pp. 147–148.

8. *Let History Judge,* pp. 408–482.

9. *Let History Judge,* p. 558; also Medvedev, R., *On Stalin and Stalinism,* p. 150.

10. For the stages of the Soviet-Yugoslav dispute, see Ulam, A., *Titoism and the Cominform,* Westport, 1971, pp. 69–134.

11. For the correspondence, see *The Soviet-Yugoslav Dispute: Text of the Published Correspondence,* London, Royal Institute of International Affairs, 1948.

12. For the full text of the Resolution, ibid., pp. 61–70.

2. PRELUDE IN ALBANIA

1. For the historical background, see *Albania,* edited by Stavro Skendi, New York, 1956, pp. 1–17, and Pano, N. C., *The People's Republic of Albania,* Baltimore, 1968, pp. 3–43.

2. For a detailed account of the prewar communist splinter groups, see Pano, Baltimore, 1968, pp. 26–39. For the role of the Yugoslavs in the formation of the Albanian Communist Party, see ibid., pp. 40–43.

3. The status of Albania as a subsatellite of the Soviet Union is expressed also in the fact that its communist party was not a member of the Cominform, but rather was accepted as an appendage of the Yugoslav C.P.

4. *Albania,* pp. 85 and 119; Pano, pp. 47–50; Wolff, R., *The Balkans in Our Time,* New York, 1978, pp. 217, 234.

5. Wolff, pp. 338–341; Pano, pp. 58–66.

6. Pano, pp. 67–68.

7. A personal account of the January 1948 Moscow meeting is given in Djilas, M., *Conversations with Stalin,* New York 1962, pp. 142–147; see also Dedijer, V., *The Battle Stalin Lost,* New York, 1971, p. 194.

8. For the worsening Albanian-Yugoslav relations, see Pano, pp. 68–87; Lendvai, P., *Eagles in Cobwebs,* New York, 1969, pp. 187–190; Skendi, pp. 313–314; and Wolff, pp. 275–278.

9. A rather one-sided account of the Yugoslav contribution to the Albanian economy ·is given in the *White Book of the Yugoslav Foreign Ministry,* Belgrade, 1949, chapter on Albania; Dedijer, pp. 194–196; Djilas, *Rise and Fall,* New York, 1983, pp. 145–146; and see also *Albania,* pp. 229–231.

10. Pano, pp. 78–79; Wolff, p. 276.

11. Djilas, pp. 148–149.

12. Pano, pp. 81–82.

13. Pano, pp. 83–87; Wolff, p. 379.

14. Wolff, p. 279.

15. There exists hardly any documentary report on the Xoxe trial. The following

account had to be gathered from scattered references in the literature, Albanian and Yugoslav papers, and private information furnished by Yugoslav communists.

16. In the first phase of the purge following the Xoxe trial, 14 of the 31 members of the Central Committee and 32 of the 109 deputies of the people's assembly were liquidated; in the second phase, along with Abedin Shehu, a large number of army commanders were charged with "anti-Soviet activities" and shot. See Brzezinski, Z., *The Soviet Bloc,* Cambridge, 1981, p. 387; Pano, p. 93. The Albanian papers printed short notices about secret trials of "Titoist spies" in the cities of Tirana, Durres, and Kukes; see *White Book,* p. 139.

17. Xoxe is the only prominent murder victim of the East European show trials who was never rehabilitated. In Albania, the purges continued uninterrupted by Stalin's death. Each turn in Hoxha's policy claimed its victims in the old Stalinist fashion. In the protracted quarrel with Khrushchev, first Vice-Premier Tuk Jakova was liquidated in 1955 as a "Yugoslav spy," then in 1957, in a series of new show trials, a group of "Soviet agents" were sentenced, headed by Liri Belishova, secretary of the party's almighty Secretariat, together with her husband Mazo Como, the rear-admiral Sejko, and the president of the control commission, Kotcho Tashko. After the break with China in 1974, another category of scapegoats was chosen, the "traitorous putschist group of Chinese agents," headed by General Bequir Balluku, minister of defense and member of the Politburo; together with him, Hoxha liquidated Chief of Staff Petrit Dume, and the generals Hito Cako, Rahman Perllaku, and Halim Ramohito, all of them members of the Central Committee. Immediately following, the army, top government, and party officials were purged as "saboteurs in the pay of the Chinese," among them Vice Premier Abdyl Kellezi, Minister of Industry Koco Theodhosi and Minister of Trade Kico Ngjela. The last prominent victim, for the time being, was Mehmet Shehu, closest collaborator of Hoxha and second mightiest man in Albania. He was murdered in 1982 in the power struggle for the succession of the ailing dictator; Shehu became the "most dangerous traitor" and an agent of the United States, the Soviet Union, and Yugoslavia at the same time. After his murder, dozens of party and state leaders were arrested and sentenced in show trials, among them Shehu's wife, Fiqret, and a number of his relatives, the Minister of Defense Kadri Hasbiu, and the Minister of Foreign Affairs Nesti Nase.

3. THE KOSTOV TRIAL

1. See Bell, J., *The Bulgarian Communist Party,* Stanford, 1986, pp. 15–17; and Ulam, A., *Titoism and the Cominform,* Westport, 1971, pp. 86–89.

2. See Barker, E., *Macedonia,* London, 1950, esp. pp. 48–49; Wolff, R., *The Balkans in Our Time,* New York, 1978, pp. 87–88 and 145–147; and Lendvai, P., *Eagles in Cobwebs,* New York, 1969, pp. 31–37.

3. Ulam, pp. 91–93.

4. For the progress and failure of the federation plan, see Wolff, pp. 314–322; Ulam, pp. 90–95; Dedijer, V., *The Battle Stalin Lost,* New York, 1971, pp. 31–33, 101, 186–190; Djilas, M., *Conversations with Stalin,* New York, 1962, pp. 173–186; Bell, pp. 99–101; Brzezinski, Z., *The Soviet Bloc,* Cambridge, 1981, pp. 55–57; and Djilas, M., *Rise and Fall,* New York, 1983, pp. 129–132 and 163–171.

5. Dimitrov felt genuine respect and friendship for Tito. Shortly before the open break between Stalin and Tito, on April 19, 1948, he had the courage to tell Djilas in confidence: "Hold out! Hold out! . . . You must remain steadfast. The rest will follow." Djilas, *Rise and Fall*, p. 188.

6. Devedjiev, H., *Stalinization of the Bulgarian Society*, Philadelphia, 1975, pp. 15–17.

7. For the life of Kostov, see Devedjiev, pp. 21–23.

8. Djilas, *Conversations*, p. 183; Dedijer, V., *Tito*, New York, 1953, pp. 318–319; Wolff, p. 385; and Devedjijev, p. 26. Bell, p. 104, relates that "Stalin approached Kostov, removed Kostov's glasses to stare him directly in his eyes, called him a swindler and stormed out of the meeting cursing."

9. Devedjiev, pp. 23–25; Lendvai, p. 222.

10. Devedjiev, p. 27; Wolff, p. 386; Dedijer, *The Battle*, pp. 139–140 and 228.

11. Soon after the Central Committee meeting, state security arrested Kiril Slavov, a prominent communist economic official. He was the first victim prepared in prison for the upcoming show trial, extorting from him false depositions against Kostov. He was tortured to death during his interrogation: Bell, p. 104.

12. Devedjiev, pp. 28–29; Bell, p. 105; and Ulam, p. 206. See also the article of Kolarov in the issue of May 15, 1949, in the Cominform journal *For a Lasting Peace*.

13. Devedjiev, p. 29.

14. Devedjiev, pp. 29–34; Dewar, H., *The Modern Inquisition*, London, 1953, pp. 180–187.

15. Devedjiev, p. 34.

16. According to Bell, p. 106, Beria's Minister of State Security V. J. Abakumov and the Soviet ambassador Mikhail Bodrov supervised the interrogations.

17. The following account of the trial is based on the official protocol *The Trial of Traicho Kostov and His Group*, Sofia 1949. See also Devedjiev, pp. 34–45; and Ulam, pp. 214–215.

18. Devedjiev, pp. 49–51. Seventeen of the forty members of the Central Committee were purged (Brzezinski, p. 94).

19. Devedjiev, pp. 53–55; Bell, p. 108; Wolff, p. 389; and Ulam, pp. 215–217.

4. THE FIELD CONNECTION

1. Also in Western countries, in France and in Austria, communists were expelled from the party because their names were mentioned in the fabricated protocols extorted from victims of the Rajk and the Slánský trials. They were lucky to live outside the reach of the Stalinist security services.

The waves of the Field affair reached even the United States. In the memoirs of George Charney, a former American communist, he recounts the story of John Lautner, a member of the control commission and head of the party's security apparatus in New York. "Word had come from the fraternal Hungarian party, from Rákosi's party, that Lautner was an agent of the FBI. No facts were ever supplied to substantiate the charge, save from a veiled reference to his services in the O.S.S. during the war in Italy and Yugoslavia. The mere mention of Yugoslavia was sufficient to condemn him. . . . The trial of Rajk . . . had created an atmosphere of unusual suspicion, and we were ready to believe that this heinous conspiracy had penetrated our own ranks. . . . Lautner was interrogated daily for some time, but no further facts were disclosed. He was in a state of shock and could only mumble incoherent answers. . . . After the official interrogation had revealed nothing, a rendezvous was arranged in the cellar of a private home in Cleveland. Here, Lautner was confronted by three men assigned to the role of extracting the truth by any means. Lautner was stripped naked and then was tormented with accusations, threatened with bodily injury, confronted with a deadly weapon. . . . He was finally released, driven to another part of town, and instructed to meet his accusers on the following day. And Lautner returned! There was no one to meet him, however. The ordeal was over and Lautner was finished, cast out, damned forever as a despicable agent." See Charney, George, *A Long Journey,* Chicago, 1968, pp. 219–221.

Joseph Starobin gives the account of a meeting with Rákosi in Budapest in 1951, where the Hungarian communist leader accused a top American party functionary, Louis Weinstock, of being a government agent. When asked for evidence, Rákosi explained that Weinstock visited Hungary in 1949 and, soon after, his wife came to Hungary as well, and that there was an old Hungarian saying: "When you don't have a horse, send an ass." After Starobin's return, the accusation was discussed in the party leadership, but the charges were dismissed. Starobin, J., *American Communism in Crisis, 1943–1957,* Cambridge, 1972, pp. 218–219.

2. Most of the biographical data in this chapter are drawn from the thoroughly researched, excellent book, Lewis, Flora, *The Red Pawn: The Story of Noel Field,* New York, 1965.

3. Field's alleged recruitment by Hede Massing to the Soviet espionage is closely linked to the Hiss case and, in the same way, unproven. There can be no doubt that the Soviet intelligence tried to take advantage of Field's position in the State Department and his communist sympathies, but even the FBI found no solid evidence and never charged him with divulging any secret information. It is also fairly reliably documented that the Soviet NKVD contacted Field in Switzerland in 1936 through an agent named Ignatz Reiss, who next year was murdered by his comrades in Switzerland as a Trotzkyist traitor, and later by the military intelligence officer General Walter Krivitsky, who after his defection to the United States in 1937 was assassinated in Washington by Soviet agents. It seems, however, that the Soviet agents did not trust Field, they rejected him as a romantic and an idealist. Lewis, pp. 91–97.

This interpretation is confirmed by Karel Kaplan, a member of the Czechoslovak commission to reexamine the political trials. He found, among the documents in the secret archives of the Central Committee, documents of the Czech and Hungarian security services that showed that though Soviet agents had contacted Field several times, he was not drawn into their espionage organization. They characterized him as a "progressive American intellectual, an admirer of the Soviet Union, but a dreamer and politically naive." Kaplan, K., *Dans les archives du Comité Central,* Paris, 1978, p. 144. Doubtlessly, his association with Trotzkyists and defectors played a role in the fact that after 1937, the Soviet intelligence kept aloof from Field.

4. Steven, Stewart, *Operation Splinter Factor,* New York, 1974.

5. *Operation,* pp. 22–24.

6. In the Polish emigre periodical *Kultura* (Paris, No. 10, pp. 29–33), a pseudonymous X.Y.Z. advances the equally improbably assertion that Swiatło was dispatched

abroad by the MVD with falsified documents in order to present the Western media with half-truths, to shift away the blame from the real culprits of the Stalinist purge.

7. According to some sources within the CIA, Frank Wiesner, director of the Office of Policy Coordination, an organization created in 1948 for covert operations and funded by the CIA, did try to put into effect such a splitting action; he even included Noel Field in his plans. Wiesner was a friend of Dulles and worked with him in the OSS; he certainly knew about Field's wartime role. That Steven's distorted account of an Operation Splinter Factor might contain a kernel of truth is indicated also by the fact that inquiries by Flora Lewis with American and British intelligence agencies about Noel Field were fruitless; she was denied any information as containing "sensitive material." See Lewis, p. 16.

5. THE ROAD TO THE RAJK TRIAL

1. See Chapter 4, pp. 62–68.

2. Here, as well as throughout this chapter and the following two chapters of the Hungarian purge, substantial parts are based on confidential information from purge victims, former State Security officers, and communist functionaries with privileged insight into the events.

3. Another provocative use of letters by the MVD is revealed in Kaplan's book on Czechoslovakia. From Switzerland, a copy of a letter written by Field to Dulles at the end of the war emerged in 1948 in the East European headquarters of the MVD in Vienna. General Byelkin forwarded it to Gottwald in Prague and to Rakosi in Budapest. The text of the letter was completely innocuous, without any allusion to espionage, proving only the contact between the two men, well known to the Soviet, Czech, and Hungarian parties and security services. Gottwald discarded it as meaningless, while Rakosi used it later as a further evidence for preparing the arrest of Szőnyi and the Swiss group. See Kaplan, K., *Dans les archives du Comité Central*, Paris, 1978, pp. 145–147.

4. Gyurkó, L., *Arcképvázlat történelmi háterrel* (Outline of a Portrait with Historical Background), Budapest, 1982, pp. 180–181.

5. For a detailed account, see Conquest, R., *The Great Terror*, London, 1971, pp. 300–302.

6. See Chapter 9, pp. 165–166.

7. The connections of both men to the Soviet security services reaches back to the time of their exile in the USSR. The role of Farkas as an NKVD trustee was common knowledge among the emigres. Gerő, under the pseudonym of "Pedro," was probably the most feared NKVD officer among the Comintern advisors in the Spanish Civil War; his main task was to organize the mass liquidation of alleged Trotzkyists. See also Molnár, M., *Budapest 1956*, London, 1971, p. 272.

8. See also Shawcross, W., *Crime and Compromise*, New York, 1974, p. 58.

9. A very cautious account of the organized political campaign within the Politburo is given in the theoretical organ *Társadalmi Szemle*, 5/1983, Budapest.

10. May 29 was a Sunday; Rajk and his wife Julia spent it at Lake Balaton. Monday morning, Rajk went to Budapest; during the whole afternoon, Rakosi called his wife to inquire if he had come back yet. Rajk returned at eight in the evening. After dinner, the AVH came to arrest him. Julia was not allowed to leave the summer house for a week; then she, too, was arrested. See her interview in *Élet és irodalom*, pp. 12, 20, 1985.

11. For a detailed account on how the trap was set for Field, see *The Czechoslovak Political Trials*, edited by Pelikán, J., Stanford, 1971, pp. 70–73.

6. PREPARATIONS FOR THE MODEL TRIAL

1. The details in this chapter are gathered from information furnished by purge victims and former AVH officers and from personal experiences.

2. One of the few mistakes in the stage direction of the show trial was to show Szőnyi three pictures at the court hearing. Szőnyi recognized the first, that of Noel Field. When the president of the court asked him about the second one, Szőnyi said: "I don't know him. This man I don't know." The president: "You don't recognize Allan Dulles here?" Szőnyi: "Oh yes, I do recognize him. At that time, he did not wear spectacles." The President: "He did not wear spectacles. That must have confused you." Szőnyi: "Yes." *László Rajk and his accomplices before the People's Court*, Budapest, 1949, p. 159.

3. The confrontation is described in the excellent memoirs of the purge victim Béla Szász, writing under the pseudonym Vincent Savarius, *Minden kényszer nélkül*, Brussels, 1963, pp. 25–27. His book is translated into English under the title *Volunteers for the Gallows*.

4. Kopácsi, p. 39.

5. Kádár is, of course, denying his role, but there cannot be any doubt in the authenticity of his involvement. It is corroborated by informations from Rajk's cellmates and by participants at the Central Committee meeting where the tape had been played back. It fits also the general practice in the Stalinist show trials; in Bulgaria it was Chervenkov; in Czechoslovakia, Bacilek; in East Germany, Mielke who performed similar services.

6. After-the Rajk trial, Jankó was arrested and tortured to death.

7. A fourth communist witness, András Kálmán, committed suicide in the prison.

7. THE RAJK TRIAL

1. *László Rajk and his accomplices before the People's Court*, Budapest, 1949, pp. 253–254, 270–271. Those and all the following quotes are from the English transcript of the proceedings, hereafter Trial.

2. Trial, pp. 47–53.

3. Trial, pp. 165–168.

4. Trial, pp. 115–119.

5. Trial, p. 295.

6. Trial, p. 289.

7. Their bodies were buried in complete secrecy in a wood outside of Budapest. Six years later, before the solemn reburial of the rehabilitated victims, the authorities had great difficulty in finding the grave site and identifying the bodies.

8. Trial, pp. 102–103.

9. Trial, pp. 123, 125–126.

10. Trial, pp. 162–163.

11. There were bridges built reaching out from the Rajk trial to the subsequent trials of the Social Democrats and of the communist generals; for the first group, Justus and the

Central Committee member Zoltán Horváth led the way; for the second, Dezső Németh and Otto Horváth, the two generals who were executed together with Pálffy.

For the arrest, interrogation, and trial of the Social Democrats, see the excellent memoirs of the socialist writer and journalist Ignotus, Pal, *Political Prisoner*, London, 1959.

Some details of the purge of the generals are inserted in the courageous book *A tábornok* (The General), by György Száraz, Budapest, 1984, a biography of Pálffy, of which only the first volume could be published, about his youth until 1933. Száraz, pp. 309–310.

12. In Hungary, the Kádár trial belongs even now to the forbidden subjects. In his authorized biography by Gyurkó, Kádár makes only the most superficial remarks about his arrest and incarceration (Gyurkó, pp. 190–193). Some details are revealed in the book of András Hegedüs, *Im Schatten einer Idee*, Zurich 1986. The book of the former prime minister of Hungary, now living in retirement, is banned in his country.

13. Downfall and trial of Péter are among the forbidden subjects in post-Stalinist Hungary. The verdicts were published on March 13, 1954, in the party newspaper *Szabad Nép*. Neither then nor since were any details given.

8. THE UNLEASHED TERROR IN PRAGUE

1. In contrast to all the other people's democracies, in Czechoslovakia the final report of the commission, headed by Jan Piller and set up in April 1968 by the Central Committee to investigate the show trials, had been published in the West. (In Czechoslovakia, it is still suppressed.) *The Czechoslovak Political Trials 1950–1954*, Stanford, 1971, hereafter *Piller Report*.

Another report was published in Paris, written by a member of the Piller commission, the historian Kaplan, Karel, *Dans les archives du Comité Central*, Paris, 1978.

Those two documents offer a unique insight into the hidden background of the show trials, and serve, together with the memoirs of the purge victims and private, confidential information gathered by the author, the main source material of the two chapters about the Czechoslovak purges.

2. Quoted in Slanská, Josefá, *Report on My Husband*, New York, 1979, pp. 4–6.

3. For details on the initial "Fieldist" phase of the purge, see *Piller Report*, pp. 70–78; Kaplan, pp. 140–147.

4. *Piller Report*, p. 74.

5. *Piller Report*, p. 77.

6. For the joint party and security investigation of the Fieldists, see also London, A., *The Confession*, New York, 1970, pp. 25–32; and Loebl, E., *My Mind on Trial*, New York, 1976, pp. 26–38.

7. *Piller Report*, pp. 75–76.

8. *Piller Report*, p. 76. The Polish pressure on Gottwald was also confirmed by the defected security officer Swiatło in his broadcast on Radio Free Europe.

9. *Piller Report*, pp. 80, 104.

10. For details on the first purge segment, see *Piller Report*, pp. 79–101.

11. For the anti-Semitic turn in the purges, see Kaplan, pp. 158–162; Lendvai, P., *Anti-Semitism Without Jews*, New York, 1971, pp. 243–259; Fejtö, F., *Histoire des*

démocraties populaires, Paris, 1978, pp. 286–288, and especially his book *Les Juifs et l'antisemitisme dans les pays communistes,* Paris, 1960; Oren, M., *Prisonnier politique à Prague,* Paris, 1960, the memoirs of an Israeli purge victim.

12. *Piller Report,* pp. 194–105.

13. *Piller Report,* p. 106; for Gottwald's fear of arrest, see Kaplan, p. 204.

14. For the "Great Crossing Sweeper" letter, see Kaplan, pp. 173–178. Falsification also played a role in the case of Otto Šling, when the MVD planted in his apartment a forged letter addressed to the "American intelligence officer" Voska, as "evidence" of his espionage activities (*Piller Report,* p. 93; Kaplan, p. 151). For the use of forged documents in the Hungarian purges, see Chapter 5, pp. 33–35.

15. Lobl, p. 142.

16. In *Confession,* A. London mentions espresso coffee, ultraviolet ray treatment, and calcium shots, and quotes his remark to his interrogator: "You remind me of my grandmother when she stuffed her geese for Christmas" (p. 218). See also Lobl, pp. 159–162, 178–187.

17. For the complicity and subservience of the judiciary, see Kaplan, pp. 197–201; *Piller Report,* pp. 224–226, 256–258.

18. Lobl, p. 192; London, p. 225. The utter cynicism of the party leadership is revealed in the interview of Kaplan when, years later, he asked Security Minister Karol Bacilek about his prison visits. "My visits went smoothly," he answered. "Novomesky (sentenced to ten years as a Slovak bourgeois nationalist) was surprised when he saw me enter his cell, 'My poor Karol, you too?', he exclaimed, thinking that it was now my turn to be arrested. I ordered sandwiches and wine and we reminisced about our common fight in the Slovak uprising." Kaplan, p. 122.

19. *Piller Report,* p. 111.

9. THE SLÁNSKÝ TRIAL

1. The quotes in this chapter are from the transcript of the proceedings, *Trial of Rudolf Slánský,* transcript of the proceedings broadcast in Radio Prague, published by Radio Free Europe, Munich, 1952. Excerpts are also cited in London, pp. 237–277, and in Löbl, E., *Die Revolution rehabilitiert ihre Kinder,* Vienna, 1960, pp. 87–190.

2. Their bodies were immediately cremated, the ashes filled in sacks and scattered on an icy side road in the outskirts of Prague. Kaplan, p. 212.

3. For the details of the follow-up trials, see *Piller Report,* pp. 121–127.

4. Many other victims also signed confessions under torture but retracted them afterwards. Pavel, Taussigová, Švermová and Smrkovsky could not be brought to trial in the main period because there was no guarantee that they would not spoil the carefully staged performances. *Piller Report,* p. 128.

10. THE REINTERPRETED SHOW TRIALS IN ROMANIA

1. For the influence of the national minority factions on the development of the prewar communist party, see King, R., *History of the Rumanian Communist Party,* Stanford, 1980, pp. 27–38; Fischer-Galati, S., *20th Century Rumania,* New York, 1970, pp. 73–76; and above all, Ionescu, G., *Communism in Rumania 1944–1962,* Westport,

1976, pp. 2–28, 41–43; his book is, by far, the most thorough, best documented work on the subject of this chapter. See also Lendvai, P., *Eagles in Cobwebs*, New York, 1969, pp. 280–282; Silvain, N., *Rumania*, in *Jews in the Soviet Satellites*, New York, 1953.

2. About the life and role of Ana Pauker, see the very biased book, Ring, Camil, *Staline m'a dit*, Paris, 1952.

3. For the coup of August 23, 1944 against Antonescu, see Ionescu, pp. 83–86; Fischer-Galati, pp. 70–72; King, pp. 39–46. See also, from a Cold War perspective, Markham, R., *Rumania Under the Soviet Yoke*, Boston, 1949.

4. Ionescu, pp. 78–81; Lendvai, pp. 282–283.

5. The downfall, arrest, and trial of Patrascanu is very poorly documented in the Western literature. In the only English-language history of the Romanian communist party by King and in the monography of Fischer-Galati, two sentences deal with his case; both take the official charges at their face value and treat Patrascanu as a nationalist, "in opposition to Stalinist imperialism." In Brzezinski, Z., *The Soviet Bloc*, Cambridge, 1981, and in Ulam, A., *Titoism and the Cominform*, Westport, 1971, just his name is mentioned. The exception is again Ionescu, who devotes a short chapter to it (pp. 151–156). The following analysis had to rely heavily on confidential sources of former Romanian communists.

6. Quoted from *Resolutions of the Central Committee of the R.C.P., II* (in Romanian).

7. Ionescu, pp. 155–156.

8. Resolutions *II.*, Central Committee meeting of November 28, 1961.

9. An eyewitness account in the Romanian exile publication *Vocea Libertati*, Athens, May 1958, cited in Ionescu, p. 156.

10. For the purge of the Pauker-Luca faction, see Fischer-Galati, S., *The New Rumania*. Cambridge, 1967, pp. 17–43; Ionescu, pp. 208–214; King, pp. 92–94; Wolff, R. L., *The Balkans in Our Time*, pp. 467–469; Fejto, F., *Histoire des démocraties populaires*, Paris, 1979, pp. 289–293.

11. The equivocal meaning of the Pauker-Luca purge and its external and internal roots are discussed also in Lendvai, pp. 288–289; Ionescu, pp. 213–214.

12. *Cominform Journal*, June 23, 1950.

13. For the anti-Semitic campaign, see *The Jews in the Soviet Satellites*, pp. 533–550.

14. For the stages of the purge, see Ionescu, pp. 208–215; *Resolutions II.*, Central Committee meetings of February 29 and May 26, 1952; *Scinteia*, June 3, 1952.

15. See also Fricke, K. W., *Warten auf Gerechtigkeit*, Cologne, 1970, p. 45.

16. The anti-Semitic factor is also discussed in Ionescu, p. 213; Lendvai, P., *Anti-Semitism Without Jews*, New York, 1971, p. 336.

17. *Scinteia*, December 7, 1961.

18. Decision of the Supreme Court on September 18, 1968. Previously, the April 1968 plenum of the Central Committee discussed the first stage of the show trials, Ceausescu blamed Gheorghiu-Dej and the Minister of Interior Draghici for allowing and instigating "unfounded, gross fabrications" in the investigation. All criminal charges against Patrascanu were dismissed, the execution of Foris was declared illegal, and both were exonerated politically, as well as criminally. In May 1968, the Central Committee, on recommendation of the commission of inquiry, declared the criminal charges against Luca and his codefendants as null and void; a political rehabilitation was, however, denied. Lendvai, *Eagles*, pp. 323–324; Fricke, p. 46.

11. THE INTERRUPTED SHOW TRIALS IN EAST GERMANY

1. *László Rajk and his accomplices before the People's Court*, Budapest, 1949, pp. 149 and 163.

2. On the activities of the German group in Swiss exile, see Brandt, P., et al., *Karrieren eines Aussenseiters*, Berlin, 1983, pp. 85–122. The book is a well-researched political biography of the purge victim Leo Bauer and includes many details of the purge period. Valuable information about the Swiss group, though heavily distorted by a communist perspective, is contained in Teubner, H., *Exilland Schweiz 1933–1945*, East Berlin, 1975.

3. This, as well as many other facts throughout this chapter, is relying on confidential information gathered from purge victims.

4. For the judicial system, the role and organization of the East German and the Soviet authorities in the political persecution in the Soviet occupation zone, see Fricke, K. W., *Politik und Justiz in der DDR*, Cologne, 1970, Chapter II.

5. Fricke, pp. 100–104.

6. For a background of the party purge, see Stern, C., *Portrait einer bolschewistischen Partei*, Cologne, 1957, pp. 113–119. Stern (a pseudonym) was teaching Marxism-Leninism in East Berlin and defected to the West. She offers an insider's view on the Stalinization of the East German party.

7. Brandt, et al., pp. 187–188.

8. For a portrait of Bauer, as he would like to present himself, see his contribution in *Das Ende einer Utopie*, edited by Krüger, H., Olten, 1963, an anthology of former German communists, pp. 73–87.

9. Her story is presented in the honest, deeply moving book Wallach, E., *Light at Midnight*, New York, 1967. For luring her to East Berlin, see also Brandt, et al., pp. 190–191.

10. Quoted from *Dokumente der Sozialistischen Einheitspartei Deutschlands*, III. East Berlin, 1952, pp. 104 ff.

11. *Dokumente*, III, pp. 197 ff. See also *Neues Deutschland*, August 31, 1950.

12. Seliger, K., *Der Fall Sperling*, in: *Deutschland Archiv*, Nr. 3/1971, p. 277 ff. See also Fricke, K. W., *Warten auf Gerechtigkeit*, Cologne, 1971, pp. 86–87.

13. For the background and fate of Müller, see the article in *Der Spiegel*, January 30, 1957, pp. 30–37. Also Fricke, *Warten*, pp. 85–86.

14. Bauer, Leo, *Die Partei hat immer recht*, in *Das Parlament*, July 4, 1956, p. 409; E. Wallach, *Light at Midnight*, pp. 82–96.

15. This refers only to the victims of the Field connection. The number of communists purged in the years 1949–1954 is estimated to exceed one thousand. Following the reexamination of the terror trials, the officially acknowledged number of political prisoners released, until June 1956, is given as close to twelve thousand. See Lewis, F., *The Red Pawn*, New York, 1965; Fricke, *Warten*, p. 100.

16. See Chapter 8, pp. 159–160.

17. Brzezinski, Z., in *The Soviet Bloc*, New York, 1981, pp. 96–97, argues that the show trial was discarded because of the weakness of the East German party, a rather unbelievable conclusion in view of total Soviet domination; his hint about "considerations for left wing West German elements" is more to the point. Unsatisfactory is also the reason given by Leo Bauer in his essay *Die Partei hat immer recht* (pp. 412–413), that it

was the stupidity and ineptitude of the interrogators and his own resistance to confess that thwarted a public show trial. More pertinent as a contributing factor to Stalin's decision is the timing of the planned show trial: It coincided with the last Soviet proposal for a united, neutralized Germany and might have had a negative effect on the West (Brandt, et al., p. 201).

18. On the secret trial, see Brandt, pp. 202–204; Wallach, pp. 168–181; Bauer, pp. 416–417. About the years in the Soviet Gulag, see Wallach, pp. 182–374.

19. Bauer, p. 414.

20. *Dokumente IV.*, p. 199 ff.

21. *Tägliche Rundschau*, January 21, 1953. On the anti-Semitic witch hunt, see Fricke, *Warten*, pp. 87–88; Brandt, Heinz, *The Search for a Third Way*, New York, 1970, pp. 166–171.

22. For the personal and political tensions between Ulbricht and Dahlem, see Stern, p. 130.

23 *Dokumente IV.*, pp. 394 ff. See also Stern, pp. 129–130.

24. Fricke, *Warten*, p. 102.

25. Fricke, *Warten*, pp. 100–109, offers a concise summary of the rehabilitations, documented on pp. 220–238.

12. THE POLISH WAY OF SHOW TRIALS

1. Brzezinski, Z., *The Soviet Bloc*, Cambridge, 1981, p. 96.

2. See Dziewanowski, M. K., *The Communist Party of Poland*, Cambridge, 1976, for the Katyn Massacre, pp. 166–168, for the Warsaw uprising, pp. 177–182.

3. The main ideologues of the national way were Anton Ackermann in East Germany and József Révai in Hungary. It was an important part of the initial concept of "people's democracy." For a theoretical analysis of the transition phase, see Brzezinski, pp. 25–37.

4. For the controversy Lenin-Luxemburg, see Dziewanowski, pp. 34–36, 61–62.

5. Dziewanowski, pp. 88–95, 125, 131.

6. Dziewanowski, pp. 114–154.

7. Gomułka's best biography is written by Bethell, N., *Gomulka*, London, 1972. It offers, also, an understanding and detailed story of his purge.

8. For the obscure history of the underground party, see Ulam, A., *Titoism and the Cominform*, Westport, 1971, pp. 149–154; Bethell, pp. 49–79; Dziewanowski, pp. 149–154.

Many details in this chapter are based on the broadcasts of Josef Swiatło by Radio Free Europe. Swiatło was a lieutenant colonel in the security services Bezpieka, the assistant head of its Tenth Department, and defected in December 1953 to the West. His revelations offer an invaluable source material for the purges. His information, however, had to be weighed critically, trying to separate the factual events from the propagandistic, disinformational aspects and the mental distortions inflicted by a long service as a Stalinist policeman. See Swiatło, J., *Za kulisami Bezpieki i Partii*, 1954/55, Radio Free Europe. Partial mimeographed English translations are available from Radio Free Europe, Munich (*Inside Story of Bezpieka and Party*), and in *News from Behind the Iron Curtain*.

9. According to Dziewanowski, Gomułka strongly disapproved the collaboration between the party and the Gestapo (p. 383).

10. For the June 3 speech, see Bethell, pp. 142–143; Dziewanowski, p. 209; Ulam, pp. 164–165. Carefully edited accounts were published in the theoretical organ *Nowe Drogi* May/June and September/October 1948.

11. For the Szklarska Poreba conference, see Bethell, pp. 136–139.

12. For the stages of Gomułka's political liquidation, see Ulam, pp. 165–188; Bethell, pp. 142–159.

13. For the purge of the Polish Field group, see several Swiatło broadcasts (in Polish transcripts); Checinski, M., *Poland,* New York, 1982, pp. 77–85, one of the best works on the subject of this book.

14. Function and organization of the 10th Department is described by Swiatło in *News,* pp. 24–26; see also Checinski, pp. 69–82. For the investigation of the Field group, the chief Soviet adviser was Colonel Soldatov. (The names under which the Soviet security officials were known are often pseudonyms. Djilas recounts in his book that in 1946–1947, the representative of the Soviet intelligence service was a Lieutenant Colonel Timofeyev. During his trip to Budapest, he met the Soviet ambassador to Hungary, Pushkin, the same man he knew from Belgrade as Timofeyev. Djilas, M., *Rise and Fall,* New York, 1983, pp. 85–86.

15. Lewis, F., *The Red Pawn,* New York, 1965, pp. 194–195; Checinski, p. 77.

16. Lewis, pp. 200–204.

17. Swiatło and Fejgin allegedly suggested to Bierut that faked evidence should be fabricated to link Gomułka to a Jewish friend of Field (probably Anna Duracz or Tonia Lechtman) and thus "prove" an espionage connection. Bierut, however, rejected the suggestion. Wanda Bronska-Pampuch, *Polen zwischen Hoffnung und Verzweiflung,* Cologne, 1958, p. 197. For the anti-Semitic turn in the interrogation of the Field group, see Checinski, pp. 79–82.

18. For the political liquidation of Spychalski, see Bethell, pp. 164–165 and 175–176; Ulam, pp. 183–185.

19. Swiatło broadcast, Polish transcript; see also *News,* pp. 15–16.

20. Bethell, p. 164.

21. Bethell, p. 165.

22. Lewis, F., *The Polish Volcano,* London, 1959, p. 33.

23. For the arrest and interrogation of Spychalski, see Swiatło, in *News,* p. 18; Bethell, p. 176; Lewis, p. 33.

24. For the show trial of Tatar and its connection to Gomułka and Spychalski, see Bethell, pp. 177–180; Checinski, pp. 54–56.

25. Checinski, p. 56.

26. Quoted in Bethell, p. 181.

27. For those arrests, see the Polish transcripts of the Swiatło broadcasts; also Swiatło in *News,* pp. 31–32. Dubiel might have become a genuine Gestapo collaborator in the Nazi concentration camp (Bronska-Pampuch, p. 197).

28. For the initial phase of the Stalinist anti-Semitic purges, see Checinski, pp. 89–90.

29. Swiatło broadcast, Polish transcript.

30. The Komar trial is described in Checinski, pp. 79, 85.

31. Swiatło broadcast, Polish transcript.

32. For the arrest and interrogation of Gomułka, see Swiatło in *News,* pp. 17–18; Bethell, pp. 180–184.

33. Brzezinski, p. 97.

34. Bethell, p. 184; Swiatło in *News*, p. 19. Checiski, p. 74. Jakub Berman probably told part of the truth when he credited Bierut with saving the life of Gomułka and his own. "In 1949, Field gave evidence in Budapest, mentioning his letter to me and his acquaintance with comrade Anna Duracz. These matters came to the ears of Beria and Stalin, and from that time, accusations began to pour in, charging me with espionage and treason. . . . Comrade Bierut defended me from the slanderous charges for a number of years, he did it with complete dedication and self-sacrifice. . . .There is no doubt that had comrade Bierut not defended my case so well, I could, at the most, be exhumed today." (*Nowe Drogi*, October 1956). Years later, the president of the republic, Ochab, confirmed that "it was Bierut who saved comrade Gomułka in spite of strong pressure from Beria and Stalin" (*Polityka*, November 31, 1981). Dziewanowski concluded that "the party had managed to save from destruction the former underground leaders" (p. 257).

35. Lewis, *The Polish Volcano*, p. 32.

36. *Trybuna Ludu*, November 1, 1951.

37. See Bethell, pp. 188–190.

38. Swiatło broadcasts, Polish transcript.

39. Lewis, F., *The Red Pawn*, pp. 241–243. Summoned to the Central Committee for a rehabilitation hearing, Tonia Lechtman recounts how she was pressured to give evidence against her torturers, but only torturers of Jewish descent, ignoring the crimes of non-Jewish security officers (Checinski, p. 98).

13. CONSEQUENCES AND CONCLUSIONS

1. Cohen, Stephen F., *Rethinking the Soviet Experience*, New York, 1985, offers a fascinating theory about the Bukharinist alternative in the Soviet Union.

2. In this group, Géza Losonczy could not be brought to the post-Stalinist Nagy trial; he was murdered in the Soviet interrogation prison.

SELECTED BIBLIOGRAPHY

GENERAL WORKS

Ambrose, Stephen. *Rise to Globalism.* London, 1980.

Antonov-Ovseyenko, Anton. *The Time of Stalin.* New York, 1981.

Armstrong, Hamilton F. *Tito and Goliath.* New York, 1951.

Brzezinski, Zbigniew K. *The Soviet Bloc: Unity and Conflict.* Cambridge, 1981.

Carr, Edward H. *Twilight of the Comintern.* New York, 1982.

Cohen, Stephen F. *Bukharin and the Bolshevik Revolution.* New York, 1973.

———. *Rethinking the Soviet Experience: Politics and History Since 1917.* New York, 1985.

Conquest, Robert. *The Great Terror: Stalin's Purge of the Thirties.* New York, 1968.

Crossman, Richard, ed. *The God That Failed.* New York, 1949.

Dallin, Alexander, and Breslauer, George. *Political Terror in Communist Systems.* Stanford, 1970.

Fejtö, François. *Histoire des démocraties populaires.* 2 vols. Paris, 1969.

———. *Les Juifs et l'antisemitisme dans les pays communistes.* Paris, 1960.

Gluckstein, Yigael. *Stalin's Satellites in Europe.* London, 1952.

Kołakowski, Leszek. *Main Currents of Marxism.* 3 vols. New York, 1965.

Lendvai, Paul. *Anti-Semitism Without Jews: Communist Eastern Europe.* New York, 1971.

———. *Eagles in Cobwebs: Nationalism and Communism in the Balkans.* New York, 1969.

McVicker, C. P. *Titoism.* New York, 1957.

Medvedev, Roy. *On Stalin and Stalinism.* New York, 1979.

———. *Let History Judge: The Origins and Consequences of Stalinism.* New York, 1971.

Medwedew, R.; Havemann, R.; Steffen, J.; et al. *Entstalinisierung: Der XX. Parteitag der KPdSU und seine Folgen.* Frankfurt, 1977.

Meyer, Peter, ed. *Jews in the Soviet Satellites.* Syracuse, 1953.

Royal Institute of International Affairs. *The Soviet-Yugoslav Dispute: Text of the Published Correspondence.* London, 1948.

Seton-Watson, Hugh. *The East European Revolution.* New York, 1956.

———. *The Pattern of Communist Revolution.* London, 1953.

Ulam, Adam B. *Titoism and the Cominform.* Westport, 1971.

Urban, G. R., ed. *Stalinism: Its Impact on Russia and the World.* London, 1982.

Warriner, Doreen. *Revolution in Eastern Europe.* London, 1950.

Wolff, Robert L. *The Balkans in Our Time*. Revised edition. New York, 1978.
Ministry of Foreign Affairs of the Federal People's Republic of Yugoslavia. *White Book on Aggressive Activities by the Governments of the USSR, Poland, Czechoslovakia, Hungary, Rumania, Bulgaria and Albania*. Belgrade, 1951.

FOR *NOEL FIELD*

Lewis, Flora. *Red Pawn: The Story of Noel Field*. New York, 1965.
Powers, Thomas. *The Man Who Kept the Secrets: Richard Helms and the CIA*. New York, 1979.
Steven, Stewart. *Operation Splinter Factor*. New York, 1974.

FOR *ALBANIA*

Albania. Edited by Skendi, Stavro. New York, 1956.
Amery, Julian. *Sons of the Eagle*. London, 1948.
Bethell, Nicholas. *The Great Betrayal: The Untold Story of Kim Philby's Greatest Coup*. London, 1984.
Dedijer, Vladimir. *Tito*. New York, 1953.
————. *The Battle Stalin Lost*. New York, 1971.
Djilas, Milovan. *Conversations with Stalin*. New York, 1962.
————. *Rise and Fall*. New York, 1982.
Pano, N. C. *The People's Republic of Albania*. New York, 1968.
Prifti, Peter. *The Labor Party of Albania;* in: The Communist Parties of Eastern Europe, edited by S. Fischer-Galati. New York, 1979.

FOR *HUNGARY*

Fejtö, François. *La tragédie hongroise*. Paris, 1956.
Galgóczy, Erzsébet. *Vidravas* [Trap]. Budapest, 1984.
Gyurkó, László. *Arcképvázlat történelmi háttérrel* [Outline of a portrait with historical background]. Budapest, 1982.
Hegedüs, András. *Im Schatten einer Idee*. Zurich, 1986.
Hungary. Edited by Helmreich, E. New York, 1958.
Ignotus, Pál. *Political Prisoner*. London, 1957.
Kopácsi, Sándor. *Die ungarische Tragödie*. Stuttgart, 1979. *László Rajk and his accomplices before the People's Court*. Budapest, 1949.
Páloczy-Horváth, György. *The Undefeated*. London, 1959.
Shawcross, William. *Crime and Compromise: János Kádár and the Politics of Hungary Since Revolution*. New York, 1974.
Savarius, Vincent [Szász, Béla]. *Volunteers for the Gallows*. London, 1971.
Száraz, György. *A tábornok* [The general]. Budapest, 1984.

FOR *BULGARIA*

Bell, John D. *The Bulgarian Communist Party*. Stanford, 1985.
Brown, J. F. *Bulgaria Under Communist Rule*. London, 1970.

Bulgaria. Edited by Dellin, L.A.D. New York, 1965.
Devedjiev, Hristo H. *Stalinization of the Bulgarian Society 1949–1953.* Philadelphia, 1975.
Dewar, Hugo. *The Modern Inquisition.* London, 1953.
Moser, Charles. *Dimitrov of Bulgaria.* Ottawa, Ill., 1979.
Oren, Nissan. *Bulgarian Communism: The Road to Power.* New York.
Pundeff, Marin. *Nationalismus und Kommunismus in Bulgarien.* Munich, 1970.
Semerjeev, Peter. *Sudebny protsess Traicho Kostova v Bulgarii* [The trial of Traicho Kostov in Bulgaria]. Jerusalem, 1980.
The Trial of Traicho Kostov and His Group. Sofia, 1949.

FOR *CZECHOSLOVAKIA*

Czechoslovakia. Edited by Busek. V. New York, 1957.
Czechoslovak Political Trials, The, 1950–1954: The Suppressed Report of the Dubček Government's Commission of Inquiry, 1968. Edited by Jiři Pelikán. Stanford, 1971.
Kaplan, Karel. *Dans les archives du Comité Central.* Paris, 1978.
Loebl, Eugen. *My Mind on Trial.* New York, 1976.
Löbl, Eugen. *Die Revolution rehabilitiert ihre Kinder.* Vienna, 1976.
London, Artur. *The Confession.* New York, 1971.
Oren, Mordekhai. *Prisonnier politique à Prague.* Paris, 1960.
Slanská, Josefá. *Report on My Husband.* New York, 1969.
Slingová, Marian. *Truth Will Prevail.* London, 1968.
Taborsky, Edward. *Communism in Czechoslovakia.* Princeton, 1971.
Trial of Rudolf Slánský, The. Transcript of Prague Radio broadcasts, from the files of Radio Free Europe. Munich, 1952.
Ulc, Otto. *The Communist Party of Czechoslovakia.* New York, 1972.
Szulc, Tad. *Czechoslovakia Since World War II.* New York, 1971.

FOR *RUMANIA*

Captive Rumania. Edited by Cretzianu, Alexandre. New York, 1956.
Ionescu, Ghita. *Communism in Rumania 1944–1962.* Westport, 1976.
Jowitt, Kenneth. *Revolutionary Breakthrough: The Case of Rumania.* Berkeley, 1971.
King, Robert R. *History of the Rumanian Communist Party.* Stanford, 1980.
Markham, Reuben H. *Rumania Under the Soviet Yoke.* Boston, 1949.
Ring, Camil: *Staline m'a dit: Ana Pauker et la Roumanie.* Paris, 1952.
Romania. Edited by Fischer-Galati, S. New York, 1957.

FOR *EAST GERMANY*

Bauer, Leo. In: *Das Ende einer Utopie.* Edited by Krueger, H. Olten, 1963.
Bauer, Leo: *Die Partei hat immer recht.* In: Das Parlament, 27/56, July 4, 1956.
Brandt, Heinz. *The Search for a Third Way.* New York, 1970.
Brandt, P.: Schumacher, J; Schwarzrock, G; and Suhl, K. *Karrieren eines Aussenseiters: Leo Bauer zwischen Kommunismus und Sozialdemokratie.* Berlin, 1983.

DDR 1945-1970. Edited by Deuerlein, E. Munich, 1971.
Dokumente der Sozialistischen Einheitspartei Deutschlands: Beschlüsse und Erklä-rungen. Vols. II, III. East Berlin, 1952-1954.
Duhnke, Horst. *Stalinismus in Deutschland*. Cologne, 1955.
Fortsch, Eckart. *Die SED*. Stuttgart, 1969.
Fricke, Karl W. *Die DDR Staatssicherheit*. Cologne, 1984.
————. *Politik und Justiz in der DDR*. Cologne, 1978.
————. *Warten auf Gerechtigkeit: Kommunistische Säuberungen und Rehabilitierungen*. Cologne, 1979.
Gniffke, Erich W. *Jahre mit Ulbricht*. Cologne, 1966.
Leonhard, Wolfgang. *Child of the Revolution*. Chicago, 1958.
Ludz, Peter Christian. *Changing Party Elite in East Germany*. Cambridge, 1972.
Stern, Carola pseud. *Portrait einer bolschewistischen Partei*. Cologne, 1957.
————. *Ulbricht: A Political Biography*. New York, 1965.
Teubner, Hans. *Exilland Schweiz 1933-1945*. East Berlin, 1975.
Wallach, Erica. *Light at Midnight*. New York, 1967.

FOR *POLAND*

Bethell, Nicholas. *Gomulka: His Poland and His Communism*. London, 1972.
Bronska-Pampuch, Wanda. *Polen zwischen Hoffnung und Verzweiflung*. Cologne, 1958.
Checinski, Michael. *Poland: Communism, Nationalism, Anti-Semitism*. New York, 1982.
Dziewanowski, M. K. *The Communist Party of Poland*. New York, 1976.
Lewis, Flora. *The Polish Volcano*. London, 1959.
Poland. Edited by Halecky, O. New York, 1958.
Polonski, A.; and Drukiev, B. *The Beginnings of Communist Rule in Poland*. London, 1980.
Starr, Richard F. *Poland: The Sovietization of a Captive People*.New Orleans, 1962.
Swiatło, Josef. *Za kulisami Bezpieki i Partii* [Behind the scene of the Bezpieka and the Party]. Mimeographed. Munich, 1954. Partial transcripts of the broadcasts in: *News Behind the Iron Curtain*, vol. 4, No. 3, March 1955, Free Europe Press, New York.
Zinner, Paul E. *National Communist and Popular Revolt in Eastern Europe*. New York, 1956.

INDEX

ABOUT THE AUTHOR

GEORGE H. HODOS was born in Hungary. He spent the war years in Switzerland in emigration and while there joined the communist party. He began his studies at the University of Zurich and concluded them at the University of Budapest, after returning to Hungary in 1945. He was arrested in 1949 in the show trial of Rajk, released and rehabilitated in 1954. After the suppression of the Hungarian revolution he emigrated first to Austria, then, in 1969, to the United States. In Hungary, he worked as a journalist and as an editor of English-American literature in a publishing house. In Austria and in the United States, his contributions and essays were published in Austrian, German, Swiss and American newspapers, periodicals and journals.